Porter County Public Library

Teachers' Contracts

ISBN/EAN: 9783744642323

Printed in Europe, USA, Canada, Australia, Japan

Cover: Foto ©Andreas Hilbeck / pixelio.de

More available books at **www.hansebooks.com**

TEACHER'S CONTRACT.

This Agreement, Between ......_Wm A Bond_...... School Trustee of

Washington School Township, in Porter County, and State of Indiana,

of the first part, and ......_Cora Benham_...... a legally qualified teacher in said

County of the second part, certifies that the said teacher hereby agrees to teach the public school in District No. ...._1_...,

Grade........, in said Township, for the term commencing on the ...._3_.... day of ...._Sep_....

A. D. 1 _900_ , for the consideration of.........................._Two_........ Dollars and

.... Cents per { day, year, } to be paid _As Called for_

(State here when all or parts of salary will be paid.)

The said.........._Cora Benham_..........further agrees faithfully to perform

all the duties of teacher in said school; using only such text-books as are prescribed by the Trustees in accordance wi h the law, except supplementary reading, such as Young People's Reading Circle books, etc., and other works recommended by the County Superintendent, and observing all Rules and Regulations of the County Board of Education, and all instructions of the County Superintendent of Schools; that S..he will attend and participate in the exercises of each Institute or other teachers' meetings that may be appointed for the teachers of said township, or for each day's absence therefrom, forfeit a sum equal to one day's wages, unless such absence shall be occasioned by sickness, that S..he will accurately keep and use all registers and blanks placed in _her_ hands by said Trustee; that S..he will make a complete and accurate report at the close of the school term, the blank for which is provided on the back of this sheet; that S..he will make all other reports required of _her_ by said Trustee, the County Superintendent, or the laws of Indiana, at the proper time and manner and in good order; that S..he will exercise due diligence in the preservation of school buildings, grounds, furniture, apparatus, books, blanks and other school property committed to _her_ care, and turn the same over to the Trustee, or his representative, at the close of the term of school, in as good condition as when received, damage and wear by use excepted.

The said School Trustee agrees to keep the school buildings in good repair, and to furnish the necessary fuel, furniture, apparatus, books and blanks, and such other appliances as may be necessary for the systematic and proper conduct of said school.

And the said School Trustee, for and in behalf of said Township, further agrees to pay the said.........................._Cora Benham_........for services as teacher of said school, either a sum equal to the whole number of days taught at the rate of the above named sum per day, as agreed upon, or the salary for the year in the event of a yearly consideration, as agreed upon, when the said teacher shall have filled all the stipulations of this contract.

The said School Trustee further agrees to pay said teacher one day's wages for each day's attendance at the Township Institute, according to the Acts of 1889.

PROVIDED, That in case the said.........._Cora Benham_..........should be dismissed from said school by said Trustee, or his successor in office, for incompetency, cruelty, gross immorality, neglect of business, or a violation of any of the stipulations of this contract, or in case _her_ license should be annulled by the County Superintendent or State Superintendent, S..he shall not be entitled to any compensation after notice of dismissal, or notice of annulment of license.

PROVIDED FURTHER, That the teacher shall have a duplicate of this Contract.

IN WITNESS WHEREOF, We have hereunto subscribed our names this ...._1st_....

day of...._Sep_.... A. D. 1 _900_

...._Cora Benham_...._Teacher._

...._Wm A Bond_...._School Trustee._

NOTES:—

    (1.) Full authority is given the Trustee to substitute the words "principal," "supervisor" or "superintendent" for the word "teacher" in the event the Contract should be so made.

    (2.) This Contract is the official blank, made by the State Superintendent of Public Instruction, under the provisions of H. B. No. 139, Acts of 1899.

Teacher's or Principal's Report to Township Trustee.

NOTE.—This report must be made by each teacher having charge of the attendance of pupils. A high school teacher who works under the direction of a principal will not need to make the report in case the principal reports for the entire high school. In graded grammar schools each teacher should report for the pupils directly under his charge. The principal of a graded grammar school should report only for the pupils directly under his charge.

REPORT of.................... .... { teacher } of...........................District
{ principal }

WASHINGTON TOWNSHIP, PORTER COUNTY, INDIANA,

to the Township Trustee, for the school term beginning................................ ....and

closing ....: ....

FOR ALL TEACHERS WHO HAVE CHARGE OF ATTENDANCE OF PUPILS.

1. Number of days school was in session,
2. " " pupils enrolled during year, Male, ...; female,................; total,................
3. " " " withdrawn during year, " " "
4. " " " suspended " " " " "
5. " " " expelled " " " " "
6. " " " re-entered " " " " "
7. " " " remaining in school close of year, " " "
8. " " " " neither tardy nor absent during year, " " "
9. " " cases of tardiness during year, " " "
10. " " pupils tardy during year, " " "
11. Total days of attendance by all pupils for year,
12. * " " " absence " " " " "
13. Total cases of tardiness,............................ Time lost by tardiness,
14. †Average daily attendance for year,
15. Per cent. of attendance—$11 \div (11+12)$,
16. Number of pupils promoted to
    (a) Second year,
    (b) Third "
    (c) Fourth "
    (d) Fifth "
    (e) Sixth "
    (f) Seventh "
    (g) Eighth "
    (h) High School,
17. Number of graduates from the common branches and receiving diplomas,
    Male,...............; female,................; total,................
18. Number of graduates from non-commissioned township high schools,
    Male,...............; female,................; total,................
19. Number of graduates from commissioned township high schools,
    Male,...............; female,................; total,................
20. How many books in school library (not including reading circle books) at beginning of year?
21. How many books were added to library (not including reading circle books) during year?
22. Total now in school library (not including reading circle books),
23. How many reading circle books were added during year?
24. How many pupils read one or more school library or reading circle books during year?
25. Do patrons read school library books?
26. Number of visits to school, Parents,...............; officials, ...; others, ...; total,................
27. Number of teachers employed (if school be high school), Male,...............; female, ...; total,................
28. Number of days teacher attended township institute,
29. Books and apparatus left in school room at end of term,

I,.., do solemnly swear that the above report is true to the best of my knowledge and belief.

    { Teacher.
.... { Principal.

NOTES:—
    *(1.) After three days of absence the pupil should be withdrawn, and his absence counted no more for that period of absence. After being withdrawn, he is not a pupil of the school, and can not be again until he is re-entered, as in item 6.
    †(2.) To find average daily attendance divide the whole number of days of attendance made by all the pupils by the number of days of school taught.

TEACHER'S CONTRACT.

This Agreement, Between _W. A. Bond_ School Trustee of

Washington School Township, In Porter County, and State of Indiana,

of the first part, and _Cora Bowers_ a legally qualified teacher in said

County of the second part, certifies that the said teacher hereby agrees to teach the public school in District No. _6_,

Grade _____, in said Township, for the term commencing on the _Sep 3_ day of _Sep_

A. D. 1 _900_, for the consideration of _Two_ Dollars and

_____ Cents per { day, / year, } to be paid _As Called for_ (State here when all or parts of salary will be paid.)

The said _Cora Bowers_ further agrees faithfully to perform

all the duties of teacher in said school; using only such text-books as are prescribed by the Trustees in accordance with the law, except supplementary reading, such as Young People's Reading Circle books, etc., and other works recommended by the County Superintendent, and observing all Rules and Regulations of the County Board of Education, and all instructions of the County Superintendent of Schools; that S_he will attend and participate in the exercises of each Institute or other teachers' meetings that may be appointed for the teachers of said township, or for each day's absence therefrom, forfeit a sum equal to one day's wages, unless such absence shall be occasioned by sickness, that S_he will accurately keep and use all registers and blanks placed in _her_ hands by said Trustee; that S_he will make a complete and accurate report at the close of the school term, the blank for which is provided on the back of this sheet; that S_he will make all other reports required of _her_ by said Trustee, the County Superintendent, or the laws of Indiana, at the proper time and manner and in good order; that S_he will exercise due diligence in the preservation of school buildings, grounds, furniture, apparatus, books, blanks and other school property committed to _her_ care, and turn the same over to the Trustee, or his representative, at the close of the term of school, in as good condition as when received, damage and wear by use excepted.

The said School Trustee agrees to keep the school buildings in good repair, and to furnish the necessary fuel, furniture, apparatus, books and blanks, and such other appliances as may be necessary for the systematic and proper conduct of said school.

And the said School Trustee, for and in behalf of said Township, further agrees to pay the said _____

Cora Bowers for services as teacher of said school, either a sum equal to the whole number of days taught at the rate of the above named sum per day, as agreed upon, or the salary for the year in the event of a yearly consideration, as agreed upon, when the said teacher shall have filled all the stipulations of this contract.

The said School Trustee further agrees to pay said teacher one day's wages for each day's attendance at the Township Institute, according to the Acts of 1889.

PROVIDED, That in case the said _Cora Bowers_ should be dismissed from said school by said Trustee, or his successor in office, for incompetency, cruelty, gross immorality, neglect of business, or a violation of any of the stipulations of this contract, or in case _her_ license should be annulled by the County Superintendent or State Superintendent, S_he shall not be entitled to any compensation after notice of dismissal, or notice of annulment of license.

PROVIDED FURTHER, That the teacher shall have a duplicate of this Contract.

IN WITNESS WHEREOF, We have hereunto subscribed our names, this _1st_

day of _Sep_ A. D. 1 _900_

Cora Bowers Teacher.

W. A. Bond School Trustee.

NOTES:—
　(1.) Full authority is given the Trustee to substitute the words "principal," "supervisor" or "superintendent" for the word "teacher" in the event the Contract should be so made.
　(2.) This Contract is the official blank, made by the State Superintendent of Public Instruction, under the provisions of H. B. No. 139 Acts of 1899.

Teacher's or Principal's Report to Township Trustee.

NOTE.—This report must be made by each teacher having charge of the attendance of pupils. A high school teacher who works under the direction of a principal will not need to make the report in case the principal reports for the entire high school. In graded grammar schools each teacher should report for the pupils directly under his charge. The principal of a graded grammar school should report only for the pupils directly under his charge.

REPORT of........................ .... { teacher } { principal } of........................District

WASHINGTON TOWNSHIP, PORTER COUNTY, INDIANA,

to the Township Trustee, for the school term beginning..and

closing ....: ....

FOR ALL TEACHERS WHO HAVE CHARGE OF ATTENDANCE OF PUPILS.

1. Number of days school was in session, - - - - - - -
2. " " pupils enrolled during year, - Male, ...; female,....................; total,........................
3. " " " withdrawn during year, - - " " "
4. " " " suspended " " - - " " "
5. " " " expelled " " - " " "
6. " " " re-entered " " - " " "
7. " " " remaining in school close of year, " " "
8. " " " " neither tardy nor absent during year, " " "
9. " " cases of tardiness during year, - " " .... "
10. " " pupils tardy during year, - - " .... " "
11. Total days of attendance by all pupils for year, - - -
12. * " " " absence " " " " " - -
13. Total cases of tardiness,.................... Time lost by tardiness, -
14. †Average daily attendance for year, - -
15. Per cent. of attendance—$11 \div (11+12)$, -
16. Number of pupils promoted to -
    (a) Second year,
    (b) Third "
    (c) Fourth "
    (d) Fifth " -
    (e) Sixth "
    (f) Seventh " -
    (g) Eighth "
    (h) High School, -
17. Number of graduates from the common branches and receiving diplomas,
    Male,....................; female, ...; total,........................
18. Number of graduates from non-commissioned township high schools,
    Male,....................; female,....................; total,........................
19. Number of graduates from commissioned township high schools,
    Male,....................; female,....................; total,........................
20. How many books in school library (not including reading circle books) at beginning of year?
21. How many books were added to library (not including reading circle books) during year?
22. Total now in school library (not including reading circle books), - - -
23. How many reading circle books were added during year? - - -
24. How many pupils read one or more school library or reading circle books during year? -
25. Do patrons read school library books? -
26. Number of visits to school, Parents,....................; officials, ...; others, ...; total,........................
27. Number of teachers employed (if school be high school), Male,....................; female, ...; total,........................
28. Number of days teacher attended township institute, -
29. Books and apparatus left in school room at end of term, -

I,.., do solemnly swear that the above report is true to the best of my knowledge and belief.

.... { Teacher. { Principal.

NOTES:—
*(1.) After three days of absence the pupil should be withdrawn, and his absence counted no more for that period of absence. After being withdrawn, he is not a pupil of the school, and can not be again until he is re-entered, as in item 6.
†(2.) To find average daily attendance divide the whole number of days of attendance made by all the pupils by the number of days of school taught.

TEACHER'S CONTRACT.

This Agreement, Between *Wm. A. Bond* School Trustee of

Washington School Township, in Porter County, and State of Indiana,

of the first part, and *Maud Casbon* a legally qualified teacher in said

County of the second part, certifies that the said teacher hereby agrees to teach the public school in District No. **2**,

Grade ...., in said Township, for the term commencing on the . . . . . . **3** day of. **Sep**

A. D. 1. **900**, for the consideration of. . . . . **Two** Dollars and

Cents per { day, } { year } to be paid. **As culled for**
(State here when all or parts of salary will be paid.)

The said **Maud Casbon** further agrees faithfully to perform

all the duties of teacher in said school; using only such text-books as are prescribed by the Trustees in accordance with the law, except supplementary reading, such as Young People's Reading Circle books, etc., and other works recommended by the County Superintendent, and observing all Rules and Regulations of the County Board of Education, and all instructions of the County Superintendent of Schools; that S.he will attend and participate in the exercises of each Institute or other teachers' meetings that may be appointed for the teachers of said township, or for each day's absence therefrom, forfeit a sum equal to one day's wages, unless such absence shall be occasioned by sickness, that S.he will accurately keep and use all registers and blanks placed in her hands by said Trustee; that S.he will make a complete and accurate report at the close of the school term, the blank for which is provided on the back of this sheet; that S.he will make all other reports required of her by said Trustee, the County Superintendent, or the laws of Indiana, at the proper time and manner and in good order; that S.he will exercise due diligence in the preservation of school buildings, grounds, furniture, apparatus, books, blanks and other school property committed to her care, and turn the same over to the Trustee, or his representative, at the close of the term of school, in as good condition as when received, damage and wear by use excepted.

The said School Trustee agrees to keep the school buildings in good repair, and to furnish the necessary fuel, furniture, apparatus, books and blanks, and such other appliances as may be necessary for the systematic and proper conduct of said school.

And the said School Trustee, for and in behalf of said Township, further agrees to pay the said. . . . . **Maud Casbon** for services as teacher of said school, either a sum equal to the whole number of days taught at the rate of the above named sum per day, as agreed upon, or the salary for the year in the event of a yearly consideration, as agreed upon, when the said teacher shall have filled all the stipulations of this contract.

The said School Trustee further agrees to pay said teacher one day's wages for each day's attendance at the Township Institute, according to the Acts of 1889.

PROVIDED, That in case the said. . . . . . . **Maud Casbon** should be dismissed from said school by said Trustee, or his successor in office, for incompetency, cruelty, gross immorality, neglect of business, or a violation of any of the stipulations of this contract, or in case her license should be annulled by the County Superintendent or State Superintendent, S.he shall not be entitled to any compensation after notice of dismissal, or notice of annulment of license.

PROVIDED FURTHER, That the teacher shall have a duplicate of this Contract.

IN WITNESS WHEREOF, We have hereunto subscribed our names, this. **1st**

day of. . . . . **Sep** . . . . A. D. 1. **900**

Maud Easton . . . . Teacher.

Wm. A. Bond . . . . School Trustee.

NOTES:—
    (1.) Full authority is given theTrustee to substitute the words "principal," "supervisor" or "superintendent" for the word "teacher" in the event the Contract should be so made.
    (2.) This Contract is the official blank, made by the State Superintendent of Public Instruction, under the provisions of H. B. No, 139, Acts of 1899.

Teacher's or Principal's Report to Township Trustee.

NOTE.—This report must be made by each teacher having charge of the attendance of pupils. A high school teacher who works under the direction of a principal will not need to make the report in case the principal reports for the entire high school. In graded grammar schools each teacher should report for the pupils directly under his charge. The principal of a graded grammar school should report only for the pupils directly under his charge.

REPORT of................................... ....{ teacher }................................District
{ principal } of

WASHINGTON TOWNSHIP, PORTER COUNTY, INDIANA,

to the Township Trustee, for the school term beginning............................. ....and

closing ....

FOR ALL TEACHERS WHO HAVE CHARGE OF ATTENDANCE OF PUPILS.

1. Number of days school was in session,   -   -   -   -   -   -   -   -
2. "   " pupils enrolled during year,   -   Male, ...; female,...................; total,...................... ...
3. "   "   "   withdrawn during year, -   -   "   "   "
4. "   "   "   suspended   "   "   -   - "   "   "
5. "   "   "   expelled   "   "   -   . "   "   "
6. "   "   "   re-entered   "   "   .   "   "   "
7. "   "   "   remaining in school close of year, "   "   "
8. "   "   " "neither tardy nor absent during year, "   "   "
9. "   " cases of tardiness during year,   -   "   "   "
10. "   " pupils tardy during year,   -   - "   .... "   "
11. Total days of attendance by all pupils for year,   -   -   -   -   -
12. * "   "   " absence   " "   "   " "   -   -   -   -
13. Total cases of tardiness,.......................   Time lost by tardiness,   -   -   -   ... .
14. †Average daily attendance for year,   -   -   -   -   -
15. Per cent. of attendance—11 ÷ (11 + 12),   -   -   -   -
16. Number of pupils promoted to   -   -   -   -   -
        (a) Second year,
        (b) Third   "   -
        (c) Fourth   "
        (d) Fifth   "   -
        (e) Sixth   "   -   -   -   -
        (f) Seventh   "   -   -
        (g) Eighth   "   -   -   -
        (h) High School,   -   -   -   -   -
17. Number of graduates from the common branches and receiving diplomas,
                    Male,.................; female,...................; total,... ..
18. Number of graduates from non-commissioned township high schools,
                    Male,.................; female,...................; total,..................... .
19. Number of graduates from commissioned township high schools,
                    Male,.................; female,...................; total,..........
20. How many books in school library (not including reading circle books) at beginning of year?
21. How many books were added to library (not including reading circle books) during year?
22. Total now in school library (not including reading circle books),   -   -   -
23. How many reading circle books were added during year?   -   -   -
24. How many pupils read one or more school library or reading circle books during year?   -
25. Do patrons read school library books?   -   -   -   -
26. Number of visits to school,   Parents,...............; officials,................; others,.............; total,...........
27. Number of teachers employed (if school be high school), Male,.............; female,...........; total,......... ....
28. Number of days teacher attended township institute,   -   -   -   -   -
29. Books and apparatus left in school room at end of term,   -   -   -

I,.. .. .., do solemnly swear that the above report is true to the best of my knowledge and belief.

....{ Teacher.
                                                        { Principal.

NOTES:—

   *(1.) After three days of absence the pupil should be withdrawn, and his absence counted no more for that period of absence. After being withdrawn, he is not a pupil of the school, and can not be again until he is re-entered, as in item 6.
   †(2.) To find average daily attendance divide the whole number of days of attendance made by all the pupils by the number of days of school taught.

TEACHER'S CONTRACT.

This Agreement, Between _____ *W. A. Bond* _____ School Trustee of

Washington School Township, In Porter County, and State of Indiana,

of the first part, and _____ *W. E. Seymour* _____ a legally qualified teacher in said

County of the second part, certifies that the said teacher hereby agrees to teach the public school in District No. _____

Grade _____ , in said Township, for the term commencing on the _____ *3rd* _____ day of _____ *Sep* _____

A. D. 1 *900* , for the consideration of _____ *Two* _____ Dollars and

_____ Cents per { day, / year, } to be paid *As called for* (State here when all or parts of salary will be paid.)

The said _____ *W. E. Seymour* _____ further agrees faithfully to perform

all the duties of teacher in said school; using only such text-books as are prescribed by the Trustees in accordance with the law, except supplementary reading, such as Young People's Reading Circle books, etc., and other works recommended by the County Superintendent, and observing all Rules and Regulations of the County Board of Education, and all instructions of the County Superintendent of Schools; that _____ he will attend and participate in the exercises of each Institute or other teachers' meetings that may be appointed for the teachers of said township, or for each day's absence therefrom, forfeit a sum equal to one day's wages, unless such absence shall be occasioned by sickness, that _____ he will accurately keep and use all registers and blanks placed in *his* hands by said Trustee; that _____ he will make a complete and accurate report at the close of the school term, the blank for which is provided on the back of this sheet; that _____ he will make all other reports required of *him* by said Trustee, the County Superintendent, or the laws of Indiana, at the proper time and manner and in good order; that _____ he will exercise due diligence in the preservation of school buildings, grounds, furniture, apparatus, books, blanks and other school property committed to *his* care, and turn the same over to the Trustee, or his representative, at the close of the term of school, in as good condition as when received, damage and wear by use excepted.

The said School Trustee agrees to keep the school buildings in good repair, and to furnish the necessary fuel, furniture, apparatus, books and blanks, and such other appliances as may be necessary for the systematic and proper conduct of said school.

And the said School Trustee, for and in behalf of said Township, further agrees to pay the said _____

_____ *W. E. Seymour* _____ for services as teacher of said school, either a sum equal to the whole number of days taught at the rate of the above named sum per day, as agreed upon, or the salary for the year in the event of a yearly consideration, as agreed upon, when the said teacher shall have filled all the stipulations of this contract.

The said School Trustee further agrees to pay said teacher one day's wages for each day's attendance at the Township Institute, according to the Acts of 1889.

PROVIDED, That in case the said _____ *W. E. Seymour* _____ should be dismissed from said school by said Trustee, or his successor in office, for incompetency, cruelty, gross immorality, neglect of business, or a violation of any of the stipulations of this contract, or in case *his* license should be annulled by the County Superintendent or State Superintendent, _____ he shall not be entitled to any compensation after notice of dismissal, or notice of annulment of license.

PROVIDED FURTHER, That the teacher shall have a duplicate of this Contract.

IN WITNESS WHEREOF, We have hereunto subscribed our names, this _____ *1* _____

day of _____ *Sep* _____ A. D. 1 *900* _____

_____ *W. E. Seymour* _____ Teacher.

_____ *Wm. A. Bond* _____ School Trustee.

NOTES:—
(1.) Full authority is given the Trustee to substitute the words "principal," "supervisor" or "superintendent" for the word "teacher" in the event the Contract should be so made.
(2.) This Contract is the official blank, made by the State Superintendent of Public Instruction, under the provisions of H. B. No. 139, Acts of 1899.

Teacher's or Principal's Report to Township Trustee.

NOTE.--This report must be made by each teacher having charge of the attendance of pupils. A high school teacher who works under the direction of a principal will not need to make the report in case the principal reports for the entire high school. In graded grammar schools each teacher should report for the pupils directly under his charge. The principal of a graded grammar school should report only for the pupils directly under his charge.

REPORT of _A. E. Seymour_ { teacher / principal } of _Fourth_ District

WASHINGTON TOWNSHIP, PORTER COUNTY, INDIANA,

to the Township Trustee, for the school term beginning _Sept 3, 1900_ and closing _May 16, 1901._

FOR ALL TEACHERS WHO HAVE CHARGE OF ATTENDANCE OF PUPILS.

1. Number of days school was in session, - - - - - - _179_
2. " " pupils enrolled during year, Male, _20_ ; female, _23_ ; total, _43_
3. " " " withdrawn during year, - - " ____ " ____ "
4. " " " suspended " " - - " _0_ " ____ "
5. " " " expelled " " - - " _0_ " ____ "
6. " " " re-entered " " - " ____ " ____ "
7. " " " remaining in school close of year, " _20_ " ____ "
8. " " " " neither tardy nor absent during year, " ____ " ____ "
9. " " " cases of tardiness during year, - " _94_ " ____ "
10. " " " pupils tardy during year, - " ____ " ____ "
11. Total days of attendance by all pupils for year, - - - - _3609_
12. * " " " absence " " " " " - - - _407_
13. Total cases of tardiness, _94_ Time lost by tardiness, ____
14. †Average daily attendance for year, - - - - - - _21_
15. Per cent. of attendance—11÷(11+12), - - - - - - _89_
16. Number of pupils promoted to - - - - -
    (a) Second year, - - - - - _4_
    (b) Third " - - - - -
    (c) Fourth . " - - - - - _4_
    (d) Fifth " - - - - - _5_
    (e) Sixth " - - - - -
    (f) Seventh " - - - - -
    (g) Eighth " - - - - -
    (h) High School, - - - - - _1_
17. Number of graduates from the common branches and receiving diplomas,
    Male, _1_ ; female, _0_ ; total, _1_
18. Number of graduates from non-commissioned township high schools,
    Male, ____ ; female, ____ ; total, ____
19. Number of graduates from commissioned township high schools,
    Male, ____ ; female, ____ ; total, ____
20. How many books in school library (not including reading circle books) at beginning of year?
21. How many books were added to library (not including reading circle books) during year?
22. Total now in school library (not including reading circle books), - - - -
23. How many reading circle books were added during year? - - - - _0_
24. How many pupils read one or more school library or reading circle books during year? - _11_
25. Do patrons read school library books? - - - - - -
26. Number of visits to school, Parents, _0_ ; officials, _1_ ; others, _4_ ; total, _5_
27. Number of teachers employed (if school be high school), Male, _1_ ; female, ____ ; total, ____
28. Number of days teacher attended township institute, - - - - - _9_
29. Books and apparatus left in school room at end of term, - _1_ - - - _Yes Sir_

I, _A. Edgar Seymour_ , do solemnly swear that the above report is true to the best of my knowledge and belief.

A. E. Seymour { Teacher. / Principal.

NOTES:—
*(1.) After three days of absence the pupil should be withdrawn, and his absence counted no more for that period of absence. After being withdrawn, he is not a pupil of the school, and can not be again until he is re-entered, as in item 6.
†(2.) To find average daily attendance divide the whole number of days of attendance made by all the pupils by the number of days of school taught.

TEACHER'S CONTRACT.

Wm. A. Boud

This Agreement, Between *Henry W Davis* School Trustee of

Washington School Township, in Porter County, and State of Indiana,

of the first part, and *Henry W Davis* a legally qualified teacher in said

County of the second part, certifies that the said teacher hereby agrees to teach the public school in District No. *5* ,

Grade.......... , in said Township, for the term commencing on the. *10* day of *Sep*

A. D. 1 *900* , for the consideration of........................ *Two*..........Dollars and

................................Cents per { day, year, } to be paid *As Called for* (State here when all or parts of salary will be paid.)

The said *Henry W Davis* further agrees faithfully to perform

all the duties of teacher in said school; using only such text-books as are prescribed by the Trustees in accordance with the law, except supplementary reading, such as Young People's Reading Circle books, etc., and other works recommended by the County Superintendent, and observing all Rules and Regulations of the County Board of Education, and all instructions of the County Superintendent of Schools; that .....he will attend and participate in the exercises of each Institute or other teachers' meetings that may be appointed for the teachers of said township, or for each day's absence therefrom, forfeit a sum equal to one day's wages, unless such absence shall be occasioned by sickness, that .....he will accurately keep and use all registers and blanks placed in *his* hands by said Trustee; that .....he will make a complete and accurate report at the close of the school term, the blank for which is provided on the back of this sheet; that ......he will make all other reports required of *him* .by said Trustee, the County Superintendent, or the laws of Indiana, at the proper time and manner and in good order; that ......he will exercise due diligence in the preservation of school buildings, grounds, furniture, apparatus, books, blanks and other school property committed to *his* . care, and turn the same over to the Trustee, or his representative, at the close of the term of school, in as good condition as when received, damage and wear by use excepted.

The said School Trustee agrees to keep the school buildings in good repair, and to furnish the necessary fuel, furniture, apparatus, books and blanks, and such other appliances as may be necessary for the systematic and proper conduct of said school.

And the said School Trustee, for and in behalf of said Township, further agrees to pay the said.......... ....
Henry W Davis for services as teacher of said school, either a sum equal to the whole number of days taught at the rate of the above named sum per day, as agreed upon, or the salary for the year in the event of a yearly consideration, as agreed upon, when the said teacher shall have filled all the stipulations of this contract.

The said School Trustee further agrees to pay said teacher one day's wages for each day's attendance at the Township Institute, according to the Acts of 1889. *Henry W Davis*

PROVIDED), That in case the said *Henry W Davis* should be dismissed from said school by said Trustee, or his successor in office, for incompetency, cruelty, gross immorality neglect of business, or a violation of any of the stipulations of this contract, or in case *his* license should b annulled by the County Superintendent or State Superintendent, ...he shall not be entitled to any compensation afte notice of dismissal, or notice of annulment of license.

PROVIDED FURTHER, That the teacher shall have a duplicate of this Contract.

IN WITNESS WHEREOF, We have hereunto subscribed our names, this *10th*

day of........*Sep*............ A D. 1 *900*

Henry W Davis Teache

Wm. A. Boud School Truste

NOTES:—
(1.) Full authority is given the Trustee to substitute the words "principal," "supervisor" or "superintendent" for the word "teache in the event the Contract should be so made.
(2.) This Contract is the official blank, made by the State Superintendent of Public Instruction, under the provisions of H. B. No. 1 Acts of 1899.

Teacher's or Principal's Report to Township Trustee.

NOTE.—This report must be made by each teacher having charge of the attendance of pupils. A high school teacher who works under the direction of a principal will not need to make the report in case the principal reports for the entire high school. In graded grammar schools each teacher should report for the pupils directly under his charge. The principal of a graded grammar school should report only for the pupils directly under his charge.

REPORT of............................ .... { teacher } { principal } of............................District

WASHINGTON TOWNSHIP, PORTER COUNTY, INDIANA,

to the Township Trustee, for the school term beginning............................ ....and

closing ...: ....

FOR ALL TEACHERS WHO HAVE CHARGE OF ATTENDANCE OF PUPILS.

1. Number of days school was in session,   -   -   -   -   -   -   -   -
2. " " pupils enrolled during year,   -   Male, ...; female,....................; total,.............. ...
3. " " " withdrawn during year, -   -   "   "   "
4. " " " suspended " "   -   . "   "   "
5. " " " expelled " "   -   . "   "   "
6. " " " re-entered " "   .   "   "   "
7. " " " remaining in school close of year, "   "   "
8. " " " " neither tardy nor absent during year, "   "   "
9. " " cases of tardiness during year,   -   "   "   "
10. " " pupils tardy during year,   -   - "   "   "
11. Total days of attendance by all pupils for year,   -   .   -   .   -
12. * " " " absence " " " " "   .   -   .   -   .
13. Total cases of tardiness,........................   Time lost by tardiness,   -   .   -   ... - . ..
14. †Average daily attendance for year,   -   .   -   -   .   -
15. Per cent. of attendance—$11 \div (11+12)$,   -   -   -   -   -
16. Number of pupils promoted to   -   -   -   -   -
    - (a) Second year,   -   -   .   -   -   -
    - (b) Third "   -   .   -   -   .
    - (c) Fourth "   -   -   -   -   ....
    - (d) Fifth "   -   -   -   .   ...
    - (e) Sixth "   -   -   -   -   ....
    - (f) Seventh "   -   -   -   -   -
    - (g) Eighth "   -   -   -   -   -
    - (h) High School,   -   -   -   -   ....
17. Number of graduates from the common branches and receiving diplomas,
    Male,....................; female, ...; total,... . ..   -   . ...
18. Number of graduates from non-commissioned township high schools,
    Male,....................; female,.................; total,..... ....
19. Number of graduates from commissioned township high schools,
    Male,....................; female,.................; total,.......
20. How many books in school library (not including reading circle books) at beginning of year?
21. How many books were added to library (not including reading circle books) during year?
22. Total now in school library (not including reading circle books),   -   -   -
23. How many reading circle books were added during year?   -   -   -   ....
24. How many pupils read one or more school library or reading circle books during year?   -   ....
25. Do patrons read school library books?   ....
26. Number of visits to school,   Parents,....................; officials, ...; others, ...; total, ...
27. Number of teachers employed (if school be high school), Male,...............; female, ...; total,...... . ...
28. Number of days teacher attended township institute,   -   -   -   -   -
29. Books and apparatus left in school room at end of term,   -   -   -   ....

I,... ...., do solemnly swear that the above report is true to the best of my knowledge and belief.

{ Teacher.
{ Principal.
....

NOTES:—

*(1.) After three days of absence the pupil should be withdrawn, and his absence counted no more for that period of absence. After being withdrawn, he is not a pupil of the school, and can not be again until he is re-entered, as in item 6.

†(2.) To find average daily attendance divide the whole number of days of attendance made by all the pupils by the number of days of school taught.

15A

TEACHER'S CONTRACT.

This Agreement, Between *L W Gan* .... School Trustee of

Washington School Township, in Porter County, and State of Indiana,

of the first part, and *Lucinda Ott* ....a legally qualified teacher in said

County of the second part, certifies that the said teacher hereby agrees to teach the public school in District No. ....,

Grade............, in said Township, for the term commencing on the *Twenty First* day of *Jany*

A. D. 1 *901* , for the consideration of............... *Two* ....Dollars and

.... Cents per { day, { to be paid *as called for*

{ year, { (State here when all or parts of salary will be paid.)

The said *Lucinda Ott* ....further agrees faithfully to perform

all the duties of teacher in said school; using only such text-books as are prescribed by the Trustees in accordance with the law, except supplementary reading, such as Young People's Reading Circle books, etc., and other works recom-mended by the County Superintendent, and observing all Rules and Regulations of the County Board of Education, and all instructions of the County Superintendent of Schools; that ......he will attend and participate in the exercises of each Institute or other teachers' meetings that may be appointed for the teachers of said township, or for each day's absence therefrom, forfeit a sum equal to one day's wages, unless such absence shall be occasioned by sickness, that ......he will accurately keep and use all registers and blanks placed in *her* ......hands by said Trustee; that ......he will make a complete and accurate report at the close of the school term, the blank for which is provided on the back of this sheet; that ......he will make all other reports required of *her* ......by said Trustee, the County Superintendent, or the laws of Indiana, at the proper time and manner and in good order; that ......he will exercise due diligence in the preservation of school buildings, grounds, furniture, apparatus, books, blanks and other school property committed to *her* ......care, and turn the same over to the Trustee, or his representative, at the close of the term of school, in as good condition as when received, damage and wear by use excepted.

The said School Trustee agrees to keep the school buildings in good repair, and to furnish the necessary fuel, furniture, apparatus, books and blanks, and such other appliances as may be necessary for the systematic and proper conduct of said school.

And the said School Trustee, for and in behalf of said Township, further agrees to pay the said............... *Lucinda Ott* ....for services as teacher of said school, either a sum equal to the whole number of days taught at the rate of the above named sum per day, as agreed upon, or the salary for the year in the event of a yearly consideration, as agreed upon, when the said teacher shall have filled all the stipulations of this contract.

The said School Trustee further agrees to pay said teacher one day's wages for each day's attendance at the Town-ship Institute, according to the Acts of 1889.

PROVIDED, That in case the said *Lucinda Ott* ....should be dismissed from said school by said Trustee, or his successor in office, for incompetency, cruelty, gross immorality, neglect of business, or a violation of any of the stipulations of this contract, or in case......license should be annulled by the County Superintendent or State Superintendent, ...he shall not be entitled to any compensation after notice of dismissal, or notice of annulment of license.

PROVIDED FURTHER, That the teacher shall have a duplicate of this Contract.

IN WITNESS WHEREOF, We have hereunto subscribed our names, this *17th* ....

day of *Jany* .... A. D. 1 *901* *Lucinda Ott*, Teacher.

L W Gan, School-Trustee.

NOTES:—
　(1.) Full authority is given the Trustee to substitute the words "principal," "supervisor" or "superintendent" for the word "teacher" in the event the Contract should be so made.
　(2.) This Contract is the official blank, made by the State Superintendent of Public Instruction, under the provisions of H. B. No. 139 Acts of 1899.

Teacher's or Principal's Report to Township Trustee.

NOTE.—This report must be made by each teacher having charge of the attendance of pupils. A high school teacher who works under the direction of a principal will not need to make the report in case the principal reports for the entire high school. In graded grammar schools each teacher should report for the pupils directly under his charge. The principal of a graded grammar school should report only for the pupils directly under his charge.

REPORT of.................................   .... { teacher } of...........................District
                                                                              { principal }

WASHINGTON TOWNSHIP, PORTER COUNTY, INDIANA,

to the Township Trustee, for the school term beginning.. ....and

closing ....

FOR ALL TEACHERS WHO HAVE CHARGE OF ATTENDANCE OF PUPILS.

1. Number of days school was in session,   -   -   -   -   -   -   -   -
2. "   " pupils enrolled during year,   -   Male, ...; female,....................; total,.......................
3. "   "   " withdrawn during year, -   -   "   "   "
4. "   "   " suspended "   "   -   - "   "   "
5. "   "   " expelled   "   "   -   - "   "   "
6. "   "   " re-entered "   "   -   "   "   "
7. "   "   " remaining in school close of year, "   "   "
8. "   "   " "neither tardy nor absent during year, "   "   "
9. "   " cases of tardiness during year,   -   "   "   "
10. "   " pupils tardy during year,   -   - "   "   "
11. Total days of attendance by all pupils for year,   -   -   -   -
12. * "   "   " absence   " "   "   " "   -   -   -
13. Total cases of tardiness,.................. Time lost by tardiness,   -   -   -
14. †Average daily attendance for year,   -   -   -   -
15. Per cent. of attendance—$11 \div (11+12)$,   -   -   -
16. Number of pupils promoted to   -   -   -   -
      (a) Second year,   -   -   -   -
      (b) Third   "   -   -   -
      (c) Fourth   "   -   -   -
      (d) Fifth   "   -   -   -
      (e) Sixth   "   -   -   -
      (f) Seventh   "   -   -   -
      (g) Eighth   "   -   -   -
      (h) High School,   -   -   -   -   -
17. Number of graduates from the common branches and receiving diplomas,
                              Male,..................; female,.................; total,...... ..
18. Number of graduates from non-commissioned township high schools,
                              Male,..................; female,.................; total,...... ..
19. Number of graduates from commissioned township high schools,
                              Male,..................; female,.................; total,.......
20. How many books in school library (not including reading circle books) at beginning of year?
21. How many books were added to library (not including reading circle books) during year?
22. Total now in school library (not including reading circle books),   -   -   -   -
23. How many reading circle books were added during year?   -   -   -
24. How many pupils read one or more school library or reading circle books during year?   -
25. Do patrons read school library books?   -   -   -   -   -
26. Number of visits to school,   Parents,................; officials,...............; others, ...; total,...................
27. Number of teachers employed (if school be high school), Male,.............; female, ...; total,..................
28. Number of days teacher attended township institute,   -   -   -   -
29. Books and apparatus left in school room at end of term,   -   -   -

I,... ...., do solemnly swear that the above report is true to the best of my knowledge and belief.

                                                        { Teacher.
.... { Principal.

NOTES:—
   *(1.) After three days of absence the pupil should be withdrawn, and his absence counted no more for that period of absence. After being withdrawn, he is not a pupil of the school, and can not be again until he is re-entered, as in item 6.
   †(2.) To find average daily attendance divide the whole number of days of attendance made by all the pupils by the number of days of school taught.

TEACHER'S CONTRACT.

This Agreement, Between _L. M. Green_   School Trustee of

Washington School Township, in Porter County, and State of Indiana,

of the first part, and _W. E. Seymour_, a legally qualified teacher in said County of the second part, certifies that the said teacher hereby agrees to teach the public school in District No.____, Grade____, in said Township, for the term commencing on the _2nd_ day of _September_ A. D. 190_1_, for the consideration of _Two and 25_ Dollars and ____ Cents per { day, { year, } to be paid _as wanted_

(State here when all or parts of salary will be paid.)

The said _W. E. Seymour_ further agrees faithfully to perform all the duties of teacher in said school; using only such text-books as are prescribed by the Trustees in accordance with the law, except supplementary reading, such as Young People's Reading Circle books, etc., and other works recommended by the County Superintendent, and observing all Rules and Regulations of the County Board of Education, and all instructions of the County Superintendent of Schools; that ___ he will attend and participate in the exercises of each Institute or other teachers' meetings that may be appointed for the teachers of said township, or for each day's absence therefrom, forfeit a sum equal to one day's wages, unless such absence shall be occasioned by sickness, that ____ he will accurately keep and use all registers and blanks placed in _his_ hands by said Trustee; that ___ he will make a complete and accurate report at the close of the school term, the blank for which is provided on the back of this sheet; that ____ he will make all other reports required of _him_ by said Trustee, the County Superintendent, or the laws of Indiana, at the proper time and manner and in good order; that ____ he will exercise due diligence in the preservation of school buildings, grounds, furniture, apparatus, books, blanks and other school property committed to _his_ care, and turn the same over to the Trustee, or his representative, at the close of the term of school, in as good condition as when received, damage and wear by use excepted.

The said School Trustee agrees to keep the school buildings in good repair, and to furnish the necessary fuel, furniture, apparatus, books and blanks, and such other appliances as may be necessary for the systematic and proper conduct of said school.

And the said School Trustee, for and in behalf of said Township, further agrees to pay the said____

____ for services as teacher of said school, either a sum equal to the whole number of days taught at the rate of the above named sum per day, as agreed upon, or the salary for the year in the event of a yearly consideration, as agreed upon, when the said teacher shall have filled all the stipulations of this contract.

The said School Trustee further agrees to pay said teacher one day's wages for each day's attendance at the Township Institute, according to the Acts of 1889.

PROVIDED, That in case the said _W. E. Seymour_ should be dismissed from said school by said Trustee, or his successor in office, for incompetency, cruelty, gross immorality, neglect of business, or a violation of any of the stipulations of this contract, or in case _his_ license should be annulled by the County Superintendent or State Superintendent, ____ he shall not be entitled to any compensation after notice of dismissal, or notice of annulment of license.

PROVIDED FURTHER, That the teacher shall have a duplicate of this Contract.

IN WITNESS WHEREOF, We have hereunto subscribed our names, this _17th_ day of _August_ A. D. 190_1_

W. E. Seymour - Teacher.

L. M. Green School Trustee.

NOTES:—
   (1.) Full authority is given the Trustee to substitute the words "principal," "supervisor" or "superintendent" for the word "teacher" in the event the Contract should be so made.
   (2.) This Contract is the official blank, made by the State Superintendent of Public Instruction, under the provisions of H. B. No. 139, Acts of 1899.

Teacher's or Principal's Report to Township Trustee.

NOTE.—This report must be made by each teacher having charge of the attendance of pupils. A high school teacher who works under the direction of a principal will not need to make the report in case the principal reports for the entire high school. In graded grammar schools each teacher should report for the pupils directly under his charge. The principal of a graded grammar school should report only for the pupils directly under his charge.

REPORT of.. .... { teacher } of...........................District
{ principal }

WASHINGTON TOWNSHIP, PORTER COUNTY, INDIANA,

to the Township Trustee, for the school term beginning..and

closing ....

FOR ALL TEACHERS WHO HAVE CHARGE OF ATTENDANCE OF PUPILS.

1. Number of days school was in session, - - - - - - - -
2. "   " pupils enrolled during year, - Male, ...; female,.....................; total,......................
3. "   "   " withdrawn during year, - - " " "
4. "   "   " suspended " " - - " " "
5. "   "   " expelled " " - " " "
6. "   "   " re-entered " " - " " "
7. "   "   " remaining in school close of year, " " "
8. "   "   " neither tardy nor absent during year, " " "
9. "   " cases of tardiness during year, - " " "
10. "   " pupils tardy during year, - - " " "
11. Total days of attendance by all pupils for year, - - - - -
12. * "   "   " absence " " " " " - - - - -
13. Total cases of tardiness,..................... Time lost by tardiness, - - - ...   ...
14. †Average daily attendance for year, - - - - -
15. Per cent. of attendance—$11 \div (11+12)$, - - - -
16. Number of pupils promoted to - - - - -
    (a) Second year, - - - -
    (b) Third " - - -
    (c) Fourth " - - -
    (d) Fifth " - - -
    (e) Sixth " - - -
    (f) Seventh " - - -
    (g) Eighth " - - -
    (h) High School, - - - - - - -
17. Number of graduates from the common branches and receiving diplomas,
    Male,..................; female,.....................; total,......   ...
18. Number of graduates from non-commissioned township high schools,
    Male,..................; female,.....................; total,........ .
19. Number of graduates from commissioned township high schools,
    Male,..................; female,.....................; total,.......
20. How many books in school library (not including reading circle books) at beginning of year?
21. How many books were added to library (not including reading circle books) during year?
22. Total now in school library (not including reading circle books), - - - -
23. How many reading circle books were added during year? - - -
24. How many pupils read one or more school library or reading circle books during year? -
25. Do patrons read school library books?
26. Number of visits to school, Parents,..................; officials, ...; others, ...; total,.............
27. Number of teachers employed (if school be high school), Male,.............; female, ...; total,......... ....
28. Number of days teacher attended township institute, - - - - -
29. Books and apparatus left in school room at end of term, - - -

I,.., do solemnly swear that the above report is

true to the best of my knowledge and belief.

{ Teacher.
.... { Principal.

NOTES:—
    *(1.) After three days of absence the pupil should be withdrawn, and his absence counted no more for that period of absence. After being withdrawn, he is not a pupil of the school, and can not be again until he is re-entered, as in item 6.
    †(1a.) To find average daily attendance divide the whole number of days of attendance made by all the pupils by the number of days of school taught.

For Township Trustees.   Wade Bros. & Wise, Printers.

TEACHER'S CONTRACT.

This Agreement, Between *L M Green* ....School Trustee of

Washington School Township, in Porter County, and State of Indiana,

of the first part, and *Cora Benham* ....a legally qualified teacher in said

County of the second part, certifies that the said teacher hereby agrees to teach the public school in District No. *Two*

Grade...., in said Township, for the term commencing on the *2nd* day of *September*

A. D. 1.*901*, for the consideration of *Two* ....Dollars and

Twenty Cents per { day, { year, } to be paid *As called for*
(State here when all or parts of salary will be paid.)

The said *Cora Benham* ....further agrees faithfully to perform

all the duties of teacher in said school; using only such text-books as are prescribed by the Trustees in accordance with the law, except supplementary reading, such as Young People's Reading Circle books, etc., and other works recommended by the County Superintendent, and observing all Rules and Regulations of the County Board of Education, and all instructions of the County Superintendent of Schools; that she will attend and participate in the exercises of each Institute or other teachers' meetings that may be appointed for the teachers of said township, or for each day's absence therefrom, forfeit a sum equal to one day's wages, unless such absence shall be occasioned by sickness, that .....he will accurately keep and use all registers and blanks placed in *her* hands by said Trustee; that ....he will make a complete and accurate report at the close of the school term, the blank for which is provided on the back of this sheet; that ....he will make all other reports required of *his* .. by said Trustee, the County Superintendent, or the laws of Indiana, at the proper time and manner and in good order; that ..... he will exercise due diligence in the preservation of school buildings, grounds, furniture, apparatus, books, blanks and other school property committed to *her* care, and turn the same over to the Trustee, or his representative, at the close of the term of school, in as good condition as when received, damage and wear by use excepted.

The said School Trustee agrees to keep the school buildings in good repair, and to furnish the necessary fuel, furniture, apparatus, books and blanks, and such other appliances as may be necessary for the systematic and proper conduct of said school.

And the said School Trustee, for and in behalf of said Township, further agrees to pay the said.............. ... .
Cora Benham for services as teacher of said school, either a sum equal to the whole number of days taught at the rate of the above named sum per day, as agreed upon, or the salary for the year in the event of a yearly consideration, as agreed upon, when the said teacher shall have filled all the stipulations of this contract.

The said School Trustee further agrees to pay said teacher one day's wages for each day's attendance at the Township Institute, according to the Acts of 1889.

PROVIDED, That in case the said *Cora B enham* ....should be dismissed from said school by said Trustee, or his successor in office, for incompetency, cruelty, gross immorality, neglect of business, or a violation of any of the stipulations of this contract, or in case ....license should be annulled by the County Superintendent or State Superintendent, S he shall not be entitled to any compensation after notice of dismissal, or notice of annulment of license.

PROVIDED FURTHER, That the teacher shall have a duplicate of this Contract.

IN WITNESS WHEREOF, We have hereunto subscribed our names, this *27th*
day of *August* A. D. 1 *901*

Cora Benham ......Teacher.
L M Green ....School Trustee.

Teacher's or Principal's Report to Township Trustee.

NOTE.—This report must be made by each teacher having charge of the attendance of pupils. A high school teacher who works under the direction of a principal will not need to make the report in case the principal reports for the entire high school. In graded grammar schools each teacher should report for the pupils directly under his charge. The principal of a graded grammar school should report only for the pupils directly under his charge.

REPORT of............................ .... { teacher } of........................District
.... { principal }

WASHINGTON TOWNSHIP, PORTER COUNTY, INDIANA,

to the Township Trustee, for the school term beginning...and

closing....

FOR ALL TEACHERS WHO HAVE CHARGE OF ATTENDANCE OF PUPILS.

1. Number of days school was in session,   -   -   -   -   -   -   -
2.   "   "   pupils enrolled during year,   -   Male, ...; female,....................; total,....................
3.   "   "   "   withdrawn during year, -   -   "   "   "
4.   "   "   "   suspended   "   "   -   - "   "   "
5.   "   "   "   expelled   "   "   -   "   "   "
6.   "   "   "   re-entered   "   "   -   "   "   "
7.   "   "   "   remaining in school close of year, "   "   "
8.   "   "   "   "neither tardy nor absent during year, "   "   "
9.   "   "   cases of tardiness during year,   -   "   "   "
10.   "   "   pupils tardy during year,   -   - "   "   "
11. Total days of attendance by all pupils for year,   -   -   -   -   -   -
12. * "   "   "   absence   "   "   "   "   "   -   -   -   -   -
13. Total cases of tardiness,......................   Time lost by tardiness,   -   -   -   ... - - -
14. †Average daily attendance for year,   -   -   -   -   -   -
15. Per cent. of attendance—$11 \div (11+12)$,   -   -   -   -
16. Number of pupils promoted to   -   -

    (a) Second year,
    (b) Third   "   -
    (c) Fourth   "   -   -   -   -
    (d) Fifth   "   -   -   -   -
    (e) Sixth   "   -   -   -   -   -
    (f) Seventh   "   -   -   -   -   -
    (g) Eighth   "   -   -   -   -   -
    (h) High School,   -   -   -   -   -

17. Number of graduates from the common branches and receiving diplomas,
    Male,.................; female,.................; total,.................
18. Number of graduates from non-commissioned township high schools,
    Male,.................; female,.................; total,.................
19. Number of graduates from commissioned township high schools,
    Male,.................; female,.................; total,.................
20. How many books in school library (not including reading circle books) at beginning of year?
21. How many books were added to library (not including reading circle books) during year?
22. Total now in school library (not including reading circle books),   -   -   -
23. How many reading circle books were added during year?   -   -   -
24. How many pupils read one or more school library or reading circle books during year?   -
25. Do patrons read school library books?   -
26. Number of visits to school,   Parents,.................; officials,.................; others,.................; total,.................
27. Number of teachers employed (if school be high school), Male,.................; female,.................; total,.................
28. Number of days teacher attended township institute,   -   -   -   -
29. Books and apparatus left in school room at end of term,   -   -   -

I,..., do solemnly swear that the above report is
true to the best of my knowledge and belief.
.... { Teacher.
{ Principal.

NOTES:—
*(1.) After three days of absence the pupil should be withdrawn, and his absence counted no more for that period of absence. After being withdrawn, he is not a pupil of the school, and can not be again until he is re-entered, as in item 6.
†(2.) To find average daily attendance divide the whole number of days of attendance made by all the pupils by the number of days of school taught.

TEACHER'S CONTRACT.

This Agreement, Between _ZM Green_ .... School Trustee of

Washington School Township, in Porter County, and State of Indiana,

of the first part, and _Cora Bowers_ .... a legally qualified teacher in said County of the second part, certifies that the said teacher hereby agrees to teach the public school in District No. _6_, Grade ...., in said Township, for the term commencing on the _2ond_ day of _Sept_ A. D. 1 _901_ , for the consideration of _Two_ .... Dollars and _Twenty_ Cents per { day, year, } to be paid _as called for_ (State here when all or parts of salary will be paid.)

The said _Cora Bowers_ .... further agrees faithfully to perform all the duties of teacher in said school; using only such text-books as are prescribed by the Trustees in accordance with the law, except supplementary reading, such as Young People's Reading Circle books, etc., and other works recommended by the County Superintendent, and observing all Rules and Regulations of the County Board of Education, and all instructions of the County Superintendent of Schools; that _s_he will attend and participate in the exercises of each Institute or other teachers' meetings that may be appointed for the teachers of said township, or for each day's absence therefrom, forfeit a sum equal to one day's wages, unless such absence shall be occasioned by sickness, that _s_he will accurately keep and use all registers and blanks placed in _her_ hands by said Trustee; that _s_ he will make a complete and accurate report at the close of the school term, the blank for which is provided on the back of this sheet; that _s_ he will make all other reports required of _her_ by said Trustee, the County Superintendent, or the laws of Indiana, at the proper time and manner and in good order; that ......he will exercise due diligence in the preservation of school buildings, grounds, furniture, apparatus, books, blanks and other school property committed to _her_ care, and turn the same over to the Trustee, or his representative, at the close of the term of school, in as good condition as when received, damage and wear by use excepted.

The said School Trustee agrees to keep the school buildings in good repair, and to furnish the necessary fuel, furniture, apparatus, books and blanks, and such other appliances as may be necessary for the systematic and proper conduct of said school.

And the said School Trustee, for and in behalf of said Township, further agrees to pay the said................. _Cora Bowers_ .... for services as teacher of said school, either a sum equal to the whole number of days taught at the rate of the above named sum per day, as agreed upon, or the salary for the year in the event of a yearly consideration, as agreed upon, when the said teacher shall have filled all the stipulations of this contract.

The said School Trustee further agrees to pay said teacher one day's wages for each day's attendance at the Township Institute, according to the Acts of 1889.

PROVIDED, That in case the said _Cora Bowers_ .... should be dismissed from said school by said Trustee, or his successor in office, for incompetency, cruelty, gross immorality, neglect of business, or a violation of any of the stipulations of this contract, or in case _her_ license should be annulled by the County Superintendent or State Superintendent, _s_ he shall not be entitled to any compensation after notice of dismissal, or notice of annulment of license.

PROVIDED FURTHER, That the teacher shall have a duplicate of this Contract.

IN WITNESS WHEREOF, We have hereunto subscribed our names, this _27th_ day of _Sept_ A. D. 1 _901_

Cora Bowers Teacher
ZM Green School Trustee.

NOTES:—
    (1.) Full authority is given the Trustee to substitute the words "principal," "supervisor" or "superintendent" for the word "teacher" in the event the Contract should be so made.
    (2.) This Contract is the official blank, made by the State Superintendent of Public Instruction, under the provisions of H. B. No. 139, Acts of 1899.

Teacher's or Principal's Report to Township Trustee.

NOTE.—This report must be made by each teacher having charge of the attendance of pupils. A high school teacher who works under the direction of a principal will not need to make the report in case the principal reports for the entire high school. In graded grammar schools each teacher should report for the pupils directly under his charge. The principal of a graded grammar school should report only for the pupils directly under his charge.

REPORT of................................ .... { teacher } { principal } of............................District

WASHINGTON TOWNSHIP, PORTER COUNTY, INDIANA,

to the Township Trustee, for the school term beginning.................. ....and

closing ....

FOR ALL TEACHERS WHO HAVE CHARGE OF ATTENDANCE OF PUPILS.

1. Number of days school was in session,   -   -   -   -   -   -   -   -
2. "   "   pupils enrolled during year,   -   Male, ...; female,.....................; total,....... ...
3. "   "   "   withdrawn during year,   -   -   "   "   "
4. "   "   "   suspended   "   "   -   . "   "   ....   "
5. "   "   "   expelled   "   "   -   . "   "   "
6. "   "   "   re-entered   "   "   .   "   "   "
7. "   "   "   remaining in school close of year, "   "   "
8. "   "   "   "neither tardy nor absent during year, "   "   "
9. "   "   cases of tardiness during year,   -   "   "   ....   "
10. "   "   pupils tardy during year,   -   . "   ....   "   "
11. Total days of attendance by all pupils for year,   -   -   -   -   -
12. * "   "   "   absence   " "   "   " "   -   -   -   -   -
13. Total cases of tardiness,...................   Time lost by tardiness,   -   -   -   ... .. - ..
14. †Average daily attendance for year,   -   -   -   -   -   -
15. Per cent. of attendance—11÷(11+12),   -   -   -   -   -
16. Number of pupils promoted to   -   -   -   -   -   -
        (a) Second year,   -   -   -   -   -   -   -
        (b) Third   "   -   -   -   -   -   -   -
        (c) Fourth   "   -   -   -   -   -   ....
        (d) Fifth   "   -   -   -   -   -   ....
        (e) Sixth   "   -   -   -   -   -   ....
        (f) Seventh   "   -   -   -   -   -
        (g) Eighth   "   -   -   -   -   -
        (h) High School,   -   -   -   -   -   ....
17. Number of graduates from the common branches and receiving diplomas,
        Male,................; female,..................; total,...... .. ..
18. Number of graduates from non-commissioned township high schools,
        Male,...................; female,....................; total,............. .
19. Number of graduates from commissioned township high schools,
        Male,...................; female,....................; total,..........
20. How many books in school library (not including reading circle books) at beginning of year?
21. How many books were added to library (not including reading circle books) during year?
22. Total now in school library (not including reading circle books),   -   -   -   -
23. How many reading circle books were added during year?   -   -   -   -
24. How many pupils read one or more school library or reading circle books during year?   -   ....
25. Do patrons read school library books?   -   -   -   -   ....
26. Number of visits to school,   Parents,...................; officials,...................; others, ...; total,....................
27. Number of teachers employed (if school be high school), Male,...................; female,...................; total,...................
28. Number of days teacher attended township institute,   -   -   -   -
29. Books and apparatus left in school room at end of term,   -   -   -   ....

I,... .   . .., do solemnly swear that the above report is true to the best of my knowledge and belief.

.... { Teacher. } { Principal.

NOTES:—
        *(1.) After three days of absence the pupil should be withdrawn, and his absence counted no more for that period of absence. After being withdrawn, he is not a pupil of the school, and can not be again until he is re-entered, as in item 6.
        †(2.) To find average daily attendance divide the whole number of days of attendance made by all the pupils by the number of days of school taught.

For Township Trustees.   Wade Bros. & Wise, Printers

TEACHER'S CONTRACT.

This Agreement, Between X. W. Green .... School Trustee of

Washington School Township, In Porter County, and State of Indiana,

of the first part, and ....Ethel Collins.......................a legally qualified teacher in said

County of the second part, certifies that the said teacher hereby agrees to teach the public school in District No. ....

Grade........, in said Township, for the term commencing on the....2 ond........ day of....Sept........

A. D. 19.01......, for the consideration of...........Two.................................., Dollars and

.....Sixteen..... Cents per { day, year, } to be paid....as called for..... (State here when all or parts of salary will be paid.)

The said............Ethel Collins...........................further agrees faithfully to perform

all the duties of teacher in said school; using only such text-books as are prescribed by the Trustees in accordance with the law, except supplementary reading, such as Young People's Reading Circle books, etc., and other works recommended by the County Superintendent, and observing all Rules and Regulations of the County Board of Education, and all instructions of the County Superintendent of Schools; that ...he will attend and participate in the exercises of each Institute or other teachers' meetings that may be appointed for the teachers of said township, or for each day's absence therefrom, forfeit a sum equal to one day's wages, unless such absence shall be occasioned by sickness, that ....she will accurately keep and use all registers and blanks placed in ....her.... hands by said Trustee; that ...she will make a complete and accurate report at the close of the school term, the blank for which is provided on the back of this sheet; that ....she will make all other reports required of ...her..., by said Trustee, the County Superintendent, or the laws of Indiana, at the proper time and manner and in good order; that ......he will exercise due diligence in the preservation of school buildings, grounds, furniture, apparatus, books, blanks and other school property committed to ....her.... care, and turn the same over to the Trustee, or his representative, at the close of the term of school, in as good condition as when received, damage and wear by use excepted.

The said School Trustee agrees to keep the school buildings in good repair, and to furnish the necessary fuel, furniture, apparatus, books and blanks, and such other appliances as may be necessary for the systematic and proper conduct of said school.

And the said School Trustee, for and in behalf of said Township, further agrees to pay the said.............. .....Ethel Collins.............for services as teacher of said school, either a sum equal to the whole number of days taught at the rate of the above named sum per day, as agreed upon, or the salary for the year in the event of a yearly consideration, as agreed upon, when the said teacher shall have filled all the stipulations of this contract.

The said School Trustee further agrees to pay said teacher one day's wages for each day's attendance at the Township Institute, according to the Acts of 1889.

PROVIDED, That in case the said............Ethel Collins...........................should be dismissed from said school by said Trustee, or his successor in office, for incompetency, cruelty, gross immorality, neglect of business, or a violation of any of the stipulations of this contract, or in case ...her... license should be annulled by the County Superintendent or State Superintendent, ...she shall not be entitled to any compensation after notice of dismissal, or notice of annulment of license.

PROVIDED FURTHER, That the teacher shall have a duplicate of this Contract.

IN WITNESS WHEREOF, We have hereunto subscribed our names, this....27th...............

day of......Aug........ A. D. 19....

..........E thel Collins...........................Teacher.

..........X. W. Green......................School Trustee.

NOTES:—
(1.) Full authority is given the Trustee to substitute the words "principal," "supervisor" or "superintendent" for the word "teacher" in the event the Contract should be so made.
(2.) This Contract is the official blank, made by the State Superintendent of Public Instruction, under the provisions of H. B. No. 139, Acts of 1899.

Teacher's or Principal's Report to Township Trustee.

NOTE.—This report must be made by each teacher having charge of the attendance of pupils. A high school teacher who works under the direction of a principal will not need to make the report in case the principal reports for the entire high school. In graded grammar schools each teacher should report for the pupils directly under his charge. The principal of a graded grammar school should report only for the pupils directly under his charge.

REPORT of............................ .... { teacher } of ....District
{ principal }

WASHINGTON TOWNSHIP, PORTER COUNTY, INDIANA,

to the Township Trustee, for the school term beginning............. . ... and

closing ....: ....

FOR ALL TEACHERS WHO HAVE CHARGE OF ATTENDANCE OF PUPILS.

1. Number of days school was in session,   -   -   -   -   -   -   -   -
2.   "   " pupils enrolled during year,   -   Male, ...; female,.................; total,........................
3.   "   "   "   withdrawn during year, -   -   "   "   "
4.   "   "   "   suspended   "   "   -   .   "   "   "
5.   "   "   "   expelled   "   "   .   "   "   "
6.   "   "   "   re-entered   "   "   .   "   "   "
7.   "   "   "   remaining in school close of year, "   "   "
8.   "   "   " neither tardy nor absent during year, "   "   "
9.   "   "   cases of tardiness during year,   -   "   "   "
10.   "   "   pupils tardy during year,   -   .   "   ....   "   "
11. Total days of attendance by all pupils for year,   -   -   -   -   -
12. * "   "   " absence   "   "   "   "   "   -   -   -   -   -
13. Total cases of tardiness,.................   Time lost by tardiness,   -   -   -   ... ...
14. †Average daily attendance for year,   -   -   -   -   -
15. Per cent. of attendance—11÷(11+12),   -   -   -   -
16. Number of pupils promoted to   -   -   -   -   -   -
    (a) Second year,
    (b) Third   "   -
    (c) Fourth   "   -
    (d) Fifth   "   -
    (e) Sixth   "   -
    (f) Seventh   "   -
    (g) Eighth   "
    (h) High School,   -   -   -   -   -
17. Number of graduates from the common branches and receiving diplomas,
    Male,......................; female, ... ; total,... . ..
18. Number of graduates from non-commissioned township high schools,
    Male,......................; female,........................; total,........ ... .
19. Number of graduates from commissioned township high schools,
    Male,......................; female,........................; total,........
20. How many books in school library (not including reading circle books) at beginning of year?
21. How many books were added to library (not including reading circle books) during year?
22. Total now in school library (not including reading circle books),   -   -   -   -
23. How many reading circle books were added during year?   -   -   -   -
24. How many pupils read one or more school library or reading circle books during year?   -
25. Do patrons read school library books?
26. Number of visits to school,   Parents,......................; officials, ...; others, ... ; total, ...
27. Number of teachers employed (if school be high school), Male,..................; female, ...; total,................. ...
28. Number of days teacher attended township institute,   -   -
29. Books and apparatus left in school room at end of term,   -   -   -   -

I,... . .. ., do solemnly swear that the above report is true to the best of my knowledge and belief.

{ Teacher.
.... { Principal.

NOTES:—

*(1.) After three days of absence the pupil should be withdrawn, and his absence counted no more for that period of absence. After being withdrawn, he is not a pupil of the school, and can not be again until he is re-entered, as in item 6.

†(14.) To find average daily attendance divide the whole number of days of attendance made by all the pupils by the number of days of school taught.

Teacher's or Principal's Report to Township Trustee.

NOTE.—This report must be made by each teacher having charge of the attendance of pupils. A high school teacher who works under the direction of a principal will not need to make the report in case the principal reports for the entire high school. In graded grammar schools each teacher should report for the pupils directly under his charge. The principal of a graded grammar school should report only for the pupils directly under his charge.

REPORT of .... { teacher } of .... District
{ principal }

WASHINGTON TOWNSHIP, PORTER COUNTY, INDIANA,

to the Township Trustee, for the school term beginning .... and

closing ...

FOR ALL TEACHERS WHO HAVE CHARGE OF ATTENDANCE OF PUPILS.

1. Number of days school was in session,
2. "   " pupils enrolled during year, -   Male, ...; female, ...; total, ...
3. "   "   " withdrawn during year, -   -   "   "   "
4. "   "   " suspended   "   "   -   "   "   "
5. "   "   " expelled   "   "   -   "   "   "
6. "   "   " re-entered   "   "   -   "   "   "
7. "   "   " remaining in school close of year, "   "   "
8. "   "   " neither tardy nor absent during year, "   "   "
9. "   " cases of tardiness during year, -   "   "   "
10. "   " pupils tardy during year, -   -   "   "   "
11. Total days of attendance by all pupils for year, -   -   -   -
12. " "   "   " absence   "   "   "   "
13. Total cases of tardiness, ...   Time lost by tardiness,
14. †Average daily attendance for year, -   -   -   -
15. Per cent. of attendance—11÷(11+12),
16. Number of pupils promoted to   -   -   -   -
       (a) Second year, -   -   -   -
       (b) Third   "   -
       (c) Fourth   "   -   -   -   -
       (d) Fifth   "   -   -   -   -
       (e) Sixth   "
       (f) Seventh   "   -
       (g) Eighth   "
       (h) High School, -   -   -   -
17. Number of graduates from the common branches and receiving diplomas,
       Male, ...; female, ...; total, ...
18. Number of graduates from non-commissioned township high schools,
       Male, ...; female, ...; total, ...
19. Number of graduates from commissioned township high schools,
       Male, ...; female, ...; total, ...
20. How many books in school library (not including reading circle books) at beginning of year?
21. How many books were added to library (not including reading circle books) during year?
22. Total now in school library (not including reading circle books),   -   -   -   -
23. How many reading circle books were added during year?   -   -   -   -
24. How many pupils read one or more school library or reading circle books during year?   -
25. Do patrons read school library books?   -   -   -   -   -
26. Number of visits to school,   Parents, ...; officials, ...; others, ...; total, ...
27. Number of teachers employed (if school be high school), Male, ...; female, ...; total, ...
28. Number of days teacher attended township institute,   -   -   -   -   -
29. Books and apparatus left in school room at end of term,   -   -   -   -   -

I, ..., do solemnly swear that the above report is true to the best of my knowledge and belief.

                               { Teacher.
...., { Principal.

NOTES:—

  *(1.) After three days of absence the pupil should be withdrawn, and his absence counted no more for that period of absence. After being withdrawn, he is not a pupil of the school, and can not be again until he is re-entered, as in item 6.

  †(2.) To find average daily attendance divide the whole number of days of attendance made by all the pupils by the number of days of school taught.

For Township Trustees.   Wade Bros. & Wise, Printers

TEACHER'S CONTRACT.

This Agreement, Between *S M Green*   School Trustee of

Washington School Township, in Porter County, and State of Indiana,

of the first part, and *Bessie Finney* ... _a legally qualified teacher in said

County of the second part, certifies that the said teacher hereby agrees to teach the public school in District No.......,

Grade........., in said Township, for the term commencing on the _20 20/_ day of _Sept_ ..

A. D. 1_90/_, for the consideration of _Two_ Dollars and

Twenty Cents per { day, { to be paid _(State here when all or parts of salary will be paid.)_
year, }

The said _Bessie Finney_ _further agrees faithfully to perform

all the duties of teacher in said school; using only such text-books as are prescribed by the Trustees in accordance with
the law, except supplementary reading, such as Young People's Reading Circle books, etc., and other works recommended by the County Superintendent, and observing all Rules and Regulations of the County Board of Education,
and all instructions of the County Superintendent of Schools; that _s_ he will attend and participate in the exercises of
each Institute or other teachers' meetings that may be appointed for the teachers of said township, or for each day's
absence therefrom, forfeit a sum equal to one day's wages, unless such absence shall be occasioned by sickness, that
_s_ he will accurately keep and use all registers and blanks placed in _her_ hands by said Trustee; that _s_ he will
make a complete and accurate report at the close of the school term, the blank for which is provided on the back of
this sheet; that _s_ he will make all other reports required of _her_ by said Trustee, the County Superintendent, or
the laws of Indiana, at the proper time and manner and in good order; that ......he will exercise due diligence in the
preservation of school buildings, grounds, furniture, apparatus, books, blanks and other school property committed to
she care, and turn the same over to the Trustee, or his representative, at the close of the term of school, in as
good condition as when received, damage and wear by use excepted.

The said School Trustee agrees to keep the school buildings in good repair, and to furnish the necessary fuel
furniture, apparatus, books and blanks, and such other appliances as may be necessary for the systematic and proper
conduct of said school.

And the said School Trustee, for and in behalf of said Township, further agrees to pay the said......................
Bessie Finney for services as teacher of said school, either a sum equal to the whole
number of days taught at the rate of the above named sum per day, as agreed upon, or the salary for the year in the
event of a yearly consideration, as agreed upon, when the said teacher shall have filled all the stipulations of this contract

The said School Trustee further agrees to pay said teacher one day's wages for each day's attendance at the Township Institute, according to the Acts of 1889.

PROVIDED, That in case the said_Bessie Finney_should be
dismissed from said school by said Trustee, or his successor in office, for incompetency, cruelty, gross immorality
neglect of business, or a violation of any of the stipulations of this contract, or in case ....license should be
annulled by the County Superintendent or State Superintendent, ...he shall not be entitled to any compensation after
notice of dismissal, or notice of annulment of license.

PROVIDED FURTHER, That the teacher shall have a duplicate of this Contract.

IN WITNESS WHEREOF, We have hereunto subscribed our names, this_27th_

day of _Aug_ A. D. 1_90/_

Bessie Finney.Teacher

S M Green.School Trustee

NOTES:—
(1.) Full authority is given the Trustee to substitute the words "principal," "supervisor" or "superintendent" for the word "teacher"
in the event the Contract should be so made.
(2.) This Contract is the official blank, made by the State Superintendent of Public Instruction, under the provisions of H. B. No. 13
Acts of 1899.

Teacher's or Principal's Report to Township Trustee.

NOTE.—This report must be made by each teacher having charge of the attendance of pupils. A high school teacher who works under the direction of a principal will not need to make the report in case the principal reports for the entire high school. In graded grammar schools each teacher should report for the pupils directly under his charge. The principal of a graded grammar school should report only for the pupils directly under his charge.

REPORT of................................ .... { teacher } { principal } of........................District

WASHINGTON TOWNSHIP, PORTER COUNTY, INDIANA,

to the Township Trustee, for the school term beginning..and

closing ...: ....

FOR ALL TEACHERS WHO HAVE CHARGE OF ATTENDANCE OF PUPILS.

1. Number of days school was in session,　-　-　-　-　-　-　-　-　-
2. "　" pupils enrolled during year,　-　Male, ...; female,....................; total,.............
3. "　"　" withdrawn during year, -　-　"　"　"
4. "　"　" suspended　"　"　-　-　"　"　"
5. "　"　" expelled　"　"　-　"　"　"
6. "　"　" re-entered　"　"　-　"　"　"
7. "　"　" remaining in school close of year, "　"　"
8. "　"　" neither tardy nor absent during year, "　"　"
9. "　" cases of tardiness during year,　-　"　"　"
10. "　" pupils tardy during year,　-　-　"　"　"
11. Total days of attendance by all pupils for year,　-　-　-　-　-
12. * "　"　" absence　"　"　"　"　"　-　-　-　-
13. Total cases of tardiness,.......................　Time lost by tardiness,　-　-　-　.........
14. †Average daily attendance for year,　-　-　-　-　-
15. Per cent. of attendance—11÷(11+12),　-　-　-
16. Number of pupils promoted to　-　-　-　-　-　-
     (a) Second year,　-　-　-　-　-　-
     (b) Third　"　-　-　-　-　-
     (c) Fourth　"　-　-　-　-　-
     (d) Fifth　"　-　-　-　-　-
     (e) Sixth　"　-　-　-　-　-
     (f) Seventh　"　-　-　-
     (g) Eighth　"　-　-　-　-
     (h) High School,　-　-　-　-
17. Number of graduates from the common branches and receiving diplomas,
     Male,......................; female,......................; total,................
18. Number of graduates from non-commissioned township high schools,
     Male,......................; female,......................; total,................
19. Number of graduates from commissioned township high schools,
     Male,......................; female,......................; total,................
20. How many books in school library (not including reading circle books) at beginning of year?
21. How many books were added to library (not including reading circle books) during year?
22. Total now in school library (not including reading circle books),　-　-　-　-　-
23. How many reading circle books were added during year?　-　-　-　-
24. How many pupils read one or more school library or reading circle books during year?　-
25. Do patrons read school library books?　-　-　-　-　-　-
26. Number of visits to school,　Parents,......................; officials,....................; others,.................; total,................
27. Number of teachers employed (if school be high school), Male,....................; female,..............; total,................
28. Number of days teacher attended township institute,　-　-　-　-　-
29. Books and apparatus left in school room at end of term,　-　-　-

I,.., do solemnly swear that the above report is true to the best of my knowledge and belief.

{ Teacher.
....{ Principal.

NOTES:—

*(1.) After three days of absence the pupil should be withdrawn, and his absence counted no more for that period of absence. After being withdrawn, he is not a pupil of the school, and can not be again until he is re-entered, as in item 6.

†(2.) To find average daily attendance divide the whole number of days of attendance made by all the pupils by the number of days of school taught.

TEACHER'S CONTRACT.

This Agreement, Between _L M Gun_ .... School Trustee of

Washington School Township, in Porter County, and State of Indiana,

of the first part, and ..... _Mann Louderback_ a legally qualified teacher in said County of the second part, certifies that the said teacher hereby agrees to teach the public school in District No....... , Grade ..... , in said Township, for the term commencing on the _2nd_ day of _Sept_ A. D. 190_ , for the consideration of .... _Two_ .. Dollars and _Twenty Two_ Cents per { day, / year, } to be paid .... (State here when all or parts of salary will be paid.)

The said ..... _Mann Louderback_ ..... further agrees faithfully to perform all the duties of teacher in said school; using only such text-books as are prescribed by the Trustees in accordance with the law, except supplementary reading, such as Young People's Reading Circle books, etc., and other works recommended by the County Superintendent, and observing all Rules and Regulations of the County Board of Education, and all instructions of the County Superintendent of Schools; that _s_he will attend and participate in the exercises of each Institute or other teachers' meetings that may be appointed for the teachers of said township, or for each day's absence therefrom, forfeit a sum equal to one day's wages, unless such absence shall be occasioned by sickness, that _s_he will accurately keep and use all registers and blanks placed in _her_ hands by said Trustee; that _ he will make a complete and accurate report at the close of the school term, the blank for which is provided on the back of this sheet; that _s_he will make all other reports required of _her_ by said Trustee, the County Superintendent, or the laws of Indiana, at the proper time and manner and in good order; that _s_he will exercise due diligence in the preservation of school buildings, grounds, furniture, apparatus, books, blanks and other school property committed to care, and turn the same over to the Trustee, or his representative, at the close of the term of school, in as good condition as when received, damage and wear by use excepted.

The said School Trustee agrees to keep the school buildings in good repair, and to furnish the necessary fuel, furniture, apparatus, books and blanks, and such other appliances as may be necessary for the systematic and proper conduct of said school.

And the said School Trustee, for and in behalf of said Township, further agrees to pay the said .... _Mann Louderback_ for services as teacher of said school, either a sum equal to the whole number of days taught at the rate of the above named sum per day, as agreed upon, or the salary for the year in the event of a yearly consideration, as agreed upon, when the said teacher shall have filled all the stipulations of this contract.

The said School Trustee further agrees to pay said teacher one day's wages for each day's attendance at the Township Institute, according to the Acts of 1889.

PROVIDED), That in case the said _Mann Louderback_ ....should be dismissed from said school by said Trustee, or his successor in office, for incompetency, cruelty, gross immorality, neglect of business, or a violation of any of the stipulations of this contract, or in case _her_ license should be annulled by the County Superintendent or State Superintendent, _s_he shall not be entitled to any compensation after notice of dismissal, or notice of annulment of license.

PROVIDED FURTHER, That the teacher shall have a duplicate of this Contract.

IN WITNESS WHEREOF, We have hereunto subscribed our names, this _27th_ day of _Aug_ A. D. 190_

Mames Louderback ....Teacher.

L M Gun .... School Trustee.

NOTES:—
(1.) Full authority is given the Trustee to substitute the words "principal," "supervisor" or "superintendent" for the word "teacher" in the event the Contract should be so made.
(2.) This Contract is the official blank, made by the State Superintendent of Public Instruction, under the provisions of H. B. No. 139. Acts of 1899.

Teacher's or Principal's Report to Township Trustee.

NOTE.—This report must be made by each teacher having charge of the attendance of pupils. A high school teacher who works under the direction of a principal will not need to make the report in case the principal reports for the entire high school. In graded grammar schools each teacher should report for the pupils directly under his charge. The principal of a graded grammar school should report only for the pupils directly under his charge.

REPORT of.................... ....—...... { teacher } of...........................District
..............—....... { principal }

WASHINGTON TOWNSHIP, PORTER COUNTY, INDIANA,

to the Township Trustee, for the school term beginning.................... .. ..and

closing ....

FOR ALL TEACHERS WHO HAVE CHARGE OF ATTENDANCE OF PUPILS.

1. Number of days school was in session, - . . . .
2. " " pupils enrolled during year, - Male, ...; female,.....................; total,..................... ...
3. " " " withdrawn during year, - - " " "
4. " " " suspended " " . - " " "
5. " " " expelled " " . " " "
6. " " " re-entered " " . " " "
7. " " " remaining in school close of year, " " "
8. " " " " neither tardy nor absent during year, " " "
9. " " cases of tardiness during year, - " " "
10. " " pupils tardy during year, - - " " "
11. Total days of attendance by all pupils for year, - . . . - . .
12. * " " " absence " " " " " . - . - . .
13. Total cases of tardiness,................... Time lost by tardiness, - . ... .. - . .
14. †Average daily attendance for year, ...
15. Per cent. of attendance—$11 \div (11 + 12)$, . . .
16. Number of pupils promoted to - . . . . . .
    - (a) Second year, - . . . . . .
    - (b) Third " - . . . . .
    - (c) Fourth " - . . . . . .
    - (d) Fifth " - . . . . . .
    - (e) Sixth " . . . . . .
    - (f) Seventh " - . . . . .
    - (g) Eighth " . . . . . .
    - (h) High School, - . . . . .
17. Number of graduates from the common branches and receiving diplomas,
    Male,................; female,.................; total,... . ..   ...
18. Number of graduates from non-commissioned township high schools,
    Male,................; female,............; total,.............. .....
19. Number of graduates from commissioned township high schools,
    Male,.................; female,.................; total,..........
20. How many books in school library (not including reading circle books) at beginning of year?
21. How many books were added to library (not including reading circle books) during year?
22. Total now in school library (not including reading circle books), - . - . .
23. How many reading circle books were added during year? - . . . .
24. How many pupils read one or more school library or reading circle books during year? - ....
25. Do patrons read school library books? - . - . . .
26. Number of visits to school, Parents,.................; officials,................; others, ...; total, ...
27. Number of teachers employed (if school be high school), Male,...... ; female,...............; total, ...
28. Number of days teacher attended township institute, - . . . .
29. Books and apparatus left in school room at end of term, - . - ....

I,.. .. . ., do solemnly swear that the above report is true to the best of my knowledge and belief.

.... { Teacher.
{ Principal.

NOTES:—
*(1.) After three days of absence the pupil should be withdrawn, and his absence counted no more for that period of absence. After being withdrawn, he is not a pupil of the school, and can not be again until he is re-entered, as in item 6.
†(2.) To find average daily attendance divide the whole number of days of attendance made by all the pupils by the number of days of school taught.

For Township Trustees.   Wade Bros. & Wise, Printers.

TEACHER'S CONTRACT.

This Agreement, Between _J. W. Green_ ....School Trustee of

Washington School Township, in Porter County, and State of Indiana,

of the first part, and _Cora Benham_ a legally qualified teacher in said
County of the second part, certifies that the said teacher hereby agrees to teach the public school in District No.......
Grade ...., in said Township, for the term commencing on the _8th_ day of _Sept_
A. D. 1_902_ , for the consideration of ...._Two_................, Dollars and
......._Thirty_.......... Cents per { day, { year, } to be paid _when called for_
(State here when all or parts of salary will be paid.)

The said ...._Cora Benham_............further agrees faithfully to perform
all the duties of teacher in said school; using only such text-books as are prescribed by the Trustees in accordance with
the law, except supplementary reading, such as Young People's Reading Circle books, etc., and other works recommended by the County Superintendent, and observing all Rules and Regulations of the County Board of Education,
and all instructions of the County Superintendent of Schools; that _she_ he will attend and participate in the exercises of
each Institute or other teachers' meetings that may be appointed for the teachers of said township, or for each day's
absence therefrom, forfeit a sum equal to one day's wages, unless such absence shall be occasioned by sickness, that
...... he will accurately keep and use all registers and blanks placed in _her_ hands by said Trustee; that _she_ will
make a complete and accurate report at the close of the school term, the blank for which is provided on the back of
this sheet; that ... .he will make all other reports required of _her_ , by said Trustee, the County Superintendent, or
the laws of Indiana, at the proper time and manner and in good order; that _she_ will exercise due diligence in the
preservation of school buildings, grounds, furniture, apparatus, books, blanks and other school property committed to
her ... care, and turn the same over to the Trustee, or his representative, at the close of the term of school, in as
good condition as when received, damage and wear by use excepted.

The said School Trustee agrees to keep the school buildings in good repair, and to furnish the necessary fuel,
furniture, apparatus, books and blanks, and such other appliances as may be necessary for the systematic and proper
conduct of said school.

And the said School Trustee, for and in behalf of said Township, further agrees to pay the said ......
................for services as teacher of said school, either a sum equal to the whole
number of days taught at the rate of the above named sum per day, as agreed upon, or the salary for the year in the
event of a yearly consideration, as agreed upon, when the said teacher shall have filled all the stipulations of this contract.

The said School Trustee further agrees to pay said teacher one day's wages for each day's attendance at the Township Institute, according to the Acts of 1889.

PROVIDED, That in case the said _Cora Benham_ should be
dismissed from said school by said Trustee, or his successor in office, for incompetency, cruelty, gross immorality,
neglect of business, or a violation of any of the stipulations of this contract, or in case _her_ license should be
annulled by the County Superintendent or State Superintendent, ... he shall not be entitled to any compensation after
notice of dismissal, or notice of annulment of license.

PROVIDED FURTHER, That the teacher shall have a duplicate of this Contract.

IN WITNESS WHEREOF, We have hereunto subscribed our names, this ......
day of ......_Sept_ A. D. 1_902_

Cora Benham ...... Teacher.

J. W. Green .... School Trustee.

NOTES:—
  (1.) Full authority is given the Trustee to substitute the words "principal," "supervisor" or "superintendent" for the word "teacher"
in the event the Contract should be so made.
  (2.) This Contract is the official blank, made by the State Superintendent of Public Instruction, under the provisions of H. B. No. 139,
Acts of 1899.

Teacher's or Principal's Report to Township Trustee.

NOTE.—This report must be made by each teacher having charge of the attendance of pupils. A high school teacher who works under the direction of a principal will not need to make the report in case the principal reports for the entire high school. In graded grammar schools each teacher should report for the pupils directly under his charge. The principal of a graded grammar school should report only for the pupils directly under his charge.

REPORT of.................... .... { teacher }
                                                              .... { principal } of.............................District

WASHINGTON TOWNSHIP, PORTER COUNTY, INDIANA,

to the Township Trustee, for the school term beginning.............. ....and

closing ....: ....

FOR ALL TEACHERS WHO HAVE CHARGE OF ATTENDANCE OF PUPILS.

1. Number of days school was in session,   -   -   -   -   -   -   -   -   -   -
2.   "   " pupils enrolled during year,   -   Male, ...; female,....................; total,.................. ...
3.   "   "   " withdrawn during year, -   -   "   "   -   -   "   "
4.   "   "   " suspended   "   "   -   - "   "   .... "   "
5.   "   "   " expelled   "   "   -   - "   "   "   "
6.   "   "   " re-entered   "   "   -   "   "   "   "
7.   "   "   " remaining in school close of year, "   "   "   "
8.   "   "   " " neither tardy nor absent during year, "   "   "   "
9.   "   " cases of tardiness during year,   -   "   "   .... "   "
10.   "   " pupils tardy during year,   -   - "   .... "   "
11. Total days of attendance by all pupils for year,   -   -   -   -   -   -
12. * "   "   " absence   "   "   "   "   "   -   -   -   -   -
13. Total cases of tardiness, ...   Time lost by tardiness,   -   -   ... .
14. †Average daily attendance for year,   -   -   -   -   -   -
15. Per cent. of attendance—11÷(11+12),   -   -   -   -   -   -
16. Number of pupils promoted to   -   -   -   -   -   -   -
      (a) Second year,   -   -   -   -   -   -
      (b) Third   "   -   -   -   -   -   -
      (c) Fourth   "   -   -   -   -   -   ....
      (d) Fifth   "   -   -   -   -   -   ....
      (e) Sixth   "   -   -   -   -   -   ....
      (f) Seventh   "   -   -   -   -   -   -
      (g) Eighth   "   -   -   -   -   -
      (h) High School,   -   -   -   -   -   -   ....
17. Number of graduates from the common branches and receiving diplomas,
                        Male,.................; female, ...; total,.... ...   ...
18. Number of graduates from non-commissioned township high schools,
                        Male,.................; female,....................; total,.................
19. Number of graduates from commissioned township high schools,
                        Male,.................; female,....................; total,.............
20. How many books in school library (not including reading circle books) at beginning of year?
21. How many books were added to library (not including reading circle books) during year?
22. Total now in school library (not including reading circle books),   -   -   -   -
23. How many reading circle books were added during year?   -   -   -   -   ....
24. How many pupils read one or more school library or reading circle books during year?   -   ....
25. Do patrons read school library books?   ....
26. Number of visits to school,   Parents,....................; officials, ...; others, ...; total, ...
27. Number of teachers employed (if school be high school), Male,...............; female, ...; total,................ .. ..
28. Number of days teacher attended township institute,   -   -   -   -   -   -
29. Books and apparatus left in school room at end of term,   -   -   -   -   ....

I,... ... ., do solemnly swear that the above report is
true to the best of my knowledge and belief.
                                                      { Teacher.
.... { Principal.

NOTES:—
  *(1.) After three days of absence the pupil should be withdrawn, and his absence counted no more for that period of absence. After being withdrawn, he is not a pupil of the school, and can not be again until he is re-entered, as in item 6.
  †(2.) To find average daily attendance divide the whole number of days of attendance made by all the pupils by the number of days of school taught.

TEACHER'S CONTRACT.

This Agreement, Between _T. A. Ulfsen_ .... School Trustee of

Washington School Township, in Porter County, and State of Indiana,

of the first part, and _Ethel Collins_ .... a legally qualified teacher in said

County of the second part, certifies that the said teacher hereby agrees to teach the public school in District No. ....

Grade .... , in said Township, for the term commencing on the _4th_ day of _Sept_

A. D. _1902_ , for the consideration of _Two_ .... Dollars and

twenty Cents per { day, year, } to be paid _when called for_
(State here when all or parts of salary will be paid.)

The said _Ethel Collins_ ....further agrees faithfully to perform
all the duties of teacher in said school; using only such text-books as are prescribed by the Trustees in accordance with
the law, except supplementary reading, such as Young People's Reading Circle books, etc., and other works recommended by the County Superintendent, and observing all Rules and Regulations of the County Board of Education,
and all instructions of the County Superintendent of Schools; that _she_ will attend and participate in the exercises of
each Institute or other teachers' meetings that may be appointed for the teachers of said township, or for each day's
absence therefrom, forfeit a sum equal to one day's wages, unless such absence shall be occasioned by sickness, that
she will accurately keep and use all registers and blanks placed in _her_ hands by said Trustee; that _she_ will
make a complete and accurate report at the close of the school term, the blank for which is provided on the back of
this sheet; that _she_ will make all other reports required of _her_ by said Trustee, the County Superintendent, or
the laws of Indiana, at the proper time and manner and in good order; that ......he will exercise due diligence in the
preservation of school buildings, grounds, furniture, apparatus, books, blanks and other school property committed to
her care, and turn the same over to the Trustee, or his representative, at the close of the term of school, in as
good condition as when received, damage and wear by use excepted.

The said School Trustee agrees to keep the school buildings in good repair, and to furnish the necessary fuel,
furniture, apparatus, books and blanks, and such other appliances as may be necessary for the systematic and proper
conduct of said school.

And the said School Trustee, for and in behalf of said Township, further agrees to pay the said........ ....
....for services as teacher of said school, either a sum equal to the whole
number of days taught at the rate of the above named sum per day, as agreed upon, or the salary for the year in the
event of a yearly consideration, as agreed upon, when the said teacher shall have filled all the stipulations of this contract.

The said School Trustee further agrees to pay said teacher one day's wages for each day's attendance at the Township Institute, according to the Acts of 1889.

PROVIDED, That in case the said _Ethel Collins_ ....should be
dismissed from said school by said Trustee, or his successor in office, for incompetency, cruelty, gross immorality,
neglect of business, or a violation of any of the stipulations of this contract, or in case _her_ license should be
annulled by the County Superintendent or State Superintendent, _s_he shall not be entitled to any compensation after
notice of dismissal, or notice of annulment of license.

PROVIDED FURTHER, That the teacher shall have a duplicate of this Contract.

IN WITNESS WHEREOF, We have hereunto subscribed our names, this......_4th_
day of......_Sept_ A. D. 1_802_

Ethel Collins ....Teacher.

T. A. Ulfsen ....School Trustee.

NOTES:—
(1.) Full authority is given the Trustee to substitute the words "principal," "supervisor" or "superintendent" for the word "teacher"
in the event the Contract should be so made.
(2.) This Contract is the official blank, made by the State Superintendent of Public Instruction, under the provisions of H. B. No. 139,
Acts of 1899.

Teacher's or Principal's Report to Township Trustee.

NOTE.—This report must be made by each teacher having charge of the attendance of pupils. A high school teacher who works under the direction of a principal will not need to make the report in case the principal reports for the entire high school. In graded grammar schools each teacher should report for the pupils directly under his charge. The principal of a graded grammar school should report only for the pupils directly under his charge.

REPORT of................................ .... { teacher } { principal } of....................District

WASHINGTON TOWNSHIP, PORTER COUNTY, INDIANA,

to the Township Trustee, for the school term beginning...and

closing ....

FOR ALL TEACHERS WHO HAVE CHARGE OF ATTENDANCE OF PUPILS.

1. Number of days school was in session, - - - - - - - - -
2. "   " pupils enrolled during year,   - Male, ...; female,....................; total,.............
3. "   "   " withdrawn during year, - - "   "   "
4. "   "   " suspended   "   "   - - "   "   "
5. "   "   " expelled   "   "   - - "   "   "
6. "   "   " re-entered   "   "   - "   "   "
7. "   "   " remaining in school close of year, "   "   "
8. "   "   " neither tardy nor absent during year, "   "   "
9. "   " cases of tardiness during year,   - "   "   "
10. "   " pupils tardy during year,   - - "   ....   "   "
11. Total days of attendance by all pupils for year, - - - -
12. * "   "   " absence   "   "   "   "   " - - - -
13. Total cases of tardiness, ... Time lost by tardiness, - -
14. †Average daily attendance for year, - - - -
15. Per cent. of attendance—11÷(11+12), - -
16. Number of pupils promoted to - - - - -
    (a) Second year, - - -
    (b) Third " - - - -
    (c) Fourth " - - - -
    (d) Fifth " - - - -
    (e) Sixth " - - - -
    (f) Seventh " - - - -
    (g) Eighth " - - - -
    (h) High School, - - - -
17. Number of graduates from the common branches and receiving diplomas,
    Male, ...; female, ...; total, ...
18. Number of graduates from non-commissioned township high schools,
    Male, ...; female, ...; total, ...
19. Number of graduates from commissioned township high schools,
    Male, ...; female, ...; total, ...
20. How many books in school library (not including reading circle books) at beginning of year?
21. How many books were added to library (not including reading circle books) during year?
22. Total now in school library (not including reading circle books), - - - -
23. How many reading circle books were added during year? - - - -
24. How many pupils read one or more school library or reading circle books during year? -
25. Do patrons read school library books? - - - - -
26. Number of visits to school, Parents,....................; officials, ...; others, ...; total, ...
27. Number of teachers employed (if school be high school), Male,...................; female, ...; total, ...
28. Number of days teacher attended township institute, - - - - -
29. Books and apparatus left in school room at end of term, - - -

I,..., do solemnly swear that the above report is true to the best of my knowledge and belief.

{ Teacher.
.... { Principal.

NOTES:—
*(1.) After three days of absence the pupil should be withdrawn, and his absence counted no more for that period of absence. After being withdrawn, he is not a pupil of the school, and can not be again until he is re-entered, as in item 6.
†(2.) To find average daily attendance divide the whole number of days of attendance made by all the pupils by the number of days of school taught.

TEACHER'S CONTRACT.

This Agreement, Between _J. McGleer_ _____ School Trustee of

Washington School Township, In Porter County, and State of Indiana,

of the first part, and _Mame Louderback_ a legally qualified teacher in said

County of the second part, certifies that the said teacher hereby agrees to teach the public school in District No. ____,

Grade ____, in said Township, for the term commencing on the _8th_ day of _Sept_

A. D. 1 _9.0.2_ , for the consideration of _Two_ _____ Dollars and

twenty five Cents per { day, { year, } to be paid _when called for_
(State here when all or parts of salary will be paid.)

The said _Mame Louderback_ further agrees faithfully to perform
all the duties of teacher in said school; using only such text-books as are prescribed by the Trustees in accordance with
the law, except supplementary reading, such as Young People's Reading Circle books, etc., and other works recommended by the County Superintendent, and observing all Rules and Regulations of the County Board of Education,
and all instructions of the County Superintendent of Schools; that _she_ will attend and participate in the exercises of
each Institute or other teachers' meetings that may be appointed for the teachers of said township, or for each day's
absence therefrom, forfeit a sum equal to one day's wages, unless such absence shall be occasioned by sickness, that
_s_ he will accurately keep and use all registers and blanks placed in _his_ hands by said Trustee; that _he_ will
make a complete and accurate report at the close of the school term, the blank for which is provided on the back of
this sheet; that _s_ he will make all other reports required of _her_ by said Trustee, the County Superintendent, or
the laws of Indiana, at the proper time and manner and in good order; that _s_ he will exercise due diligence in the
preservation of school buildings, grounds, furniture, apparatus, books, blanks and other school property committed to
her care, and turn the same over to the Trustee, or his representative, at the close of the term of school, in as
good condition as when received, damage and wear by use excepted.

The said School Trustee agrees to keep the school buildings in good repair, and to furnish the necessary fuel,
furniture, apparatus, books and blanks, and such other appliances as may be necessary for the systematic and proper
conduct of said school.

And the said School Trustee, for and in behalf of said Township, further agrees to pay the said _____ _____
_____ for services as teacher of said school, either a sum equal to the whole
number of days taught at the rate of the above named sum per day, as agreed upon, or the salary for the year in the
event of a yearly consideration, as agreed upon, when the said teacher shall have filled all the stipulations of this contract.

The said School Trustee further agrees to pay said teacher one day's wages for each day's attendance at the Township Institute, according to the Acts of 1889.

PROVIDED, That in case the said _Mame Louderback_ _____ should be
dismissed from said school by said Trustee, or his successor in office, for incompetency, cruelty, gross immorality,
neglect of business, or a violation of any of the stipulations of this contract, or in case _her_ license should be
annulled by the County Superintendent or State Superintendent, _s_ he shall not be entitled to any compensation after
notice of dismissal, or notice of annulment of license.

PROVIDED FURTHER, That the teacher shall have a duplicate of this Contract.

IN WITNESS WHEREOF, We have hereunto subscribed our names, this _4th_
_____ day of _Sept_ _____ A. D. 1 _902_ _____

Mame Louderback ___ Teacher.

J. McGleer _____ School Trustee.

NOTES:—
    (1.) Full authority is given the Trustee to substitute the words "principal," "supervisor" or "superintendent" for the word "teacher"
in the event the Contract should be so made.
    (2.) This Contract is the official blank, made by the State Superintendent of Public Instruction, under the provisions of H. B. No. 139,
Acts of 1899.

Teacher's or Principal's Report to Township Trustee.

NOTE.—This report must be made by each teacher having charge of the attendance of pupils. A high school teacher who works under the direction of a principal will not need to make the report in case the principal reports for the entire high school. In graded grammar schools each teacher should report for the pupils directly under his charge. The principal of a graded grammar school should report only for the pupils directly under his charge.

REPORT of.................. .... } teacher } of.......................District
{ principal {

WASHINGTON TOWNSHIP, PORTER COUNTY, INDIANA,

to the Township Trustee, for the school term beginning.... ....and

closing ....: ....

FOR ALL TEACHERS WHO HAVE CHARGE OF ATTENDANCE OF PUPILS.

1. Number of days school was in session,   -   -   -   -   -   -   -   -   -   -
2. " " pupils enrolled during year,   -   Male, ...; female,....................; total,................. ...
3. " " " withdrawn during year, -   -   "   "   "
4. " " " suspended " "   -   - "   "   "
5. " " " expelled " "   -   "   "   "
6. " " " re-entered " "   -   "   "   "
7. " " " remaining in school close of year, "   "   "
8. " " " neither tardy nor absent during year, "   "   "
9. " " cases of tardiness during year,   -   "   "   "
10. " " pupils tardy during year,   -   - "   "   "
11. Total days of attendance by all pupils for year,   -   -   -   -   -   -   -
12. * " " " absence " " " " "   -   -   -   -   -
13. Total cases of tardiness,................. Time lost by tardiness,   -   -   -   ... .. - .. -
14. †Average daily attendance for year,   -   -   -   -   -   -   -
15. Per cent. of attendance—11÷(11+12),   -   -   -   -
16. Number of pupils promoted to   -   -   -   -   -   -   -
    (a) Second year,   -   -   -   -   -   -
    (b) Third "   -   -   -   -   -   -
    (c) Fourth "   -   -   -   -   -   -
    (d) Fifth "   -   -   -   -   -   -
    (e) Sixth "   -   -   -   -   -   -
    (f) Seventh "   -   -   -   -   -   -
    (g) Eighth "   -   -   -   -   -   -
    (h) High School,   -   -   -   -   -   -
17. Number of graduates from the common branches and receiving diplomas,
    Male,...............; female, ...; total,... .. ...
18. Number of graduates from non-commissioned township high schools,
    Male,...............; female,................; total,............ ... .
19. Number of graduates from commissioned township high schools,
    Male,...............; female,...............; total,.......
20. How many books in school library (not including reading circle books) at beginning of year?
21. How many books were added to library (not including reading circle books) during year?
22. Total now in school library (not including reading circle books),   -   -   -   -
23. How many reading circle books were added during year?   -   -   -   ....
24. How many pupils read one or more school library or reading circle books during year?   -   ....
25. Do patrons read school library books?   -   -   -   ....
26. Number of visits to school,   Parents,................; officials, ...; others, ...; total, ...
27. Number of teachers employed (if school be high school), Male,................; female, ...; total,............ .. ..
28. Number of days teacher attended township institute,   -   -   -   -   -
29. Books and apparatus left in school room at end of term, -   -   -   -   ....

I,................ ...., do solemnly swear that the above report is true to the best of my knowledge and belief.

.... { Teacher.
{ Principal.

NOTES:—
*(1.) After three days of absence the pupil should be withdrawn, and his absence counted no more for that period of absence. After being withdrawn, he is not a pupil of the school, and can not be again until he is re-entered, as in item 6.
†(2.) To find average daily attendance divide the whole number of days of attendance made by all the pupils by the number of days of school taught.

25 A

TEACHER'S CONTRACT.

This Agreement, Between _JW Ween_ ....School Trustee of

Washington School Township, in Porter County, and State of Indiana,

of the first part, and _Bessie Finny_ ....a legally qualified teacher in said County of the second part, certifies that the said teacher hereby agrees to teach the public school in District No. . Grade........, in said Township, for the term commencing on the _8th_ day of _Sep_ A. D. 1 _90_ , for the consideration of _two_ ....Dollars and _Twenty five_ .Cents per { day, year, } to be paid _when called for_ (State here when all or parts of salary will be paid).

The said _Bessie Finny_ ....further agrees faithfully to perform all the duties of teacher in said school; using only such text-books as are prescribed by the Trustees in accordance with the law, except supplementary reading, such as Young People's Reading Circle books, etc., and other works recommended by the County Superintendent, and observing all Rules and Regulations of the County Board of Education, and all instructions of the County Superintendent of Schools; that _A_ he will attend and participate in the exercises of each Institute or other teachers' meetings that may be appointed for the teachers of said township, or for each day's absence therefrom, forfeit a sum equal to one day's wages, unless such absence shall be occasioned by sickness; that _A_ he will accurately keep and use all registers and blanks placed in _her_ hands by said Trustee; that _S_ he will make a complete and accurate report at the close of the school term, the blank for which is provided on the back of this sheet; that _A_ he will make all other reports required of _her_ by said Trustee, the County Superintendent, or the laws of Indiana, at the proper time and manner and in good order; that ......he will exercise due diligence in the preservation of school buildings, grounds, furniture, apparatus, books, blanks and other school property committed to _her_ care, and turn the same over to the Trustee, or his representative, at the close of the term of school, in as good condition as when received, damage and wear by use excepted.

The said School Trustee agrees to keep the school buildings in good repair, and to furnish the necessary fuel, furniture, apparatus, books and blanks, and such other appliances as may be necessary for the systematic and proper conduct of said school.

And the said School Trustee, for and in behalf of said Township, further agrees to pay the said....

.......for services as teacher of said school, either a sum equal to the whole number of days taught at the rate of the above named sum per day, as agreed upon, or the salary for the year in the event of a yearly consideration, as agreed upon, when the said teacher shall have filled all the stipulations of this contract.

The said School Trustee further agrees to pay said teacher one day's wages for each day's attendance at the Township Institute, according to the Acts of 1889.

PROVIDED, That in case the said _Bessie Finny_ ....should be dismissed from said school by said Trustee, or his successor in office, for incompetency, cruelty, gross immorality, neglect of business, or a violation of any of the stipulations of this contract, or in case _her_ license should be annulled by the County Superintendent or State Superintendent, _S_ he shall not be entitled to any compensation after notice of dismissal, or notice of annulment of license.

PROVIDED, FURTHER, That the teacher shall have a duplicate of this Contract.

IN WITNESS WHEREOF, We have hereunto subscribed our names, this...._4th_

day of _Sept_ .... A. D. 1 8 0 2 ....

Bessie Finney .Teacher.

JW Ween .... School Trustee.

NOTES:—
    (1.) Full authority is given the Trustee to substitute the words "principal," "supervisor" or "superintendent" for the word "teacher" in the event the Contract should be so made.
    (2.) This Contract is the official blank, made by the State Superintendent of Public Instruction, under the provisions of H. B. No. 139, Acts of 1899.

Teacher's or Principal's Report to Township Trustee.

NOTE.—This report must be made by each teacher having charge of the attendance of pupils. A high school teacher who works under the direction of a principal will not need to make the report in case the principal reports for the entire high school. In graded grammar schools each teacher should report for the pupils directly under his charge. The principal of a graded grammar school should report only for the pupils directly under his charge.

REPORT of.................. .... { teacher } of..........................District
 { principal }

WASHINGTON TOWNSHIP, PORTER COUNTY, INDIANA,

to the Township Trustee, for the school term beginning.................. ....and

closing ...:   ....

FOR ALL TEACHERS WHO HAVE CHARGE OF ATTENDANCE OF PUPILS.

1. Number of days school was in session,   -   -   -   -   -   -   -
2. " " pupils enrolled during year,   -   Male, ...; female,......................; total,..................... ...
3. " " " withdrawn during year, -   -   "   "   "
4. " " " suspended " "   -   - "   "   .... "
5. " " " expelled " "   -   - "   "   "
6. " " " re-entered " "   - "   "   "
7. " " " remaining in school close of year, "   "   "
8. " " " neither tardy nor absent during year, "   "   "
9. " " cases of tardiness during year,   -   "   "   .... "
10. " " pupils tardy during year,   -   - "   ....   "   "
11. Total days of attendance by all pupils for year,   -   -   -   -   -
12. * " " " absence " " " " "   -   -   -   -   -
13. Total cases of tardiness,................. ......   Time lost by tardiness,   -   -   -   ... .. — ...
14. †Average daily attendance for year,   -   -   -   -   -
15. Per cent. of attendance—11÷(11+12),   -   -   -
16. Number of pupils promoted to   -   -   -   -   -
    (a) Second year,   -   -   -   -   -   -
    (b) Third "   -   -   -   -   -
    (c) Fourth "   -   -   -   -   -   ....
    (d) Fifth "   -   -   -   -   ....
    (e) Sixth "   -   -   -   -   -   ....
    (f) Seventh "   -   -   -   -   -   —
    (g) Eighth "   -   -   -   -   -
    (h) High School,   -   -   -   -   ....
17. Number of graduates from the common branches and receiving diplomas,
    Male,...................; female,.. ....; total,.. .. ..
18. Number of graduates from non-commissioned township high schools,
    Male,...................... ; female,.................. ; total,............ .... .
19. Number of graduates from commissioned township high schools,
    Male,....................; female,..................; total,.........
20. How many books in school library (not including reading circle books) at beginning of year?
21. How many books were added to library (not including reading circle books) during year?
22. Total now in school library (not including reading circle books),   -   -   -   -
23. How many reading circle books were added during year?   -   -   -   -   ....
24. How many pupils read one or more school library or reading circle books during year?   -   ....
25. Do patrons read school library books?   -   -   -   -   -   -   ....
26. Number of visits to school,   Parents,....................; officials, ...; others, ...; total,...........................
27. Number of teachers employed (if school be high school), Male,................; female,.............; total,.....................
28. Number of days teacher attended township institute,   -   -   -   -
29. Books and apparatus left in school room at end of term,   -   -   -   ....

I,... ..   .., do solemnly swear that the above report is true to the best of my knowledge and belief.

.... { Teacher.
 { Principal.

NOTES:—
    *(1.) After three days of absence the pupil should be withdrawn, and his absence counted no more for that period of absence. After being withdrawn, he is not a pupil of the school, and can not be again until he is re-entered, as in item 6.
    †(2.) To find average daily attendance divide the whole number of days of attendance made by all the pupils by the number of days of school taught.

TEACHER'S CONTRACT.

This Agreement, Between _J W Green_ _____ School Trustee of

Washington School Township, in Porter County, and State of Indiana,

of the first part, and _Cora Benham_ a legally qualified teacher in said

County of the second part, certifies that the said teacher hereby agrees to teach the public school in District No. _____

Grade _____, in said Township, for the term commencing on the _31st_ day of _Aug_

A. D. 19 _03_, for the consideration of _Two_ _____ Dollars and

_53_ Cents per { day, } { year, } to be paid _When called for_ (State here when all or parts of salary will be paid.)

The said _Cora Benham_ _____ further agrees faithfully to perform all the duties of teacher in said school; using only such text-books as are prescribed by the Trustees in accordance with the law, except supplementary reading, such as Young People's Reading Circle books, etc., and other works recommended by the County Superintendent, and observing all Rules and Regulations of the County Board of Education, and all instructions of the County Superintendent of Schools; that _s_ he will attend and participate in the exercises of each Institute or other teachers' meetings that may be appointed for the teachers of said township, or for each day's absence therefrom, forfeit a sum equal to one day's wages, unless such absence shall be occasioned by sickness, that _ _ he will accurately keep and use all registers and blanks placed in _her_ hands by said Trustee; that _s_ he will make a complete and accurate report at the close of the school term, the blank for which is provided on the back of this sheet; that _s_ he will make all other reports required of _her_ by said Trustee, the County Superintendent, or the laws of Indiana, at the proper time and manner and in good order; that _s_ he will exercise due diligence in the preservation of school buildings, grounds, furniture, apparatus, books, blanks and other school property committed to _her_ care, and turn the same over to the Trustee, or his representative, at the close of the term of school, in as good condition as when received, damage and wear by use excepted.

The said School Trustee agrees to keep the school buildings in good repair, and to furnish the necessary fuel, furniture, apparatus, books and blanks, and such other appliances as may be necessary for the systematic and proper conduct of said school.

And the said School Trustee, for and in behalf of said Township, further agrees to pay the said _____

_____ _____ for services as teacher of said school, either a sum equal to the whole number of days taught at the rate of the above named sum per day, as agreed upon, or the salary for the year in the event of a yearly consideration, as agreed upon, when the said teacher shall have filled all the stipulations of this contract.

The said School Trustee further agrees to pay said teacher one day's wages for each day's attendance at the Township Institute, according to the Acts of 1889.

PROVIDED, That in case the said _____ _____ should be dismissed from said school by said Trustee, or his successor in office, for incompetency, cruelty, gross immorality, neglect of business, or a violation of any of the stipulations of this contract, or in case _____ license should be annulled by the County Superintendent or State Superintendent, _____ he shall not be entitled to any compensation after notice of dismissal, or notice of annulment of license.

PROVIDED FURTHER, That the teacher shall have a duplicate of this Contract.

IN WITNESS WHEREOF, We have hereunto subscribed our names, this _26_

day of _Aug_ _____ A. D. 19 _03_ _____

Cora Benham Teacher.

J W Green _____ School Trustee.

NOTES:—

(1.) Full authority is given the Trustee to substitute the words "principal," "supervisor" or "superintendent" for the word "teacher" in the event the Contract should be so made.

(2.) This Contract is the official blank, made by the State Superintendent of Public Instruction, under the provisions of H. B. No. 139. Acts of 1899.

Teacher's or Principal's Report to Township Trustee.

NOTE.—This report must be made by each teacher having charge of the attendance of pupils. A high school teacher who works under the direction of a principal will not need to make the report in case the principal reports for the entire high school. In graded grammar schools each teacher should report for the pupils directly under his charge. The principal of a graded grammar school should report only for the pupils directly under his charge.

REPORT of............................ .... { teacher } { principal } of........................District

WASHINGTON TOWNSHIP, PORTER COUNTY, INDIANA,

to the Township Trustee, for the school term beginning.. ....and

closing ....:

FOR ALL TEACHERS WHO HAVE CHARGE OF ATTENDANCE OF PUPILS.

1. Number of days school was in session,   -   -   -   -   -   -   -   -   -
2. " " pupils enrolled during year,   -   Male, ...; female,........................; total,........ ...
3. " " " withdrawn during year,   -   -   "   "   "
4. " " " suspended " "   -   - "   "   ....   "
5. " " " expelled " "   -   " "   "   "
6. " " " re-entered " "   -   "   "   "
7. " " " remaining in school close of year, "   "   "
8. " " " neither tardy nor absent during year, "   "   "
9. " " cases of tardiness during year,   -   "   "   ....   "
10. " " pupils tardy during year,   -   - "   ....   "   "
11. Total days of attendance by all pupils for year,   -   -   -   -   -   -
12. * " " " absence " " " " " -   -   -   -   -
13. Total cases of tardiness,..................... Time lost by tardiness,   -   -   ... - ..
14. †Average daily attendance for year,   -   -   -   -   -   -
15. Per cent. of attendance—11÷(11+12),   -   -   -
16. Number of pupils promoted to   -   -   -   -   -   -   -
    (a) Second year,   -   -   -   -   -   -
    (b) Third " -   -   -   -   -   -
    (c) Fourth "   -   -   -   -   -   ....
    (d) Fifth "   -   -   -   -   -   ....
    (e) Sixth "   -   -   -   -   -   ....
    (f) Seventh " -   -   -   -   -   —
    (g) Eighth "   -   -   -   -   -
    (h) High School,   -   -   -   -   -   ....
17. Number of graduates from the common branches and receiving diplomas,
    Male,.................; female,...................; total,.... .. ..
18. Number of graduates from non-commissioned township high schools,
    Male,....................; female,...................; total,..................
19. Number of graduates from commissioned township high schools,
    Male,.................; female,....................; total,........
20. How many books in school library (not including reading circle books) at beginning of year?
21. How many books were added to library (not including reading circle books) during year?
22. Total now in school library (not including reading circle books),   -   -   -   -
23. How many reading circle books were added during year?   -   -   -   -   ....
24. How many pupils read one or more school library or reading circle books during year?   -   ....
25. Do patrons read school library books?   -   -   -   -   -   -
26. Number of visits to school,   Parents,..................; officials, ...; others, ...; total, ...
27. Number of teachers employed (if school be high school), Male,.................; female, ...; total, ...
28. Number of days teacher attended township institute,   -   -   -   -   -
29. Books and apparatus left in school room at end of term,   -   -   -   ....

I,... ...., do solemnly swear that the above report is true to the best of my knowledge and belief.

{ Teacher.
.... { Principal.

NOTES:—
*(1.) After three days of absence the pupil should be withdrawn, and his absence counted no more for that period of absence. After being withdrawn, he is not a pupil of the school, and can not be again until he is re-entered, as in item 6.
†(2.) To find average daily attendance divide the whole number of days of attendance made by all the pupils by the number of days of school taught.

27ª

TEACHER'S CONTRACT.

This Agreement, Between *L Allison* ....School Trustee of

Washington School Township, in Porter County, and State of Indiana,

of the first part, and *Maggie Bundy* a legally qualified teacher in said

County of the second part, certifies that the said teacher hereby agrees to teach the public school in District No. ____

Grade_____, in said Township, for the term commencing on the *31* day of *Aug*

A. D. 1 *903*, for the consideration of _____ *Two* _____Dollars and

31 Cents per { day, { year, } to be paid *when collected* (State here when all or parts of salary will be paid.)

The said _____ *Maggie Bundy* _____further agrees faithfully to perform
all the duties of teacher in said school; using only such text-books as are prescribed by the Trustees in accordance with
the law, except supplementary reading, such as Young People's Reading Circle books, etc., and other works recommended by the County Superintendent, and observing all Rules and Regulations of the County Board of Education,
and all instructions of the County Superintendent of Schools; that *s*...he will attend and participate in the exercises of
each Institute or other teachers' meetings that may be appointed for the teachers of said township, or for each day's
absence therefrom, forfeit a sum equal to one day's wages, unless such absence shall be occasioned by sickness, that
s...he will accurately keep and use all registers and blanks placed in *her*... hands by said Trustee; that ...he will
make a complete and accurate report at the close of the school term, the blank for which is provided on the back of
this sheet; that *s*he will make all other reports required of *her* by said Trustee, the County Superintendent, or
the laws of Indiana, at the proper time and manner and in good order; that ...he will exercise due diligence in the
preservation of school buildings, grounds, furniture, apparatus, books, blanks and other school property committed to
her..care, and turn the same over to the Trustee, or his representative, at the close of the term of school, in as
good condition as when received, damage and wear by use excepted.

The said School Trustee agrees to keep the school buildings in good repair, and to furnish the necessary fuel,
furniture, apparatus, books and blanks, and such other appliances as may be necessary for the systematic and proper
conduct of said school.

And the said School Trustee, for and in behalf of said Township, further agrees to pay the said...:....................
....for services as teacher of said school, either a sum equal to the whole
number of days taught at the rate of the above named sum per day, as agreed upon, or the salary for the year in the
event of a yearly consideration, as agreed upon, when the said teacher shall have filled all the stipulations of this contract.

The said School Trustee further agrees to pay said teacher one day's wages for each day's attendance at the Township Institute, according to the Acts of 1889.

PROVIDED, That in case the said_____ ....should be
dismissed from said school by said Trustee, or his successor in office, for incompetency, cruelty, gross immorality,
neglect of business, or a violation of any of the stipulations of this contract, or in case .... license should be
annulled by the County Superintendent or State Superintendent, ...he shall not be entitled to any compensation after
notice of dismissal, or notice of annulment of license.

PROVIDED FURTHER, That the teacher shall have a duplicate of this Contract.

IN WITNESS WHEREOF, We have hereunto subscribed our names, this *2e*.......................

day of....*Aug*...................... A. D. 1 *903*

Margaret Bundy .Teacher.

L Allison ....School Trustee.

NOTES:—
   (1.) Full authority is given theTrustee to substitute the words "principal," "supervisor" or "superintendent" for the word "teacher"
in the event the Contract should be so made.
   (2.) This Contract is the official blank, made by the State Superintendent of Public Instruction, under the provisions of H. B. No. 119,
Acts of 1899.

Teacher's or Principal's Report to Township Trustee.

NOTE.—This report must be made by each teacher having charge of the attendance of pupils. A high school teacher who works under the direction of a principal will not need to make the report in case the principal reports for the entire high school. In graded grammar schools each teacher should report for the pupils directly under his charge. The principal of a graded grammar school should report only for the pupils directly under his charge.

REPORT of............ .... } teacher } principal { of...........................District

WASHINGTON TOWNSHIP, PORTER COUNTY, INDIANA,

to the Township Trustee, for the school term beginning.......... ....and

closing ....: ....

FOR ALL TEACHERS WHO HAVE CHARGE OF ATTENDANCE OF PUPILS.

1. Number of days school was in session,   -   -   -   -   -   -   -   -
2. "   " pupils enrolled during year,   -   Male, ...; female,...................; total,...............
3. "   "   "   withdrawn during year, -   -   "   "   "
4. "   "   "   suspended   "   "   -   -   "   " .... "
5. "   "   "   expelled   "   "   -   -   "   "   "
6. "   "   "   re-entered   "   "   -   "   "   "
7. "   "   "   remaining in school close of year, "   "   "
8. "   "   "   " neither tardy nor absent during year, "   "   "
9. "   "   cases of tardiness during year,   -   "   "   "
10. "   "   pupils tardy during year,   -   "   "   "
11. Total days of attendance by all pupils for year,   -   -   -   -
12. * "   "   "   absence   "   "   "   "   "   -   -   -   -
13. Total cases of tardiness, ...   Time lost by tardiness,   -   -   ... .. - ...
14. †Average daily attendance for year,   -   -   -   -   -
15. Per cent. of attendance—11÷(11+12),   -   -   -
16. Number of pupils promoted to   -   -   -   -
    (a) Second year,   -   -   -   -   -   -
    (b) Third   "   -   -   -   -   -   -
    (c) Fourth   "   -   -   -   -   -   ....
    (d) Fifth   "   -   -   -   -   -   ....
    (e) Sixth   "   -   -   -   -   -   ....
    (f) Seventh   "   -   -   -   -   -   ...
    (g) Eighth   "   -   -   -   -   -
    (h) High School,   -   -   -   -   -   ....
17. Number of graduates from the common branches and receiving diplomas,
    Male, ...; female, ...; total, ...
18. Number of graduates from non-commissioned township high schools,
    Male,................; female,...............; total,...............
19. Number of graduates from commissioned township high schools,
    Male,................; female,...................; total,...........
20. How many books in school library (not including reading circle books) at beginning of year?
21. How many books were added to library (not including reading circle books) during year?
22. Total now in school library (not including reading circle books),   -   -   -   -
23. How many reading circle books were added during year?   -   -   -   ....
24. How many pupils read one or more school library or reading circle books during year?   -   ....
25. Do patrons read school library books?   -   -   -   -   -   ....
26. Number of visits to school,   Parents,................; officials,.............; others, ...; total, ...
27. Number of teachers employed (if school be high school), Male,................; female,.............; total,.............
28. Number of days teacher attended township institute,   -   -   -   -   -
29. Books and apparatus left in school room at end of term,   -   -   -   -   ....

I,... . ..., do solemnly swear that the above report is true to the best of my knowledge and belief.

} Teacher.
} Principal.
....

NOTES:—

*(1.) After three days of absence the pupil should be withdrawn, and his absence counted no more for that period of absence. After being withdrawn, he is not a pupil of the school, and can not be again until he is re-entered, as in item 6.

†(2.) To find average daily attendance divide the whole number of days of attendance made by all the pupils by the number of days of school taught.

For Township Trustees.   Wade Bros. & Wise, Printers.

TEACHER'S CONTRACT.

This Agreement, Between _L. U. Green_ _School Trustee of_

Washington School Township, in Porter County, and State of Indiana,

of the first part, and _Nora McNeff_ _a legally qualified teacher in said_

County of the second part, certifies that the said teacher hereby agrees to teach the public school in District No._____,

Grade_____, in said Township, for the term commencing on the _31_ _day of_ _Aug_

A. D. 1 _903_ , for the consideration of_____ _two_ _Dollars and_

~~75~~ _79_ _Cents per_ { day, } { year, } to be paid _when called for_ (State here when all or parts of salary will be paid.)

The said _Nora McNeff_ _further agrees faithfully to perform_

all the duties of teacher in said school; using only such text-books as are prescribed by the Trustees in accordance with the law, except supplementary reading, such as Young People's Reading Circle books, etc., and other works recommended by the County Superintendent, and observing all Rules and Regulations of the County Board of Education, and all instructions of the County Superintendent of Schools; that _s_ he will attend and participate in the exercises of each Institute or other teachers' meetings that may be appointed for the teachers of said township, or for each day's absence therefrom, forfeit a sum equal to one day's wages, unless such absence shall be occasioned by sickness, that _s_ he will accurately keep and use all registers and blanks placed in _her_ hands by said Trustee; that ____he will make a complete and accurate report at the close of the school term, the blank for which is provided on the back of this sheet; that ___he will make all other reports required of ___ by said Trustee, the County Superintendent, or the laws of Indiana, at the proper time and manner and in good order; that ____he will exercise due diligence in the preservation of school buildings, grounds, furniture, apparatus, books, blanks and other school property committed to _her_ care, and turn the same over to the Trustee, or his representative, at the close of the term of school, in as good condition as when received, damage and wear by use excepted.

The said School Trustee agrees to keep the school buildings in good repair, and to furnish the necessary fuel, furniture, apparatus, books and blanks, and such other appliances as may be necessary for the systematic and proper conduct of said school.

And the said School Trustee, for and in behalf of said Township, further agrees to pay the said_____

_____for services as teacher of said school, either a sum equal to the whole number of days taught at the rate of the above named sum per day, as agreed upon, or the salary for the year in the event of a yearly consideration, as agreed upon, when the said teacher shall have filled all the stipulations of this contract.

The said School Trustee further agrees to pay said teacher one day's wages for each day's attendance at the Township Institute, according to the Acts of 1889.

PROVIDED, That in case the said_____should be dismissed from said school by said Trustee, or his successor in office, for incompetency, cruelty, gross immorality, neglect of business, or a violation of any of the stipulations of this contract, or in case _____license should be annulled by the County Superintendent or State Superintendent, ____he shall not be entitled to any compensation after notice of dismissal, or notice of annulment of license.

PROVIDED FURTHER, That the teacher shall have a duplicate of this Contract.

IN WITNESS WHEREOF, We have hereunto subscribed our names, this _28th_

day of _Aug_ _A. D. 1 903_

Nora McNeff Teacher.

L. U. Green School Trustee.

NOTES:—

(1.) Full authority is given the Trustee to substitute the words "principal," "supervisor" or "superintendent" for the word "teacher" in the event the Contract should be so made.

(2.) This Contract is the official blank, made by the State Superintendent of Public Instruction, under the provisions of H. B. No. 139, Acts of 1899.

Teacher's or Principal's Report to Township Trustee.

NOTE.—This report must be made by each teacher having charge of the attendance of pupils. A high school teacher who works under the direction of a principal will not need to make the report in case the principal reports for the entire high school. In graded grammar schools each teacher should report for the pupils directly under his charge. The principal of a graded grammar school should report only for the pupils directly under his charge.

REPORT of .... { teacher { of ....District
.... { principal {

WASHINGTON TOWNSHIP, PORTER COUNTY, INDIANA,

to the Township Trustee, for the school term beginning............ ....and

closing ....

FOR ALL TEACHERS WHO HAVE CHARGE OF ATTENDANCE OF PUPILS.

1. Number of days school was in session, - - - - - - - -
2. " " pupils enrolled during year, - Male, ...; female,.................; total,................
3. " " " withdrawn during year, - - " " "
4. " " " suspended " " - " " "
5. " " " expelled " " " " "
6. " " " re-entered " " - " " "
7. " " " remaining in school close of year, " " "
8. " " " neither tardy nor absent during year, " " "
9. " " cases of tardiness during year, - " " "
10. " " pupils tardy during year, - - " .... " "
11. Total days of attendance by all pupils for year, - - - -
12. * " " " absence " " " " " - - - - -
13. Total cases of tardiness, ... Time lost by tardiness, - - - ... ...
14. †Average daily attendance for year, - - - - -
15. Per cent. of attendance—11÷(11+12), - - -
16. Number of pupils promoted to - - - - -
    (a) Second year, - - - -
    (b) Third " - - - -
    (c) Fourth " - - - - -
    (d) Fifth " - - - -
    (e) Sixth " - - - -
    (f) Seventh " - - - - -
    (g) Eighth " - - - -
    (h) High School, - - - -
17. Number of graduates from the common branches and receiving diplomas,
    Male,................; female,...............; total, ...
18. Number of graduates from non-commissioned township high schools,
    Male,................; female,................; total,... ... .
19. Number of graduates from commissioned township high schools,
    Male,................; female,................; total,........
20. How many books in school library (not including reading circle books) at beginning of year?
21. How many books were added to library (not including reading circle books) during year?
22. Total now in school library (not including reading circle books), - - - -
23. How many reading circle books were added during year? - - -
24. How many pupils read one or more school library or reading circle books during year? -
25. Do patrons read school library books? - - - - - -
26. Number of visits to school, Parents,................; officials, ...; others, ...; total,...........
27. Number of teachers employed (if school be high school), Male,...........; female,............; total,..........
28. Number of days teacher attended township institute, - - - - -
29. Books and apparatus left in school room at end of term, - - - -

I,.., do solemnly swear that the above report is true to the best of my knowledge and belief.

.... { Teacher.
.... { Principal.

NOTES:—
*(1.) After three days of absence the pupil should be withdrawn, and his absence counted no more for that period of absence. After being withdrawn, he is not a pupil of the school, and can not be again until he is re-entered, as in item 6.
†(2.) To find average daily attendance divide the whole number of days of attendance made by all the pupils by the number of days of school taught.

TEACHER'S CONTRACT.

This Agreement, Between _J. W. McGee_ ....School Trustee of

Washington School Township, in Porter County, and State of Indiana,

of the first part, and _Bessie Finney_ a legally qualified teacher in said

County of the second part, certifies that the said teacher hereby agrees to teach the public school in District No. ....,

Grade........., in said Township, for the term commencing on the _31st_ day of _Aug_

A. D. 1 _803_ , for the consideration of..................._Two_ ....Dollars and

_75_ Cents per { day, / year, } to be paid.._when collected_
(State here when all or parts of salary will be paid.)

The said.........._Bessie Finney_ ....further agrees faithfully to perform all the duties of teacher in said school; using only such text-books as are prescribed by the Trustees in accordance with the law, except supplementary reading, such as Young People's Reading Circle books, etc., and other works recommended by the County Superintendent, and observing all Rules and Regulations of the County Board of Education, and all instructions of the County Superintendent of Schools; that..._s_..he will attend and participate in the exercises of each Institute or other teachers' meetings that may be appointed for the teachers of said township, or for each day's absence therefrom, forfeit a sum equal to one day's wages, unless such absence shall be occasioned by sickness, that _s_..he will accurately keep and use all registers and blanks placed in.._her_...hands by said Trustee; that..._s_..he will make a complete and accurate report at the close of the school term, the blank for which is provided on the back of this sheet; that..._s_...he will make all other reports required of..._her_...by said Trustee, the County Superintendent, or the laws of Indiana, at the proper time and manner and in good order; that .....he will exercise due diligence in the preservation of school buildings, grounds, furniture, apparatus, books, blanks and other school property committed to _her_ care, and turn the same over to the Trustee, or his representative, at the close of the term of school, in as good condition as when received, damage and wear by use excepted.

The said School Trustee agrees to keep the school buildings in good repair, and to furnish the necessary fuel, furniture, apparatus, books and blanks, and such other appliances as may be necessary for the systematic and proper conduct of said school.

And the said School Trustee, for and in behalf of said Township, further agrees to pay the said..............................
..................for services as teacher of said school, either a sum equal to the whole number of days taught at the rate of the above named sum per day, as agreed upon, or the salary for the year in the event of a yearly consideration, as agreed upon, when the said teacher shall have filled all the stipulations of this contract.

The said School Trustee further agrees to pay said teacher one day's wages for each day's attendance at the Township Institute, according to the Acts of 1889.

PROVIDED, That in case the said...should be dismissed from said school by said Trustee, or his successor in office, for incompetency, cruelty, gross immorality, neglect of business, or a violation of any of the stipulations of this contract, or in case............license should be annulled by the County Superintendent or State Superintendent, ...he shall not be entitled to any compensation after notice of dismissal, or notice of annulment of license.

PROVIDED FURTHER, That the teacher shall have a duplicate of this Contract.

IN WITNESS WHEREOF, We have hereunto subscribed our names, this _28_

day of..............._Aug_ ....A. D. 1 _803_ ....

Bess Finney ....Teacher

J. W. McGee ....School Trustee

NOTES:—
   (1.) Full authority is given the Trustee to substitute the words "principal," "supervisor" or "superintendent" for the word "teacher" in the event the Contract should be so made.
   (2.) This Contract is the official blank, made by the State Superintendent of Public Instruction, under the provisions of H. B. No. 132 Acts of 1899.

Teacher's or Principal's Report to Township Trustee.

NOTE.—This report must be made by each teacher having charge of the attendance of pupils. A high school teacher who works under the direction of a principal will not need to make the report in case the principal reports for the entire high school. In graded grammar schools each teacher should report for the pupils directly under his charge. The principal of a graded grammar school should report only for the pupils directly under his charge.

REPORT of.................................. .... { teacher } { principal } of........................District

WASHINGTON TOWNSHIP, PORTER COUNTY, INDIANA,

to the Township Trustee, for the school term beginning.................. ....and

closing ....:   ....

FOR ALL TEACHERS WHO HAVE CHARGE OF ATTENDANCE OF PUPILS.

1. Number of days school was in session,   -   -   -   -   -   -   -

2. "   " pupils enrolled during year,   -   Male, ...; female,........................; total,............ ...

3. "   "   " withdrawn during year, -   -   "   "   "

4. "   "   " suspended   "   "   -   -   "   "   ....   "

5. "   "   " expelled   "   "   -   -   "   "   "

6. "   "   " re-entered   "   "   -   "   "   "

7. "   "   " remaining in school close of year, "   "   "

8. "   "   " neither tardy nor absent during year, "   "   "

9. "   "   " cases of tardiness during year,   -   "   "   ....   "

10. "   "   " pupils tardy during year,   -   -   "   ....   "   "

11. Total days of attendance by all pupils for year,   -   -   -   -   -

12. * "   "   " absence   "   "   "   "   "   -   -   -

13. Total cases of tardiness,....................   Time lost by tardiness,   -   -   ... .

14. †Average daily attendance for year,   -   -   -   -   -

15. Per cent. of attendance—$11 \div (11+12)$,   -   -   -

16. Number of pupils promoted to   -   -   -   -   -

   (a) Second year,   -   -   -   -   -   -

   (b) Third   "   -   -   -   -

   (c) Fourth   "   -   -   -   -   ....

   (d) Fifth   "   -   -   -   ....

   (e) Sixth   "   -   -   -   ....

   (f) Seventh   "   -   -   -   -   _

   (g) Eighth   "   -   -   -   -

   (h) High School,   -   -   -   -   -   -   ....

17. Number of graduates from the common branches and receiving diplomas,

   Male, ...; female,.................. ; total,... .. ...

18. Number of graduates from non-commissioned township high schools,

   Male,....................; female,.................. ; total,................. .

19. Number of graduates from commissioned township high schools,

   Male,....................; female,.................. ; total,..........

20. How many books in school library (not including reading circle books) at beginning of year?

21. How many books were added to library (not including reading circle books) during year?

22. Total now in school library (not including reading circle books),   -   -   -   -

23. How many reading circle books were added during year?   -   -   -   -

24. How many pupils read one or more school library or reading circle books during year?   -   ....

25. Do patrons read school library books?   -   -   -   -   -

26. Number of visits to school,   Parents,................; officials, ...; others, ...; total,......................

27. Number of teachers employed (if school be high school), Male,................; female, ...; total,............ .

28. Number of days teacher attended township institute,   -   -   -   -

29. Books and apparatus left in school room at end of term,   -   -   ....

I,... ... ., do solemnly swear that the above report is true to the best of my knowledge and belief.

{ Teacher.
.... { Principal.

NOTES:—

*(1.) After three days of absence the pupil should be withdrawn, and his absence counted no more for that period of absence. After being withdrawn, he is not a pupil of the school, and can not be again until he is re-entered, as in item 6.

†(2.) To find average daily attendance divide the whole number of days of attendance made by all the pupils by the number of days of school taught.

TEACHER'S CONTRACT.

This Agreement, Between _Wm A. Boud_ School Trustee of

Washington School Township, In Porter County, and State of Indiana,

of the first part, and _Cora Benham_ a legally qualified teacher in said

County of the second part, certifies that the said teacher hereby agrees to teach the public school in District No. _1_,

Grade _____, in said Township, for the term commencing on the _4th_ day of _Sep_

A. D. 1 _899_, for the consideration of _Two_ Dollars and

_____ Cents per { day, / year, } to be paid _When Called for_ (State here when all or parts of salary will be paid.)

The said _Cora Benham_ further agrees faithfully to perform all the duties of teacher in said school; using only such text-books as are prescribed by the Trustees in accordance with the law, except supplementary reading, such as Young People's Reading Circle books, etc., and other works recommended by the County Superintendent, and observing all Rules and Regulations of the County Board of Education, and all instructions of the County Superintendent of Schools; that S_he will attend and participate in the exercises of each Institute or other teachers' meetings that may be appointed for the teachers of said township, or for each day's absence therefrom, forfeit a sum equal to one day's wages, unless such absence shall be occasioned by sickness, that S_he will accurately keep and use all registers and blanks placed in _her_ hands by said Trustee; that S_he will make a complete and accurate report at the close of the school term, the blank for which is provided on the back of this sheet; that S_he will make all other reports required of _her_ by said Trustee, the County Superintendent, or the laws of Indiana, at the proper time and manner and in good order; that S_he will exercise due diligence in the preservation of school buildings, grounds, furniture, apparatus, books, blanks and other school property committed to _her_ care, and turn the same over to the Trustee, or his representative, at the close of the term of school, in as good condition as when received, damage and wear by use excepted.

The said School Trustee agrees to keep the school buildings in good repair, and to furnish the necessary fuel, furniture, apparatus, books and blanks, and such other appliances as may be necessary for the systematic and proper conduct of said school.

And the said School Trustee, for and in behalf of said Township, further agrees to pay the said _____ _Cora Benham_ for services as teacher of said school, either a sum equal to the whole number of days taught at the rate of the above named sum per day, as agreed upon, or the salary for the year in the event of a yearly consideration, as agreed upon, when the said teacher shall have filled all the stipulations of this contract.

The said School Trustee further agrees to pay said teacher one day's wages for each day's attendance at the Township Institute, according to the Acts of 1889.

PROVIDED, That in case the said _Cora Benham_ should be dismissed from said school by said Trustee, or his successor in office, for incompetency, cruelty, gross immorality, neglect of business, or a violation of any of the stipulations of this contract, or in case _her_ license should be annulled by the County Superintendent or State Superintendent, S_he shall not be entitled to any compensation after notice of dismissal, or notice of annulment of license.

PROVIDED FURTHER, That the teacher shall have a duplicate of this Contract.

IN WITNESS WHEREOF, We have hereunto subscribed our names, this _Eight_

day of _Aug_ A. D. 18 _99_

Cora Benham .Teacher.

Wm A. Boud School Trustee.

NOTES:—
   (1.) Full authority is given the Trustee to substitute the words "principal," "supervisor" or "superintendent" for the word "teacher" in the event the Contract should be so made.
   (2.) This Contract is the official blank, made by the State Superintendent of Public Instruction, under the provisions of H. B. No. 130 Acts of 1899.

Teacher's or Principal's Report to Township Trustee.

NOTE.—This report must be made by each teacher having charge of the attendance of pupils. A high school teacher who works under the direction of a principal will not need to make the report in case the principal reports for the entire high school. In graded grammar schools each teacher should report for the pupils directly under his charge. The principal of a graded grammar school should report only for the pupils directly under his charge.

REPORT of .... { teacher } of .... District
                                                                            { principal }

WASHINGTON TOWNSHIP, PORTER COUNTY, INDIANA,

to the Township Trustee, for the school term beginning .... and

closing ..

FOR ALL TEACHERS WHO HAVE CHARGE OF ATTENDANCE OF PUPILS.

1. Number of days school was in session,   -   -   -   -   -   -   -
2. " " pupils enrolled during year,   - Male, ...; female, ...; total, ...
3. " " " " withdrawn during year, -   -   "   "   "
4. " " " " suspended " "   -   - "   "   "
5. " " " " expelled " "   -   "   "   "
6. " " " " re-entered " "   -   "   "   "
7. " " " " remaining in school close of year, "   "   "
8. " " " " neither tardy nor absent during year, "   "   "
9. " " " cases of tardiness during year,   -   "   "   "
10. " " pupils tardy during year,   -   - "   __   "   "
11. Total days of attendance by all pupils for year,   -   -   -   -   -
12. " " " " absence " " " " " "
13. Total cases of tardiness, ... Time lost by tardiness,   -   -   -
14. †Average daily attendance for year,   -   -   -   -   -   -   -
15. Per cent. of attendance—11 ÷ (11 + 12),   -   -   -   -
16. Number of pupils promoted to   -   -   -   -   -   -
    (a) Second year,   -   -   -   -   -   -   -
    (b) Third "   -   -   -   -   -
    (c) Fourth "   -   -   -   -   -   -   ....
    (d) Fifth "   -   -   -   -   -   ....
    (e) Sixth "   -   -   -   -   -   -
    (f) Seventh "   -   -   -   -   -   ....
    (g) Eighth "   -   -   -   -   -   -
    (h) High School,   -   -   -   -   -   -   ....
17. Number of graduates from the common branches and receiving diplomas,
                    Male, ...; female, ...; total, ...
18. Number of graduates from non-commissioned township high schools,
                    Male, ...; female, ...; total, ...
19. Number of graduates from commissioned township high schools,
                    Male, ...; female, ...; total, ...
20. How many books in school library (not including reading circle books) at beginning of year?
21. How many books were added to library (not including reading circle books) during year?
22. Total now in school library (not including reading circle books),   -   -   -
23. How many reading circle books were added during year?   -   -   -   -   ....
24. How many pupils read one or more school library or reading circle books during year?   -
25. Do patrons read school library books?   -   -   -   -   -   -   -
26. Number of visits to school,   Parents, ...; officials, ...; others, ...; total, ...
27. Number of teachers employed (if school be high school), Male, ...; female, ...; total, ...
28. Number of days teacher attended township institute,   -   -   -   -
29. Books and apparatus left in school room at end of term,   -   -   -   ....

I, ..., do solemnly swear that the above report is true to the best of my knowledge and belief.

                                                            { Teacher.
                                                            { Principal.

NOTES:—
*(1.) After three days of absence the pupil should be withdrawn, and his absence counted no more for that period of absence. After being withdrawn, he is not a pupil of the school, and can not be again until he is re-entered, as in item 6.
†(2.) To find average daily attendance divide the whole number of days of attendance made by all the pupils by the number of days of school taught.

For Township Trustees.   Wade Bros. & Wise, Printers.

TEACHER'S CONTRACT.

This Agreement, Between _L W Green_ .School Trustee of

Washington School Township, In Porter County, and State of Indiana,

of the first part, and _Geneva Pierce_ a legally qualified teacher in said

County of the second part, certifies that the said teacher hereby agrees to teach the public school in District No. ... ...

Grade......, in said Township, for the term commencing on the _31st_ day of _Aug_

A. D. 1 _913_ , for the consideration of _two_ .Dollars and

_27_ Cents per { day, year, } to be paid _when called for_ (State here when all or parts of salary will be paid.)

The said _Geneva Pierce_ .further agrees faithfully to perform all the duties of teacher in said school; using only such text-books as are prescribed by the Trustees in accordance with the law, except supplementary reading, such as Young People's Reading Circle books, etc., and other works recommended by the County Superintendent, and observing all Rules and Regulations of the County Board of Education, and all instructions of the County Superintendent of Schools; that _s_ he will attend and participate in the exercises of each Institute or other teachers' meetings that may be appointed for the teachers of said township, or for each day's absence therefrom, forfeit a sum equal to one day's wages, unless such absence shall be occasioned by sickness, that _s_ he will accurately keep and use all registers and blanks placed in _her_ hands by said Trustee; that .he will make a complete and accurate report at the close of the school term, the blank for which is provided on the back of this sheet; that _s_ he will make all other reports required of _her_ by said Trustee, the County Superintendent, or the laws of Indiana, at the proper time and manner and in good order; that ....he will exercise due diligence in the preservation of school buildings, grounds, furniture, apparatus, books, blanks and other school property committed to _her_ .care, and turn the same over to the Trustee, or his representative, at the close of the term of school, in as good condition as when received, damage and wear by use excepted.

The said School Trustee agrees to keep the school buildings in good repair, and to furnish the necessary fuel, furniture, apparatus, books and blanks, and such other appliances as may be necessary for the systematic and proper conduct of said school.

And the said School Trustee, for and in behalf of said Township, further agrees to pay the said.................................. ....for services as teacher of said school, either a sum equal to the whole number of days taught at the rate of the above named sum per day, as agreed upon, or the salary for the year in the event of a yearly consideration, as agreed upon, when the said teacher shall have filled all the stipulations of this contract.

The said School Trustee further agrees to pay said teacher one day's wages for each day's attendance at the Township Institute, according to the Acts of 1889.

PROVIDED, That in case the said................................... ....should be dismissed from said school by said Trustee, or his successor in office, for incompetency, cruelty, gross immorality, neglect of business, or a violation of any of the stipulations of this contract, or in case ....license should be annulled by the County Superintendent or State Superintendent, ...he shall not be entitled to any compensation after notice of dismissal, or notice of annulment of license.

PROVIDED FURTHER, That the teacher shall have a duplicate of this Contract.

IN WITNESS WHEREOF, We have hereunto subscribed our names, this _26_

day of _Aug_ A. D. 19 _03_

Geneva Pierce ...Teacher.

L W Green ......School Trustee.

NOTES:—
(1.) Full authority is given the Trustee to substitute the words "principal," "supervisor" or "superintendent" for the word "teacher" in the event the Contract should be so made.
(2.) This Contract is the official blank, made by the State Superintendent of Public Instruction, under the provisions of H. B. No. 130, Acts of 1899.

Teacher's or Principal's Report to Township Trustee.

NOTE.—This report must be made by each teacher having charge of the attendance of pupils. A high school teacher who works under the direction of a principal will not need to make the report in case the principal reports for the entire high school. In graded grammar schools each teacher should report for the pupils directly under his charge. The principal of a graded grammar school should report only for the pupils directly under his charge.

REPORT of.................... .... { teacher } { principal } of........................District

WASHINGTON TOWNSHIP, PORTER COUNTY, INDIANA,

to the Township Trustee, for the school term beginning.................. ....and

closing ....

FOR ALL TEACHERS WHO HAVE CHARGE OF ATTENDANCE OF PUPILS.

1. Number of days school was in session, - - - - - - - - - -
2. " " pupils enrolled during year, - Male, ...; female,....................; total,..................... ...
3. " " " withdrawn during year, - - " " "
4. " " " suspended " " - - " " .... "
5. " " " expelled " " - - " " "
6. " " " re-entered " " - " " "
7. " " " remaining in school close of year, " " "
8. " " " neither tardy nor absent during year, " " "
9. " " cases of tardiness during year, - " " .... "
10. " " pupils tardy during year, - - " .... " "
11. Total days of attendance by all pupils for year, - - - - - -
12. * " " " absence " " " " " - - - - -
13. Total cases of tardiness, ... Time lost by tardiness, - - - ....
14. †Average daily attendance for year, - - - - - -
15. Per cent. of attendance—$11 \div (11+12)$, - - - -
16. Number of pupils promoted to - - - - - -
    (a) Second year, - - - - - -
    (b) Third " - - - - -
    (c) Fourth " - - - - - ....
    (d) Fifth " - - - - - - ....
    (e) Sixth " - - - - - - ....
    (f) Seventh " - - - - - - —
    (g) Eighth " - - - - -
    (h) High School, - - - - - - ....
17. Number of graduates from the common branches and receiving diplomas,
    Male,....................; female,.................... ; total,.... .. ..   ..
18. Number of graduates from non-commissioned township high schools,
    Male,....................; female,....................; total,............ ... .
19. Number of graduates from commissioned township high schools,
    Male,....................; female,....................; total,...........
20. How many books in school library (not including reading circle books) at beginning of year?
21. How many books were added to library (not including reading circle books) during year?
22. Total now in school library (not including reading circle books), - - - - -
23. How many reading circle books were added during year? - - - - - ....
24. How many pupils read one or more school library or reading circle books during year? - ....
25. Do patrons read school library books? - - - - - - ....
26. Number of visits to school, Parents,....................; officials, ...; others, ...; total,...........................
27. Number of teachers employed (if school be high school), Male,....................; female, ...; total,........... .. ..
28. Number of days teacher attended township institute, - - - " - - -
29. Books and apparatus left in school room at end of term, - - - - ....;

I,... .. .., do solemnly swear that the above report is true to the best of my knowledge and belief.

.... { Teacher. } { Principal. }

NOTES:—
*(1.) After three days of absence the pupil should be withdrawn, and his absence counted no more for that period of absence. After being withdrawn, he is not a pupil of the school, and can not be again until he is re-entered, as in item 6.
†(2.) To find average daily attendance divide the whole number of days of attendance made by all the pupils by the number of days of school taught.

For Township Trustees.   Wade Bros. & Wise, Printers.

TEACHER'S CONTRACT.

This Agreement, Between _L. W. Green_ School Trustee of

Washington School Township, In Porter County, and State of Indiana,

of the first part, and _Harold Cornell_ a legally qualified teacher in said

County of the second part, certifies that the said teacher hereby agrees to teach the public school in District No.............

Grade........, in said Township, for the term commencing on the _31st_ day of _Aug_

A. D. 19 _03_ , for the consideration of _One_ Dollars and

_25_ Cents per { day, } { year, } to be paid _when called for_

(State here when all or parts of salary will be paid.)

The said _Harold Cornell_ further agrees faithfully to perform all the duties of teacher in said school; using only such text-books as are prescribed by the Trustees in accordance with the law, except supplementary reading, such as Young People's Reading Circle books, etc., and other works recommended by the County Superintendent, and observing all Rules and Regulations of the County Board of Education, and all instructions of the County Superintendent of Schools; that .....he will attend and participate in the exercises of each Institute or other teachers' meetings that may be appointed for the teachers of said township, or for each day's absence therefrom, forfeit a sum equal to one day's wages, unless such absence shall be occasioned by sickness, that .....he will accurately keep and use all registers and blanks placed in _his_ hands by said Trustee; that .....he will make a complete and accurate report at the close of the school term, the blank for which is provided on the back of this sheet; that .....he will make all other reports required of .._his_ by said Trustee, the County Superintendent, or the laws of Indiana, at the proper time and manner and in good order; that .....he will exercise due diligence in the preservation of school buildings, grounds, furniture, apparatus, books, blanks and other school property committed to _his_ care, and turn the same over to the Trustee, or his representative, at the close of the term of school, in as good condition as when received, damage and wear by use excepted.

The said School Trustee agrees to keep the school buildings in good repair, and to furnish the necessary fuel, furniture, apparatus, books and blanks, and such other appliances as may be necessary for the systematic and proper conduct of said school.

And the said School Trustee, for and in behalf of said Township, further agrees to pay the said.........

.. ..for services as teacher of said school, either a sum equal to the whole number of days taught at the rate of the above named sum per day, as agreed upon, or the salary for the year in the event of a yearly consideration, as agreed upon, when the said teacher shall have filled all the stipulations of this contract.

The said School Trustee further agrees to pay said teacher one day's wages for each day's attendance at the Township Institute, according to the Acts of 1889.

PROVIDED, That in case the said.. should be dismissed from said school by said Trustee, or his successor in office, for incompetency, cruelty, gross immorality, neglect of business, or a violation of any of the stipulations of this contract, or in case ....license should be annulled by the County Superintendent or State Superintendent, ...he shall not be entitled to any compensation after notice of dismissal, or notice of annulment of license.

PROVIDED FURTHER, That the teacher shall have a duplicate of this Contract.

IN WITNESS WHEREOF, We have hereunto subscribed our names, this _25_

day of _Aug_ A. D. 19 _03_

Harold Cornell Teacher.

L. W. Green School Trustee.

NOTES:—

(1.) Full authority is given the Trustee to substitute the words "principal," "supervisor" or "superintendent" for the word "teacher" in the event the Contract should be so made.

(2.) This Contract is the official blank, made by the State Superintendent of Public Instruction, under the provisions of H. B. No. 139, Acts of 1899.

Teacher's or Principal's Report to Township Trustee.

NOTE.—This report must be made by each teacher having charge of the attendance of pupils. A high school teacher who works under the direction of a principal will not need to make the report in case the principal reports for the entire high school. In graded grammar schools each teacher should report for the pupils directly under his charge. The principal of a graded grammar school should report only for the pupils directly under his charge.

REPORT of........................ .... ⎰ teacher ⎱ of........................District
.... ⎱ principal ⎰

WASHINGTON TOWNSHIP, PORTER COUNTY, INDIANA,

to the Township Trustee, for the school term beginning........................ .... _and

closing ...: ....

FOR ALL TEACHERS WHO HAVE CHARGE OF ATTENDANCE OF PUPILS.

1. Number of days school was in session,   -   -   -   -   -   -   -   -

2. "   " pupils enrolled during year,   -   Male, ...; female,........................; total,........................

3. "   "   "   " withdrawn during year,   -   -   "   "   "

4. "   "   "   " suspended   "   "   -   -   "   "   "

5. "   "   "   " expelled   "   "   -   "   "   "

6. "   "   "   " re-entered   "   "   -   "   "   "

7. "   "   "   " remaining in school close of year, "   "   "

8. "   "   "   " neither tardy nor absent during year, "   "   "

9. "   "   " cases of tardiness during year,   -   "   "   "

10. "   "   " pupils tardy during year,   -   -   "   "   "

11. Total days of attendance by all pupils for year,   -   -   -   -   -

12. *   "   "   " absence   "   "   "   "   "   -   -   -   -   -

13. Total cases of tardiness,........................   Time lost by tardiness,   -   -   -   -   -

14. †Average daily attendance for year,   -   -   -   -   -   -

15. Per cent. of attendance—11÷(11+12),   -   -   -

16. Number of pupils promoted to   -   -   -   -   -   -

      (a) Second year,   -   -   -   -   -   -

      (b) Third   "   -   -   -   -   -

      (c) Fourth   "   -   -   -   -   -

      (d) Fifth   "   -   -   -   -   -

      (e) Sixth   "   -   -   -   -   -

      (f) Seventh   "   -   -   -   -   -

      (g) Eighth   "   -   -   -   -   -

      (h) High School,   -   -   -   -   -

17. Number of graduates from the common branches and receiving diplomas,

      Male,........................; female,........................; total,........................

18. Number of graduates from non-commissioned township high schools,

      Male,........................; female,........................; total,........................

19. Number of graduates from commissioned township high schools,

      Male,........................; female,........................; total,........................

20. How many books in school library (not including reading circle books) at beginning of year?

21. How many books were added to library (not including reading circle books) during year?

22. Total now in school library (not including reading circle books),   -   -   -   -

23. How many reading circle books were added during year?   -   -   -   -

24. How many pupils read one or more school library or reading circle books during year?   -

25. Do patrons read school library books?   -   -   -

26. Number of visits to school,   Parents,........................; officials,........................; others,........................; total,........................

27. Number of teachers employed (if school be high school), Male,........................; female,........................; total,........................

28. Number of days teacher attended township institute,   -   -   -   -

29. Books and apparatus left in school room at end of term,   -   -   -   -

I,........................ ...., do solemnly swear that the above report is true to the best of my knowledge and belief.

                                       ⎰ Teacher.
....⎱ Principal.

NOTES:—
    *(1.) After three days of absence the pupil should be withdrawn, and his absence counted no more for that period of absence. After being withdrawn, he is not a pupil of the school, and can not be again until he is re-entered, as in item 6.
    †(2.) To find average daily attendance divide the whole number of days of attendance made by all the pupils by the number of days of school taught.

TEACHER'S CONTRACT.

This Agreement, Between _L M Green_ ....School Trustee of

Washington School Township, in Porter County, and State of Indiana,

of the first part, and _Thure Bowser_ ....a legally qualified teacher in said County of the second part, certifies that the said teacher hereby agrees to teach the public school in District No. ....,

Grade........, in said Township, for the term commencing on the ... _5th_ day of _Sept_

A. D. 1_904_ , for the consideration of........ _Two_ ....Dollars and

.... _Twenty Five_ Cents per { day, } to be paid........ _When called for_
....{ year, }   (State here when all or parts of salary will be paid.)

The said ... _Thure Bowser_ ....further agrees faithfully to perform all the duties of teacher in said school; using only such text-books as are prescribed by the Trustees in accordance with the law, except supplementary reading, such as Young People's Reading Circle books, etc., and other works recommended by the County Superintendent, and observing all Rules and Regulations of the County Board of Education, and all instructions of the County Superintendent of Schools; that _o_ he will attend and participate in the exercises of each Institute or other teachers' meetings that may be appointed for the teachers of said township, or for each day's absence therefrom, forfeit a sum equal to one day's wages, unless such absence shall be occasioned by sickness, that ___ he will accurately keep and use all registers and blanks placed in _her_ hands by said Trustee; that ....he will make a complete and accurate report at the close of the school term, the blank for which is provided on the back of this sheet; that ......he will make all other reports required of _her_ ....by said Trustee, the County Superintendent, or the laws of Indiana, at the proper time and manner and in good order; that ....he will exercise due diligence in the preservation of school buildings, grounds, furniture, apparatus, books, blanks and other school property committed to _her_ .care, and turn the same over to the Trustee, or his representative, at the close of the term of school, in as good condition as when received, damage and wear by use excepted.

The said School Trustee agrees to keep the school buildings in good repair, and to furnish the necessary fuel, furniture, apparatus, books and blanks, and such other appliances as may be necessary for the systematic and proper conduct of said school.

And the said School Trustee, for and in behalf of said Township, further agrees to pay the said .

....for services as teacher of said school, either a sum equal to the whole number of days taught at the rate of the above named sum per day, as agreed upon, or the salary for the year in the event of a yearly consideration, as agreed upon, when the said teacher shall have filled all the stipulations of this contract.

The said School Trustee further agrees to pay said teacher one day's wages for each day's attendance at the Township Institute, according to the Acts of 1889.

PROVIDED, That in case the said.... ....should be dismissed from said school by said Trustee, or his successor in office, for incompetency, cruelty, gross immorality, neglect of business, or a violation of any of the stipulations of this contract, or in case... .license should be annulled by the County Superintendent or State Superintendent, ...he shall not be entitled to any compensation after notice of dismissal, or notice of annulment of license.

PROVIDED FURTHER, That the teacher shall have a duplicate of this Contract.

IN WITNESS WHEREOF, We have hereunto subscribed our names, this....... _June_

day of.. _25th_ ....A. D. 1_904_

.... _Thura Bowser_ ....Teacher.

.... _L M Green_ ....School Trustee.

NOTES:—
    (1.) Full authority is given theTrustee to substitute the words "principal," "supervisor" or "superintendent" for the word "teacher" in the event the Contract should be so made.
    (2.) This Contract is the official blank, made by the State Superintendent of Public Instruction, under the provisions of H. B. No. 139. Acts of 1899.

Teacher's or Principal's Report to Township Trustee.

NOTE.—This report must be made by each teacher having charge of the attendance of pupils. A high school teacher who works under the direction of a principal will not need to make the report in case the principal reports for the entire high school. In graded grammar schools each teacher should report for the pupils directly under his charge. The principal of a graded grammar school should report only for the pupils directly under his charge.

REPORT of................ .... } teacher } of....................District
                                                                    } principal }

WASHINGTON TOWNSHIP, PORTER COUNTY, INDIANA,

to the Township Trustee, for the school term beginning.... ...._and

closing ...:   ....

FOR ALL TEACHERS WHO HAVE CHARGE OF ATTENDANCE OF PUPILS.

1. Number of days school was in session,   -   -   -   -   -   -   -
2. " " pupils enrolled during year,   -   Male,................; female,....................; total,................
3. " " " withdrawn during year, -   -   "   "   "
4. " " " suspended " "   .   - "   " ....   "
5. " " " expelled " "   . "   "   "
6. " " " re-entered " "   . "   "   "
7. " " " remaining in school close of year, "   "   "
8. " " " "neither tardy nor absent during year, "   "   "
9. " " " cases of tardiness during year,   - "   " ....   "
10. " " " pupils tardy during year,   -   - " ....   "   "
11. Total days of attendance by all pupils for year,   -   -   -   -   -
12. * " " " absence " " " " "   -   -   -   -
13. Total cases of tardiness, ...   Time lost by tardiness,   -   -   .. - . .
14. †Average daily attendance for year,   -   -   -   -   -
15. Per cent. of attendance—11÷(11+12),   -   -   -
16. Number of pupils promoted to   -   -   -   -   -
    (a) Second year,   -   -   -   -   -
    (b) Third "   -   -   -   -
    (c) Fourth "   -   -   -   -   -
    (d) Fifth "   -   -   -   -   ....
    (e) Sixth "   -   -   -   -   ....
    (f) Seventh "   -   -   -   -
    (g) Eighth "   -   -   -   -
    (h) High School,   -   -   -   -   -   ....
17. Number of graduates from the common branches and receiving diplomas,
    Male,................; female,................; total,.... .. ...
18. Number of graduates from non-commissioned township high schools,
    Male,................; female,................; total,................
19. Number of graduates from commissioned township high schools,
    Male,................; female,................; total,................
20. How many books in school library (not including reading circle books) at beginning of year?
21. How many books were added to library (not including reading circle books) during year?
22. Total now in school library (not including reading circle books),   -   -   -   -
23. How many reading circle books were added during year?   -   -   -   ....
24. How many pupils read one or more school library or reading circle books during year?   -   ....
25. Do patrons read school library books?   -   -   -   -   -   -
26. Number of visits to school,   Parents,................; officials,................; others, ...; total, ...
27. Number of teachers employed (if school be high school), Male,................; female, ...; total, ...
28. Number of days teacher attended township institute,   -   -   -   .   .   -
29. Books and apparatus left in school room at end of term,   -   -   -   ....

I,... .. . ., do solemnly swear that the above report is true to the best of my knowledge and belief.

.... } Teacher.
                                                                        } Principal.

NOTES:—
    *(1.) After three days of absence the pupil should be withdrawn, and his absence counted no more for that period of absence. After being withdrawn, he is not a pupil of the school, and can not be again until he is re-entered, as in item 6.
    †(2.) To find average daily attendance divide the whole number of days of attendance made by all the pupils by the number of days of school taught.

For Township Trustees.   Wade Bros. & Wise, Printers.

TEACHER'S CONTRACT.

This Agreement, Between *L. M. Green* ....School Trustee of

Washington School Township, in Porter County, and State of Indiana,

of the first part, and *Edna Mewhirter* ....a legally qualified teacher in said

County of the second part, certifies that the said teacher hereby agrees to teach ~~the public~~ *Music* school in District No. *1* ...,

~~(Grade.....~~ *R.No7* ~~in said~~ Township, for the term commencing on the *5th* day of......*Sept* .....

A. D. 1 *904* ...., for the consideration of......*Two* ....Dollars and

fifty .... Cents per { day, } to be paid......*when called for*
                           { year, }   (State here when all or parts of salary will be paid.)

for teaching 8 days each month for nine months.

The said .... ~~further agrees faithfully to perform~~

all the duties of teacher in said school; using only such text-books as are prescribed by the Trustees in accordance with the law, except supplementary reading, such as Young People's Reading Circle books, etc., and other works recommended by the County Superintendent, and observing all Rules and Regulations of the County Board of Education, and all instructions of the County Superintendent of Schools; that .....he will attend and participate in the exercises of each Institute or other teachers' meetings that may be appointed for the teachers of said township, or for each day's absence therefrom, forfeit a sum equal to one day's wages, unless such absence shall be occasioned by sickness, that .....he will accurately keep and use all registers and blanks placed in.................. hands by said Trustee; that .....he will make a complete and accurate report at the close of the school term, the blank for which is provided on the back of this sheet; that ....he will make all other reports required of............... by said Trustee, the County Superintendent, or the laws of Indiana, at the proper time and manner and in good order; that .....he will exercise due diligence in the preservation of school buildings, grounds, furniture, apparatus, books, blanks and other school property committed to ....care, and turn the same over to the Trustee, or his representative, at the close of the term of school, in as good condition as when received, damage and wear by use excepted.

The said School Trustee agrees to keep the school buildings in good repair, and to furnish the necessary fuel, furniture, apparatus, books and blanks, and such other appliances as may be necessary for the systematic and proper conduct of said school.

And the said School Trustee, for and in behalf of said Township, further agrees to pay the said........................

for services as teacher of said school, either a sum equal to the whole number of days taught at the rate of the above named sum per day, as agreed upon, or the salary for the year in the event of a yearly consideration, as agreed upon, when the said teacher shall have filled all the stipulations of this contract.

The said School Trustee further agrees to pay said teacher ~~one day's wages for each day's attendance at the Town-ship Institute, according to the Acts of 1889.~~

PROVIDED, That in case the said.. should be dismissed from said school by said Trustee, or his successor in office, for incompetency, cruelty, gross immorality, neglect of business, or a violation of any of the stipulations of this contract, or in case ..... license should be annulled by the County Superintendent or State Superintendent, ...he shall not be entitled to any compensation after notice of dismissal, or notice of annulment of license.

PROVIDED FURTHER, That the teacher shall have a duplicate of this Contract.

IN WITNESS WHEREOF, We have hereunto subscribed our names, this.....*1st*

day of.......*Sept*........ A. D. 1 *904*

Edna Mewhirter ....Teacher.

L. M. Green ....School Trustee.

NOTES:—
    (1.) Full authority is given the Trustee to substitute the words "principal," "supervisor" or "superintendent" for the word "teacher" in the event the Contract should be so made.
    (2.) This Contract is the official blank, made by the State Superintendent of Public Instruction, under the provisions of H. B. No. 139, Acts of 1899.

Teacher's or Principal's Report to Township Trustee.

NOTE.—This report must be made by each teacher having charge of the attendance of pupils. A high school teacher who works under the direction of a principal will not need to make the report in case the principal reports for the entire high school. In graded grammar schools each teacher should report for the pupils directly under his charge. The principal of a graded grammar school should report only for the pupils directly under his charge.

REPORT of........................ .... { teacher } { principal } of...........................District

WASHINGTON TOWNSHIP, PORTER COUNTY, INDIANA,

to the Township Trustee, for the school term beginning......................... ....and

closing ....

FOR ALL TEACHERS WHO HAVE CHARGE OF ATTENDANCE OF PUPILS.

1. Number of days school was in session,   -   -   -   -   -   -   -   -   -
2. "   " pupils enrolled during year,   -   Male, ...; female,.....................; total,........................ ...
3. "   "   "   withdrawn during year, -   -   "   "   "
4. "   "   "   suspended   "   "   -   -   "   "   ....   "
5. "   "   "   expelled   "   "   -   -   "   "   "
6. "   "   "   re-entered   "   "   -   "   "   "
7. "   "   "   remaining in school close of year, "   "   "
8. "   "   "   " neither tardy nor absent during year, "   "   "
9. "   "   cases of tardiness during year,   -   "   "   ....   "
10. "   "   pupils tardy during year,   -   - "   ....   "   "
11. Total days of attendance by all pupils for year,   -   -   -   -   -   -
12. * "   "   " absence   " "   "   "   "   -   -   -   -   -
13. Total cases of tardiness,...................... Time lost by tardiness,   -   -   -   ... .
14. †Average daily attendance for year,   -   -   -   -   -   -
15. Per cent. of attendance—11÷(11+12),   -   -   -   -   -
16. Number of pupils promoted to   -   -   -   -   -   -
    (a) Second year,   -   -   -   -   -   -   -
    (b) Third   "   -   -   -   -   -   -
    (c) Fourth   "   -   -   -   -   -   ....
    (d) Fifth   "   -   -   -   -   -   ....
    (e) Sixth   "   -   -   -   -   -   ....
    (f) Seventh "   -   -   -   -   -   —
    (g) Eighth   "   -   -   -   -   -
    (h) High School,   -   -   -   -   -   ....
17. Number of graduates from the common branches and receiving diplomas,
    Male,.....................; female, ... ; total,.... .. ..
18. Number of graduates from non-commissioned township high schools,
    Male,......................; female,....................; total,.... ... ...
19. Number of graduates from commissioned township high schools,
    Male,...................; female,....................; total,........
20. How many books in school library (not including reading circle books) at beginning of year?
21. How many books were added to library (not including reading circle books) during year?
22. Total now in school library (not including reading circle books),   -   -   -   -
23. How many reading circle books were added during year?   -   -   -   ....
24. How many pupils read one or more school library or reading circle books during year?   -   ....
25. Do patrons read school library books?   -   ....
26. Number of visits to school,   Parents,.....................; officials, ...; others, ...; total,........................
27. Number of teachers employed (if school be high school), Male,..............; female, ...; total,............... .. ...
28. Number of days teacher attended township institute,   -   *   -   -   -
29. Books and apparatus left in school room at end of term,   -   -   -   -   ....

I,.. ...., do solemnly swear that the above report is true to the best of my knowledge and belief.

.... { Teacher. { Principal.

NOTES:—
*(1.) After three days of absence the pupil should be withdrawn, and his absence counted no more for that period of absence. After being withdrawn, he is not a pupil of the school, and can not be again until he is re-entered, as in item 6.
†(2.) To find average daily attendance divide the whole number of days of attendance made by all the pupils by the number of days of school taught.

34 A

For Township Trustees.   Wade Bros. & Wise, Printers.

TEACHER'S CONTRACT.

This Agreement, Between _L M Gu_ .... School Trustee of

Washington School Township, in Porter County, and State of Indiana,

of the first part, and .... _Grant Hollett_ .... a legally qualified teacher in said

County of the second part, certifies that the said teacher hereby agrees to teach the public school in District No. .... ,

. Grade .... , in said Township, for the term commencing on the _5th_ day of _Sept_

A. D. 1 _904_ , for the consideration of .... _One_ .... Dollars and

Twenty Eight Cents per { day, year, } to be paid _When called for_
$35.20 _for 180 days teaching at dis No 1._ (State here when all or parts of salary will be paid.)

The said .... _Grant Hollett_ .... further agrees faithfully to perform

all the duties of teacher in said school; using only such text-books as are prescribed by the Trustees in accordance with
the law, except supplementary reading, such as Young People's Reading Circle books, etc., and other works recommended by the County Superintendent, and observing all Rules and Regulations of the County Board of Education,
and all instructions of the County Superintendent of Schools; that .... he will attend and participate in the exercises of
each Institute or other teachers' meetings that may be appointed for the teachers of said township, or for each day's
absence therefrom, forfeit a sum equal to one day's wages, unless such absence shall be occasioned by sickness, that
..... he will accurately keep and use all registers and blanks placed in _his_ hands by said Trustee; that .....he will
make a complete and accurate report at the close of the school term, the blank for which is provided on the back of
this sheet; that..... ...he will make all other reports required of .... by said Trustee, the County Superintendent, or
the laws of Indiana, at the proper time and manner and in good order; that .....he will exercise due diligence in the
preservation of school buildings, grounds, furniture, apparatus, books, blanks and other school property committed to
his .... care, and turn the same over to the Trustee, or his representative, at the close of the term of school, in as
good condition as when received, damage and wear by use excepted.

The said School Trustee agrees to keep the school buildings in good repair, and to furnish the necessary fuel,
furniture, apparatus, books and blanks, and such other appliances as may be necessary for the systematic and proper
conduct of said school.

And the said School Trustee, for and in behalf of said Township, further agrees to pay the said ....
Grant Hollett for services as teacher of said school, either a sum equal to the whole
number of days taught at the rate of the above named sum per day, as agreed upon, or the salary for the year in the
event of a yearly consideration, as agreed upon, when the said teacher shall have filled all the stipulations of this contract.

The said School Trustee further agrees to pay said teacher one day's wages for each day's attendance at the Township Institute, according to the Acts of 1889.

PROVIDED, That in case the said .... _Grant Hollett_ .... should be
dismissed from said school by said Trustee, or his successor in office, for incompetency, cruelty, gross immorality,
neglect of business, or a violation of any of the stipulations of this contract, or in case .... license should be
annulled by the County Superintendent or State Superintendent, ...he shall not be entitled to any compensation after
notice of dismissal, or notice of annulment of license.

PROVIDED FURTHER, That the teacher shall have a duplicate of this Contract.

IN WITNESS WHEREOF, We have hereunto subscribed our names, this _15_

day of .... _Sept_ .... A. D. 1 _904_

.... _Grant Hollett_ .... Teacher.

.... _L M Green_ .... School Trustee.

NOTES:—
    (1.) Full authority is given the Trustee to substitute the words "principal," "supervisor" or "superintendent" for the word "teacher"
in the event the Contract should he so made.
    (2.) This Contract is the official blank, made by the State Superintendent of Public Instruction, under the provisions of H. B. No. 139,
Acts of 1899.

Teacher's or Principal's Report to Township Trustee.

NOTE.—This report must be made by each teacher having charge of the attendance of pupils. A high school teacher who works under the direction of a principal will not need to make the report in case the principal reports for the entire high school. In graded grammar schools each teacher should report for the pupils directly under his charge. The principal of a graded grammar school should report only for the pupils directly under his charge.

REPORT of................................ .... { teacher } of....................District
{ principal }

WASHINGTON TOWNSHIP, PORTER COUNTY, INDIANA,

to the Township Trustee, for the school term beginning.............................. ...._and

closing ....: ....

FOR ALL TEACHERS WHO HAVE CHARGE OF ATTENDANCE OF PUPILS.

1. Number of days school was in session, - - - - - - -

2. " " pupils enrolled during year, - Male,............; female,............; total,............

3. " " " withdrawn during year, - - " " "

4. " " " suspended " " - - " " "

5. " " " expelled " " - - " " "

6. " " " re-entered " " - " " "

7. " " " remaining in school close of year, " " "

8. " " " neither tardy nor absent during year, " " "

9. " " cases of tardiness during year, - " " "

10. " " pupils tardy during year, - " " "

11. Total days of attendance by all pupils for year, - - - - -

12. * " " " absence " " " " " - - - -

13. Total cases of tardiness,................. Time lost by tardiness, - - - - -

14. †Average daily attendance for year, - - - - -

15. Per cent. of attendance—$11 \div (11 + 12)$, -

16. Number of pupils promoted to - - - - -

       (a) Second year, - - - - -

       (b) Third " - - - - -

       (c) Fourth " - - - - -

       (d) Fifth " - - - -

       (e) Sixth " - - - -

       (f) Seventh " - - - -

       (g) Eighth " - - - -

       (h) High School, - - - - - -

17. Number of graduates from the common branches and receiving diplomas,

       Male,............; female,............; total,............

18. Number of graduates from non-commissioned township high schools,

       Male,............; female,............; total,............

19. Number of graduates from commissioned township high schools,

       Male,............; female,............; total,............

20. How many books in school library (not including reading circle books) at beginning of year?

21. How many books were added to library (not including reading circle books) during year?

22. Total now in school library (not including reading circle books), - - - -

23. How many reading circle books were added during year? - - - -

24. How many pupils read one or more school library or reading circle books during year? -

25. Do patrons read school library books? - - - - - -

26. Number of visits to school, Parents,............; officials,............; others,............; total,............

27. Number of teachers employed (if school be high school), Male,............; female,............; total,............

28. Number of days teacher attended township institute, - - - -

29. Books and apparatus left in school room at end of term, - - -

I,.. do solemnly swear that the above report is true to the best of my knowledge and belief.

{ Teacher.
.... { Principal.

NOTES:—

*(1.) After three days of absence the pupil should be withdrawn, and his absence counted no more for that period of absence. After being withdrawn, he is not a pupil of the school, and can not be again until he is re-entered, as in item 6.

†(2.) To find average daily attendance divide the whole number of days of attendance made by all the pupils by the number of days of school taught.

TEACHER'S CONTRACT.

This Agreement, Between *L. W. Green* School Trustee of

Washington School Township, in Porter County, and State of Indiana,

of the first part, and *Geneva Pierce* a legally qualified teacher in said County of the second part, certifies that the said teacher hereby agrees to teach the public school in District No. , Grade , in said Township, for the term commencing on the *5th* day of *Sept* A. D. 1*904* , for the consideration of *Two* Dollars and *53* Cents per { day, year, } to be paid *when called for* (State here when all or parts of salary will be paid.)

for 180 days work computed to $455.40

The said *Geneva Pierce* further agrees faithfully to perform all the duties of teacher in said school; using only such text-books as are prescribed by the Trustees in accordance with the law, except supplementary reading, such as Young People's Reading Circle books, etc., and other works recommended by the County Superintendent, and observing all Rules and Regulations of the County Board of Education, and all instructions of the County Superintendent of Schools; that *she* will attend and participate in the exercises of each Institute or other teachers' meetings that may be appointed for the teachers of said township, or for each day's absence therefrom, forfeit a sum equal to one day's wages, unless such absence shall be occasioned by sickness, that he will accurately keep and use all registers and blanks placed in *her* hands by said Trustee; that he will make a complete and accurate report at the close of the school term, the blank for which is provided on the back of this sheet; that *she* will make all other reports required of *her* by said Trustee, the County Superintendent, or the laws of Indiana, at the proper time and manner and in good order; that he will exercise due diligence in the preservation of school buildings, grounds, furniture, apparatus, books, blanks and other school property committed to *her* care, and turn the same over to the Trustee, or his representative, at the close of the term of school, in as good condition as when received, damage and wear by use excepted.

The said School Trustee agrees to keep the school buildings in good repair, and to furnish the necessary fuel, furniture, apparatus, books and blanks, and such other appliances as may be necessary for the systematic and proper conduct of said school.

And the said School Trustee, for and in behalf of said Township, further agrees to pay the said *Geneva Pierce* for services as teacher of said school, either a sum equal to the whole number of days taught at the rate of the above named sum per day, as agreed upon, or the salary for the year in the event of a yearly consideration, as agreed upon, when the said teacher shall have filled all the stipulations of this contract.

The said School Trustee further agrees to pay said teacher one day's wages for each day's attendance at the Township Institute, according to the Acts of 1889.

PROVIDED, That in case the said should be dismissed from said school by said Trustee, or his successor in office, for incompetency, cruelty, gross immorality, neglect of business, or a violation of any of the stipulations of this contract, or in case license should be annulled by the County Superintendent or State Superintendent, he shall not be entitled to any compensation after notice of dismissal, or notice of annulment of license.

PROVIDED FURTHER, That the teacher shall have a duplicate of this Contract.

IN WITNESS WHEREOF, We have hereunto subscribed our names, this *1st* day of *Sept* A. D. 1*904*

Geneva Pierce Teacher.

L. W. Green School Trustee.

NOTES:—
(1.) Full authority is given the Trustee to substitute the words "principal," "supervisor" or "superintendent" for the word "teacher" in the event the Contract should be so made.
(2.) This Contract is the official blank, made by the State Superintendent of Public Instruction, under the provisions of H. B. No. 139, Acts of 1899.

Teacher's or Principal's Report to Township Trustee.

NOTE.—This report must be made by each teacher having charge of the attendance of pupils. A high school teacher who works under the direction of a principal will not need to make the report in case the principal reports for the entire high school. In graded grammar schools each teacher should report for the pupils directly under his charge. The principal of a graded grammar school should report only for the pupils directly under his charge.

REPORT of.................... ....-........ { teacher } of..........................District
....-........ { principal }

WASHINGTON TOWNSHIP, PORTER COUNTY, INDIANA,

to the Township Trustee, for the school term beginning.................... ......_.......................... ....and

closing ...: .... - ....

FOR ALL TEACHERS WHO HAVE CHARGE OF ATTENDANCE OF PUPILS.

1. Number of days school was in session,   -   -   -   -   -   -   -   -   -

2.   "   " pupils enrolled during year,   -   Male, ...; female,....................; total,.....................

3.   "   "   " withdrawn during year, -   -   "   "   "

4.   "   "   " suspended   "   "   -   - "   "   ....   "

5.   "   "   " expelled   "   "   -   - "   "   "

6.   "   "   " re-entered   "   "   -   "   "   "

7.   "   "   " remaining in school close of year,   "   "   "

8.   "   "   " neither tardy nor absent during year,   "   "   "

9.   "   " cases of tardiness during year,   -   "   "   ....   "

10.   "   " pupils tardy during year,   -   - "   ....   "   "

11. Total days of attendance by all pupils for year,   -   -   -   -   -   -

12. * "   "   " absence   "   "   "   "   "   -   -   -   -   -

13. Total cases of tardiness, ...   Time lost by tardiness,   -   -   -   ... ...

14. †Average daily attendance for year,   -   -   -   -   -   -

15. Per cent. of attendance—$11 \div (11 + 12)$,   -   -   -   -

16. Number of pupils promoted to   -   -   -   -   -   -

      (a) Second year,   -   -   -   -   -   -

      (b) Third   "   -   -   -   -   -   -

      (c) Fourth   "   -   -   -   -   ....

      (d) Fifth   "   -   -   -   -   -   ....

      (e) Sixth   "   -   -   -   -   -   -

      (f) Seventh   "   -   -   -   -   -   —

      (g) Eighth   "   -   -   -   -   -   -

      (h) High School,   -   -   -   -   -   ....

17. Number of graduates from the common branches and receiving diplomas,
      Male, ...; female, ...; total, ...

18. Number of graduates from non-commissioned township high schools,
      Male,....................; female,....................; total,.......... ... .

19. Number of graduates from commissioned township high schools,
      Male,....................; female,....................; total,............

20. How many books in school library (not including reading circle books) at beginning of year?

21. How many books were added to library (not including reading circle books) during year?

22. Total now in school library (not including reading circle books),   -   -   -   -

23. How many reading circle books were added during year?   -   -   -   -   ....

24. How many pupils read one or more school library or reading circle books during year?   -   ....

25. Do patrons read school library books?   -   -   -   -   -   ....

26. Number of visits to school,   Parents,....................; officials, ...; others, ...; total,........................

27. Number of teachers employed (if school be high school), Male, ...; female, ...; total,............. ...

28. Number of days teacher attended township institute,   -   *   -   -   -

29. Books and apparatus left in school room at end of term,   -   -   -   -   ....

I,.. .. .., do solemnly swear that the above report is true to the best of my knowledge and belief.

.... { Teacher.
.... { Principal.

2A

For Township Trustees.   Wade Bros. & Wise, Printers.

TEACHER'S CONTRACT.

This Agreement, Between _Wm A. Boyd_ ....School Trustee of

Washington School Township, In Porter County, and State of Indiana,

of the first part, and _Cora Benham_ ....a legally qualified teacher in said
County of the second part, certifies that the said teacher hereby agrees to teach the public school in District No. _1_,
Grade ...., in said Township, for the term commencing on the _4th_ .... day of _Sep_
A. D. 1 _899_ , for the consideration of .... _Two_ ....Dollars and
.... Cents per { day, year, } to be paid _where called for_ ....
(State here when all or parts of salary will be paid.)

The said ...._Cora Benham_ .... further agrees faithfully to perform
all the duties of teacher in said school; using only such text-books as are prescribed by the Trustees in accordance with
the law, except supplementary reading, such as Young People's Reading Circle books, etc., and other works recommended by the County Superintendent, and observing all Rules and Regulations of the County Board of Education,
and all instructions of the County Superintendent of Schools; that S he will attend and participate in the exercises of
each Institute or other teachers' meetings that may be appointed for the teachers of said township, or for each day's
absence therefrom, forfeit a sum equal to one day's wages, unless such absence shall be occasioned by sickness, that
S he will accurately keep and use all registers and blanks placed in _her_ hands by said Trustee; that S he will
make a complete and accurate report at the close of the school term, the blank for which is provided on the back of
this sheet; that S he will make all other reports required of _her_ by said Trustee, the County Superintendent, or
the laws of Indiana, at the proper time and manner and in good order; that S he will exercise due diligence in the
preservation of school buildings, grounds, furniture, apparatus, books, blanks and other school property committed to
her care, and turn the same over to the Trustee, or his representative, at the close of the term of school, in as
good condition as when received, damage and wear by use excepted.

The said School Trustee agrees to keep the school buildings in good repair, and to furnish the necessary fuel,
furniture, apparatus, books and blanks, and such other appliances as may be necessary for the systematic and proper
conduct of said school.

And the said School Trustee, for and in behalf of said Township, further agrees to pay the said........................
Cora Benham for services as teacher of said school, either a sum equal to the whole
number of days taught at the rate of the above named sum per day, as agreed upon, or the salary for the year in the
event of a yearly consideration, as agreed upon, when the said teacher shall have filled all the stipulations of this contract.

The said School Trustee further agrees to pay said teacher one day's wages for each day's attendance at the Township Institute, according to the Acts of 1889.

PROVIDED, That in case the said ...._Cora Benham_ ....should be
dismissed from said school by said Trustee, or his successor in office, for incompetency, cruelty, gross immorality,
neglect of business, or a violation of any of the stipulations of this contract, or in case _her_ license should be
annulled by the County Superintendent or State Superintendent, S he shall not be entitled to any compensation after
notice of dismissal, or notice of annulment of license.

PROVIDED FURTHER, That the teacher shall have a duplicate of this Contract.

IN WITNESS WHEREOF, We have hereunto subscribed our names, this _Eight_
day of _Aug_ .... A. D. 18 _99_
............_Cora Benham_ ....Teacher.
............_Wm A. Boyd_ ....School Trustee.

NOTES:—
(1.) Full authority is given the Trustee to substitute the words "principal," "supervisor" or "superintendent" for the word "teacher"
in the event the Contract should be so made.
(2.) This Contract is the official blank, made by the State Superintendent of Public Instruction, under the provisions of H. B. No. 139,
Acts of 1899.

Teacher's or Principal's Report to Township Trustee.

NOTE.—This report must be made by each teacher having charge of the attendance of pupils. A high school teacher who works under the direction of a principal will not need to make the report in case the principal reports for the entire high school. In graded grammar schools each teacher should report for the pupils directly under his charge. The principal of a graded grammar school should report only for the pupils directly under his charge.

REPORT of.................. .... { teacher } of..........................District
{ principal }

WASHINGTON TOWNSHIP, PORTER COUNTY, INDIANA,

to the Township Trustee, for the school term beginning.... ....and

closing ...:   ....

FOR ALL TEACHERS WHO HAVE CHARGE OF ATTENDANCE OF PUPILS.

1. Number of days school was in session, -   -   -   -   -   -   -   -   -
2. "   " pupils enrolled during year,   -   Male, ...; female,.....................; total,..................
3. "   "   " withdrawn during year, -   -   "   "   "
4. "   "   " suspended   "   "   -   -   "   "   ....   "
5. "   "   " expelled   "   "   -   -   "   "   "
6. "   "   " re-entered   "   "   -   "   "   "
7. "   "   " remaining in school close of year, "   "   "
8. "   "   " " neither tardy nor absent during year, "   "   "
9. "   " cases of tardiness during year,   -   "   "   ....   "
10. "   " pupils tardy during year,   -   -   "   ....   "   "
11. Total days of attendance by all pupils for year,   -   -   -   -   -   -
12. * "   "   " absence   "   "   "   "   "   -   -   -   -   -
13. Total cases of tardiness,......... Time lost by tardiness,   -   -   -   ... _ __ .
14. †Average daily attendance for year,   -   -   -   -   -   -
15. Per cent. of attendance—$11 \div (11+12)$,   -   ___ -   -
16. Number of pupils promoted to   -   -   -   -   -   -   -
    (a) Second year,   -   -   -   -   -   -   -
    (b) Third   "   -   -   -   -   -   -
    (c) Fourth   "   -   -   -   -   -   ....
    (d) Fifth   "   -   -   -   -   -   ....
    (e) Sixth   "   -   -   -   -   -   ....
    (f) Seventh   "   -   -   -   -   -   -
    (g) Eighth   "   -   -   -   -   -
    (h) High School,   -   -   -   -   -   -   ....
17. Number of graduates from the common branches and receiving diplomas,
    Male,....................; female, ... ; total,.. .. ..
18. Number of graduates from non-commissioned township high schools,
    Male,....................; female,...................; total,........ ... .
19. Number of graduates from commissioned township high schools,
    Male,....................; female,....................; total,.........
20. How many books in school library (not including reading circle books) at beginning of year?
21. How many books were added to library (not including reading circle books) during year?
22. Total now in school library (not including reading circle books),   -   -   -   -   -
23. How many reading circle books were added during year?   -   -   -   -   -   ....
24. How many pupils read one or more school library or reading circle books during year?   -   ....
25. Do patrons read school library books?   -   -   -   -   -   -   -   ....
26. Number of visits to school,   Parents,.................; officials, ...; others, ...; total,............................
27. Number of teachers employed (if school be high school), Male,.............; female, ...; total,............ ...
28. Number of days teacher attended township institute,   -   -   *   -   -
29. Books and apparatus left in school room at end of term,   -   -   -   -   ....

I,... . .. ., do solemnly swear that the above report is true to the best of my knowledge and belief.

{ Teacher.
{ Principal.

*(1.) After three days of absence the pupil should be withdrawn, and his absence counted no more for that period of absence. After being withdrawn, he is not a pupil of the school, and can not be again until he is re-entered, as in item 6.
†(2.) To find average daily attendance divide the whole number of days of attendance made by all the pupils by the number of days of school taught.

For Township Trustees.   Wade Bros. & Wise, Printers.

TEACHER'S CONTRACT.

This Agreement, Between *L. M. Green* .School Trustee of

Washington School Township, in Porter County, and State of Indiana,

of the first part, and *Cora Benham* a legally qualified teacher in said

County of the second part, certifies that the said teacher hereby agrees to teach the public school in District No.............,

Grade........, in said Township, for the term commencing on the.. *5th* day of *Sept*

A. D. 1 *904* .., for the consideration of........ *Two* Dollars and

Sixty ...Cents per { day, year, } to be paid.. *when called for* (State here when all or parts of salary will be paid.)

for 180 days teachg consideration $468 00

The said *Cora Benham* further agrees faithfully to perform

all the duties of teacher in said school; using only such text-books as are prescribed by the Trustees in accordance with
the law, except supplementary reading, such as Young People's Reading Circle books, etc., and other works recommended by the County Superintendent, and observing all Rules and Regulations of the County Board of Education,
and all instructions of the County Superintendent of Schools; that *s*he will attend and participate in the exercises of
each Institute or other teachers' meetings that may be appointed for the teachers of said township, or for each day's
absence therefrom, forfeit a sum equal to one day's wages, unless such absence shall be occasioned by sickness, that
*s*he will accurately keep and use all registers and blanks placed in *her* hands by said Trustee; that *s*he will
make a complete and accurate report at the close of the school term, the blank for which is provided on the back of
this sheet; that *s*he will make all other reports required of *her* by said Trustee, the County Superintendent, or
the laws of Indiana, at the proper time and manner and in good order; that *s*he will exercise due diligence in the
preservation of school buildings, grounds, furniture, apparatus, books, blanks and other school property committed to
her care, and turn the same over to the Trustee, or his representative, at the close of the term of school, in as
good condition as when received, damage and wear by use excepted.

The said School Trustee agrees to keep the school buildings in good repair, and to furnish the necessary fuel,
furniture, apparatus, books and blanks, and such other appliances as may be necessary for the systematic and proper
conduct of said school.

And the said School Trustee, for and in behalf of said Township, further agrees to pay the said............. ....
....for services as teacher of said school, either a sum equal to the whole
number of days taught at the rate of the above named sum per day, as agreed upon, or the salary for the year in the
event of a yearly consideration, as agreed upon, when the said teacher shall have filled all the stipulations of this contract.

The said School Trustee further agrees to pay said teacher one day's wages for each day's attendance at the Township Institute, according to the Acts of 1889.

PROVIDED, That in case the said... should be
dismissed from said school by said Trustee, or his successor in office, for incompetency, cruelty, gross immorality,
neglect of business, or a violation of any of the stipulations of this contract, or in case ....license should be
annulled by the County Superintendent or State Superintendent, ...he shall not be entitled to any compensation after
notice of dismissal, or notice of annulment of license.

PROVIDED FURTHER, That the teacher shall have a duplicate of this Contract.

IN WITNESS WHEREOF, We have hereunto subscribed our names, this.. *1st*

day of *Sept* A. D. 1 *804*

Cora Benham .Teacher.

J. M. Green .School Trustee.

NOTES:—
    (1.) Full authority is given the Trustee to substitute the words "principal," "supervisor" or "superintendent" for the word "teacher"
in the event the Contract should be so made.
    (2.) This Contract is the official blank, made by the State Superintendent of Public Instruction, under the provisions of H. B. No. 139,
Acts of 1899.

Teacher's or Principal's Report to Township Trustee.

NOTE.—This report must be made by each teacher having charge of the attendance of pupils. A high school teacher who works under the direction of a principal will not need to make the report in case the principal reports for the entire high school. In graded grammar schools each teacher should report for the pupils directly under his charge. The principal of a graded grammar school should report only for the pupils directly under his charge.

REPORT of............................ .... { teacher } { principal } of....................District

WASHINGTON TOWNSHIP, PORTER COUNTY, INDIANA,

to the Township Trustee, for the school term beginning.................... .... .and

closing ....: ....

FOR ALL TEACHERS WHO HAVE CHARGE OF ATTENDANCE OF PUPILS.

1. Number of days school was in session, - - - - - - - -
2. " " pupils enrolled during year, - Male, ...; female,....................; total,.............. ...
3. " " " withdrawn during year, - - " " "
4. " " " suspended " " - - " " ....
5. " " " expelled " " - " " "
6. " " " re-entered " " - " " "
7. " " " remaining in school close of year, " " "
8. " " " neither tardy nor absent during year, " " "
9. " " cases of tardiness during year, - " " ....
10. " " pupils tardy during year, - " .... " "
11. Total days of attendance by all pupils for year, - - - - - -
12. * " " " absence " " " " " - - - -
13. Total cases of tardiness,.................... Time lost by tardiness, - - ... .. - ..
14. †Average daily attendance for year, - - - - - -
15. Per cent. of attendance—11÷(11+12), - - -
16. Number of pupils promoted to - - - - - -
    - (a) Second year, - - - - -
    - (b) Third " - - - - -
    - (c) Fourth " - - - - -
    - (d) Fifth " - - - - -
    - (e) Sixth " - - - - -
    - (f) Seventh " - - - - -
    - (g) Eighth " - - - - -
    - (h) High School, - - - - -
17. Number of graduates from the common branches and receiving diplomas, Male,............; female, ...; total,.. .. ..
18. Number of graduates from non-commissioned township high schools, Male,............; female,............; total,........ ... ...
19. Number of graduates from commissioned township high schools, Male,............; female,............; total,........
20. How many books in school library (not including reading circle books) at beginning of year?
21. How many books were added to library (not including reading circle books) during year?
22. Total now in school library (not including reading circle books), - - - - -
23. How many reading circle books were added during year? - - - - -
24. How many pupils read one or more school library or reading circle books during year? -
25. Do patrons read school library books? - - - - -
26. Number of visits to school, Parents, ...; officials, ...; others, ...; total, ...
27. Number of teachers employed (if school be high school), Male,............; female, ...; total, ...
28. Number of days teacher attended township institute, - - - . - -
29. Books and apparatus left in school room at end of term, - - - -

I,............................ .... , do solemnly swear that the above report is

true to the best of my knowledge and belief.

.... { Teacher. { Principal.

NOTES:—

*(1.) After three days of absence the pupil should be withdrawn, and his absence counted no more for that period of absence. After being withdrawn, he is not a pupil of the school, and can not be again until he is re-entered, as in item 6.

†(2.) To find average daily attendance divide the whole number of days of attendance made by all the pupils by the number of days of school taught.

For Township Trustees.   Wade Bros. & Wise, Printers.

TEACHER'S CONTRACT.

This Agreement, Between _Geo Green_, _____School Trustee of

Washington School Township, In Porter County, and State of Indiana,

of the first part, and _Jennie Redding_ ____a legally qualified teacher in said County of the second part, certifies that the said teacher hereby agrees to teach the public school in District No.____, Grade____, in said Township, for the term commencing on the _5th_ ____ day of _Sept_ ____ A. D. 1 _904_, for the consideration of _Two_ ____Dollars and _20_ ____ Cents per { day, { year, } to be paid _when called for_ (State here when all or parts of salary will be paid.)

180 das at $2.20 pr day $396 00

The said _Jennie Redding_ ____ further agrees faithfully to perform all the duties of teacher in said school; using only such text-books as are prescribed by the Trustees in accordance with the law, except supplementary reading, such as Young People's Reading Circle books, etc., and other works recommended by the County Superintendent, and observing all Rules and Regulations of the County Board of Education, and all instructions of the County Superintendent of Schools; that _s_he will attend and participate in the exercises of each Institute or other teachers' meetings that may be appointed for the teachers of said township, or for each day's absence therefrom, forfeit a sum equal to one day's wages, unless such absence shall be occasioned by sickness, that _s_he will accurately keep and use all registers and blanks placed in _her_ hands by said Trustee; that ____he will make a complete and accurate report at the close of the school term, the blank for which is provided on the back of this sheet; that _s_he will make all other reports required of _her_ by said Trustee, the County Superintendent, or the laws of Indiana, at the proper time and manner and in good order; that _s_he will exercise due diligence in the preservation of school buildings, grounds, furniture, apparatus, books, blanks and other school property committed to _her_ care, and turn the same over to the Trustee, or his representative, at the close of the term of school, in as good condition as when received, damage and wear by use excepted.

The said School Trustee agrees to keep the school buildings in good repair, and to furnish the necessary fuel, furniture, apparatus, books and blanks, and such other appliances as may be necessary for the systematic and proper conduct of said school.

And the said School Trustee, for and in behalf of said Township, further agrees to pay the said____ ____for services as teacher of said school, either a sum equal to the whole number of days taught at the rate of the above named sum per day, as agreed upon, or the salary for the year in the event of a yearly consideration, as agreed upon, when the said teacher shall have filled all the stipulations of this contract.

The said School Trustee further agrees to pay said teacher one day's wages for each day's attendance at the Township Institute, according to the Acts of 1889.

PROVIDED, That in case the said____ ____should be dismissed from said school by said Trustee, or his successor in office, for incompetency, cruelty, gross immorality, neglect of business, or a violation of any of the stipulations of this contract, or in case ____ license should be annulled by the County Superintendent or State Superintendent, ____he shall not be entitled to any compensation after notice of dismissal, or notice of annulment of license.

PROVIDED FURTHER, That the teacher shall have a duplicate of this Contract.

IN WITNESS WHEREOF, We have hereunto subscribed our names, this _1st_ day of _Sept_ ____A. D. 1 _904_

Jennie Reding ____Teacher.

Geo Green ____School Trustee.

NOTES:—

(1.) Full authority is given the Trustee to substitute the words "principal," "supervisor" or "superintendent" for the word "teacher" in the event the Contract should be so made.

(2.) This Contract is the official blank, made by the State Superintendent of Public Instruction, under the provisions of H. B. No. 139, Acts of 1899.

Teacher's or Principal's Report to Township Trustee.

NOTE.—This report must be made by each teacher having charge of the attendance of pupils. A high school teacher who works under the direction of a principal will not need to make the report in case the principal reports for the entire high school. In graded grammar schools each teacher should report for the pupils directly under his charge. The principal of a graded grammar school should report only for the pupils directly under his charge.

REPORT of.................. .... { teacher } { principal } of.......................District

WASHINGTON TOWNSHIP, PORTER COUNTY, INDIANA,

to the Township Trustee, for the school term beginning.................. ....and

closing .....

FOR ALL TEACHERS WHO HAVE CHARGE OF ATTENDANCE OF PUPILS.

1. Number of days school was in session,
2. "   " pupils enrolled during year,   - Male, ...; female,......................; total,...................
3. "   "   " withdrawn during year, - -   "   "   "
4. "   "   " suspended   "   "   - -   "   "......................   "
5. "   "   " expelled   "   "   -   "   "   "
6. "   "   " re-entered   "   "   -   "   "   "
7. "   "   " remaining in school close of year,   "   "   "
8. "   "   " " neither tardy nor absent during year,   "   "   "
9. "   "   cases of tardiness during year,   -   "   "......................   "
10. "   "   pupils tardy during year,   -   -   " ....   "   "
11. Total days of attendance by all pupils for year,
12. * "   "   " absence   "   "   "   "   "   -   -   -   -   -   -
13. Total cases of tardiness,..................... Time lost by tardiness,   -   -   -   ... .
14. †Average daily attendance for year,   -   -   -   -   -
15. Per cent. of attendance—$11 \div (11+12)$,   -   -   -   -
16. Number of pupils promoted to   -   -   -   -   -   -
    (a) Second year,   -   -   -   -   -   -
    (b) Third   "   -   -   -   -   -   -
    (c) Fourth   "   -   -   -   -   -   -......................
    (d) Fifth   "   -   -   -   -   -   -......................
    (e) Sixth   "   -   -   -   -   -......................
    (f) Seventh   "   -   -   -   -   -   -
    (g) Eighth   "   -   -   -   -   -
    (h) High School,   -   -   -   -   -......................
17. Number of graduates from the common branches and receiving diplomas,
    Male,.................; female, ...; total,..... . .   ...
18. Number of graduates from non-commissioned township high schools,
    Male,.................; female,................; total,............ ... .
19. Number of graduates from commissioned township high schools,
    Male,.................; female,...................; total,.........
20. How many books in school library (not including reading circle books) at beginning of year?
21. How many books were added to library (not including reading circle books) during year?
22. Total now in school library (not including reading circle books),   -   -   -   -
23. How many reading circle books were added during year?   -   -   -   -   -......................
24. How many pupils read one or more school library or reading circle books during year?   -   ....
25. Do patrons read school library books?   -   -   -   -   -   -
26. Number of visits to school,   Parents,.................; officials, ...; others, ...; total,......................
27. Number of teachers employed (if school be high school), Male,..................; female,..................; total,... .. ..
28. Number of days teacher attended township institute,   -   -   -   "   "   -
29. Books and apparatus left in school room at end of term,   -   -   -......................

I,... ...., do solemnly swear that the above report is true to the best of my knowledge and belief.

.... { Teacher. } { Principal.

NOTES:—
*(1.) After three days of absence the pupil should be withdrawn, and his absence counted no more for that period of absence. After being withdrawn, he is not a pupil of the school, and can not be again until he is re-entered, as in item 6.
†(2.) To find average daily attendance divide the whole number of days of attendance made by all the pupils by the number of days of school taught.

For Township Trustees.   Wade Bros. & Wise, Printers.

TEACHER'S CONTRACT.

This Agreement, Between _Lewis M Sur_ School Trustee of

Washington School Township, in Porter County, and State of Indiana,

of the first part, and _Grace Maxwell_ a legally qualified teacher in said

County of the second part, certifies that the said teacher hereby agrees to teach the public school in District No.....,

Grade _____, in said Township, for the term commencing on the _5th_ day of _Sept_

A. D. 1 _904_ , for the consideration of _One_ Dollars and

_98_ Cents per { day, year, } to be paid _when called for_ (State here when all or parts of salary will be paid.)

180 days teaching consideration 35 6 40

The said _Grace Maxwell_ further agrees faithfully to perform all the duties of teacher in said school; using only such text-books as are prescribed by the Trustees in accordance with the law, except supplementary reading, such as Young People's Reading Circle books, etc., and other works recommended by the County Superintendent, and observing all Rules and Regulations of the County Board of Education, and all instructions of the County Superintendent of Schools; that _s_ he will attend and participate in the exercises of each Institute or other teachers' meetings that may be appointed for the teachers of said township, or for each day's absence therefrom, forfeit a sum equal to one day's wages, unless such absence shall be occasioned by sickness, that _s_ he will accurately keep and use all registers and blanks placed in _her_ hands by said Trustee; that _s_ he will make a complete and accurate report at the close of the school term, the blank for which is provided on the back of this sheet; that _s_ he will make all other reports required of _her_ by said Trustee, the County Superintendent, or the laws of Indiana, at the proper time and manner and in good order; that .....he will exercise due diligence in the preservation of school buildings, grounds, furniture, apparatus, books, blanks and other school property committed to _her_ care, and turn the same over to the Trustee, or his representative, at the close of the term of school, in as good condition as when received, damage and wear by use excepted.

The said School Trustee agrees to keep the school buildings in good repair, and to furnish the necessary fuel, furniture, apparatus, books and blanks, and such other appliances as may be necessary for the systematic and proper conduct of said school.

And the said School Trustee, for and in behalf of said Township, further agrees to pay the said .... for services as teacher of said school, either a sum equal to the whole number of days taught at the rate of the above named sum per day, as agreed upon, or the salary for the year in the event of a yearly consideration, as agreed upon, when the said teacher shall have filled all the stipulations of this contract.

The said School Trustee further agrees to pay said teacher one day's wages for each day's attendance at the Township Institute, according to the Acts of 1889.

PROVIDED, That in case the said..should be dismissed from said school by said Trustee, or his successor in office, for incompetency, cruelty, gross immorality, neglect of business, or a violation of any of the stipulations of this contract, or in case................license should be annulled by the County Superintendent or State Superintendent, ...he shall not be entitled to any compensation after notice of dismissal, or notice of annulment of license.

PROVIDED FURTHER, That the teacher shall have a duplicate of this Contract.

IN WITNESS WHEREOF, We have hereunto subscribed our names, this _1st_

day of _Sept_ A. D. 1 _904_

C. Grace Maxwell .Teacher.

Lewis Sur School Trustee.

NOTES:—
(1.) Full authority is given the Trustee to substitute the words "principal," "supervisor" or "superintendent" for the word "teacher" in the event the Contract should be so made.
(2.) This Contract is the official blank, made by the State Superintendent of Public Instruction, under the provisions of H. B. No. 139, Acts of 1899.

Teacher's or Principal's Report to Township Trustee.

NOTE.—This report must be made by each teacher having charge of the attendance of pupils. A high school teacher who works under the direction of a principal will not need to make the report in case the principal reports for the entire high school. In graded grammar schools each teacher should report for the pupils directly under his charge. The principal of a graded grammar school should report only for the pupils directly under his charge.

REPORT of................................ .... - .... { teacher } of..........................District
{ principal }

WASHINGTON TOWNSHIP, PORTER COUNTY, INDIANA,

to the Township Trustee, for the school term beginning.................... - ....and

closing ....: .... - ....

FOR ALL TEACHERS WHO HAVE CHARGE OF ATTENDANCE OF PUPILS.

1. Number of days school was in session, - - - - - - - - -
2. " " pupils enrolled during year, - Male, ...; female,........................; total,............... ...
3. " " " withdrawn during year, - - " " "
4. " " " suspended " " - - " " .... "
5. " " " expelled " " - " " "
6. " " " re-entered " " - " " "
7. " " " remaining in school close of year, " " "
8. " " " neither tardy nor absent during year, " " "
9. " " cases of tardiness during year, - " " .... "
10. " " pupils tardy during year, - - " .... " "
11. Total days of attendance by all pupils for year, - - - - -
12. * " " " absence " " " " " - - - - -
13. Total cases of tardiness,........................ Time lost by tardiness, - - - ... .. — ...
14. †Average daily attendance for year, - - - - -
15. Per cent. of attendance—11÷(11+12), - - -
16. Number of pupils promoted to - - - - -
    (a) Second year, - - - -
    (b) Third " - - - -
    (c) Fourth " - - - - - ....
    (d) Fifth " - - - - - ....
    (e) Sixth " - - - - - ....
    (f) Seventh " - - - - - —
    (g) Eighth " - - - - - -
    (h) High School, - - - - - .... - .
17. Number of graduates from the common branches and receiving diplomas,
    Male,.........._____ ; female, ... ; total,.. .. ..
18. Number of graduates from non-commissioned township high schools,
    Male,.................___.; female,........................; total,............... ... .
19. Number of graduates from commissioned township high schools,
    Male,......................; female,.....................; total,...........
20. How many books in school library (not including reading circle books) at beginning of year?
21. How many books were added to library (not including reading circle books) during year?
22. Total now in school library (not including reading circle books), - - - - -
23. How many reading circle books were added during year? - - - - - ....
24. How many pupils read one or more school library or reading circle books during year? - ....
25. Do patrons read school library books? - - - - - - - ....
26. Number of visits to school, Parents,.....................; officials, ...; others, ...; total,.........................
27. Number of teachers employed (if school be high school), Male,..................; female, ...; total,..................
28. Number of days teacher attended township institute, - - - - . . .
29. Books and apparatus left in school room at end of term, - - - ....

I,.., do solemnly swear that the above report is true to the best of my knowledge and belief.

.... { Teacher.
{ Principal.

NOTES:—
*(1.) After three days of absence the pupil should be withdrawn, and his absence counted no more for that period of absence. After being withdrawn, he is not a pupil of the school, and can not be again until he is re-entered, as in item 6.
†(2.) To find average daily attendance divide the whole number of days of attendance made by all the pupils by the number of days of school taught.

TEACHER'S CONTRACT.

This Agreement, Between *H. E. Seymour* ~~Wm. A. Boyd~~ School Trustee o

Washington School Township, in Porter County, and State of Indiana,

of the first part, and *W. E. Seymour* a legally qualified teacher in said

County of the second part, certifies that the said teacher hereby agrees to teach the public school in District No. 2

Grade ......, in said Township, for the term commencing on the *4th* day of *Sep.*

A. D. 1 *899* , for the consideration of................................. — *Two* Dollars and

— .... — Cents per { day, year } to be paid......*As Called For*
(State here when all or parts of salary will be paid.)

The said......*W. E. Seymour*........................further agrees faithfully to perform

all the duties of teacher in said school; using only such text-books as are prescribed by the Trustees in accordance with the law, except supplementary reading, such as Young People's Reading Circle books, etc., and other works recommended by the County Superintendent, and observing all Rules and Regulations of the County Board of Education and all instructions of the County Superintendent of Schools; that ......he will attend and participate in the exercises o each Institute or other teachers' meetings that may be appointed for the teachers of said township, or for each day's absence therefrom, forfeit a sum equal to one day's wages, unless such absence shall be occasioned by sickness, that ......he will accurately keep and use all registers and blanks placed in *his* hands by said Trustee; that he will make a complete and accurate report at the close of the school term, the blank for which is provided on the back o this sheet; that ......he will make all other reports required of *him* by said Trustee, the County Superintendent, o the laws of Indiana, at the proper time and manner and in good order; that ....he will exercise due diligence in the preservation of school buildings, grounds, furniture, apparatus, books, blanks and other school property committed to *his* ....care, and turn the same over to the Trustee, or his representative, at the close of the term of school, in a good condition as when received, damage and wear by use excepted.

The said School Trustee agrees to keep the school buildings in good repair, and to furnish the necessary fuel furniture, apparatus, books and blanks, and such other appliances as may be necessary for the systematic and prope conduct of said school.

And the said School Trustee, for and in behalf of said Township, further agrees to pay the said............................ *W. E. Seymour* ....for services as teacher of said school, either a sum equal to the whole number of days taught at the rate of the above named sum per day, as agreed upon, or the salary for the year in the event of a yearly consideration, as agreed upon, when the said teacher shall have filled all the stipulations of this contract.

The said School Trustee further agrees to pay said teacher one day's wages for each day's attendance at the Township Institute, according to the Acts of 1889. *W. E. Seymour*

PROVIDED, That in case the said......*W. E. Seymour*......should be dismissed from said school by said Trustee, or his successor in office, for incompetency, cruelty, gross immorality, neglect of business, or a violation of any of the stipulations of this contract, or in case *his* license should be annulled by the County Superintendent or State Superintendent, ... he shall not be entitled to any compensation after notice of dismissal, or notice of annulment of license.

PROVIDED FURTHER, That the teacher shall have a duplicate of this Contract.

IN WITNESS WHEREOF, We have hereunto subscribed our names, this *21st*

day of.....*June*..... A. D. 1 *899*

H. E. Seymour ....Teacher.

Wm. A. Boyd ....School Trustee.

NOTES:--
   (1.) Full authority is given the Trustee to substitute the words "principal," "supervisor" or "superintendent" for the word "teacher' in the event the Contract should be so made.
   (2.) This Contract is the official blank, made by the State Superintendent of Public Instruction, under the provisions of H. B. No. 139 Acts of 1899.

Teacher's or Principal's Report to Township Trustee.

NOTE.—This report must be made by each teacher having charge of the attendance of pupils. A high school teacher who works under the direction of a principal will not need to make the report in case the principal reports for the entire high school. In graded grammar schools each teacher should report for the pupils directly under his charge. The principal of a graded grammar school should report only for the pupils directly under his charge.

REPORT of......*H. E. Seymour*......{ teacher / principal } of... *2nd* ...District

WASHINGTON TOWNSHIP, PORTER COUNTY, INDIANA,

to the Township Trustee, for the school term beginning... *Sept. 4, 1899* ...and
closing... *May 18, 1900.*

FOR ALL TEACHERS WHO HAVE CHARGE OF ATTENDANCE OF PUPILS.

1. Number of days school was in session,			*180*
2. " " pupils enrolled during year,	Male, *8*;	female, *6*;	total, *14*
3. " " " withdrawn during year,	" *7*	" *5*	" *12*
4. " " " suspended " "	"	"	"
5. " " " expelled " "	" *1*	"	"
6. " " " re-entered " "	" *4*	" *3*	" *7*
7. " " " remaining in school close of year,	" *2*	" *2*	" *4*
8. " " " neither tardy nor absent during year,	" *0*	" *0*	"
9. " " cases of tardiness during year,	"	"	*73*
10. " " pupils tardy during year,	" *8*	" *6*	*14 73*
11. Total days of attendance by all pupils for year,			*15-28*
12. * " " " absence " " " " "			*139*
13. Total cases of tardiness, *73* Time lost by tardiness,			*29hr. 21min.*
14. †Average daily attendance for year,			*7 35/54*
15. Per cent. of attendance—11÷(11+12),			*94*

16. Number of pupils promoted to

(a) Second year, ... *1*

(b) Third "

(c) Fourth "

(d) Fifth "

(e) Sixth "

(f) Seventh " ... *1*

(g) Eighth "

(h) High School, ... *1*

17. Number of graduates from the common branches and receiving diplomas,
Male, *0*; female, *1*; total, *1*

18. Number of graduates from non-commissioned township high schools,
Male, ; female, ; total,

19. Number of graduates from commissioned township high schools,
Male, ; female, ; total,

20. How many books in school library (not including reading circle books) at beginning of year?

21. How many books were added to library (not including reading circle books) during year? ... *0*

22. Total now in school library (not including reading circle books), -

23. How many reading circle books were added during year? ... *0*

24. How many pupils read one or more school library or reading circle books during year? ... *4*

25. Do patrons read school library books? ... *yes*

26. Number of visits to school, Parents, *1*; officials, *1*; others, *2*; total, *4*

27. Number of teachers employed (if school be high school), Male, ; female, ; total, ... *7*

28. Number of days teacher attended township institute, ... *7*

29. Books and apparatus left in school room at end of term, ... *yes*

I, *H. E. Seymour*, do solemnly swear that the above report is true to the best of my knowledge and belief.

H. E. Seymour { Teacher. / Principal.

NOTES:—*(1.) After three days of absence the pupil should be withdrawn, and his absence counted no more for that period of absence. After being withdrawn, he is not a pupil of the school, and can not be again until he is re-entered, as in item 6.
†(2.) To find average daily attendance divide the whole number of days of attendance made by all the pupils by the number of days of school taught.

40

TEACHER'S CONTRACT.

This Agreement, Between *A. S. Hermance* School Trustee of

Washington School Township, in Porter County, and State of Indiana,

of the first part, and *Grant Hollett* a legally qualified teacher in said

County of the second part, certifies that the said teacher hereby agrees to teach the public school in District No. ....

Grade ...., in said Township, for the term commencing on the *Fourth* day of *September*

A. D. 1 *90 5* , for the consideration of *Two Twenty Four* Dollars and

24 Cents per { day, year, } to be paid *When Called for* (State here when all or parts of salary will be paid.)

Consideration 408 20

The said *Grant Hollett* further agrees faithfully to perform

all the duties of teacher in said school; using only such text-books as are prescribed by the Trustees in accordance with the law, except supplementary reading, such as Young People's Reading Circle books, etc., and other works recommended by the County Superintendent, and observing all Rules and Regulations of the County Board of Education, and all instructions of the County Superintendent of Schools; that ...he will attend and participate in the exercises of each Institute or other teachers' meetings that may be appointed for the teachers of said township, or for each day's absence therefrom, forfeit a sum equal to one day's wages, unless such absence shall be occasioned by sickness, that ...he will accurately keep and use all registers and blanks placed in *his* hands by said Trustee; that ...he will make a complete and accurate report at the close of the school term, the blank for which is provided on the back of this sheet; that ......he will make all other reports required of *him* by said Trustee, the County Superintendent, or the laws of Indiana, at the proper time and manner and in good order; that ....he will exercise due diligence in the preservation of school buildings, grounds, furniture, apparatus, books, blanks and other school property committed to *his* care, and turn the same over to the Trustee, or his representative, at the close of the term of school, in as good condition as when received, damage and wear by use excepted.

The said School Trustee agrees to keep the school buildings in good repair, and to furnish the necessary fuel, furniture, apparatus, books and blanks, and such other appliances as may be necessary for the systematic and proper conduct of said school.

And the said School Trustee, for and in behalf of said Township, further agrees to pay the said *Grant Hollett* for services as teacher of said school, either a sum equal to the whole number of days taught at the rate of the above named sum per day, as agreed upon, or the salary for the year in the event of a yearly consideration, as agreed upon, when the said teacher shall have filled all the stipulations of this contract.

The said School Trustee further agrees to pay said teacher one day's wages for each day's attendance at the Township Institute, according to the Acts of 1889.

PROVIDED, That in case the said *Grant Hollett* should be dismissed from said school by said Trustee, or his successor in office, for incompetency, cruelty, gross immorality, neglect of business, or a violation of any of the stipulations of this contract, or in case *his* license should be annulled by the County Superintendent or State Superintendent, ...he shall not be entitled to any compensation after notice of dismissal, or notice of annulment of license.

PROVIDED FURTHER, That the teacher shall have a duplicate of this Contract.

IN WITNESS WHEREOF, We have hereunto subscribed our names, this *28*

day of *Aug* A. D. *1905*

Grant Hollett Teacher.

A. S. Hermance School Trustee.

NOTES:—
(1.) Full authority is given the Trustee to substitute the words "principal," "supervisor" or "superintendent" for the word "teacher" in the event the Contract should be so made.
(2.) This Contract is the official blank, made by the State Superintendent of Public Instruction, under the provisions of H. B. No. 139, Acts of 1899.

Teacher's or Principal's Report to Township Trustee.

NOTE.—This report must be made by each teacher having charge of the attendance of pupils. A high school teacher who works under the direction of a principal will not need to make the report in case the principal reports for the entire high school. In graded grammar schools each teacher should report for the pupils directly under his charge. The principal of a graded grammar school should report only for the pupils directly under his charge.

REPORT of.................... ....} teacher } of..........................District
} principal }

WASHINGTON TOWNSHIP, PORTER COUNTY, INDIANA,

to the Township Trustee, for the school term beginning.................... ....and

closing ....

FOR ALL TEACHERS WHO HAVE CHARGE OF ATTENDANCE OF PUPILS.

1. Number of days school was in session,   -   -   -   -   -   -   -   -
2.   "   " pupils enrolled during year,   -   Male, ...; female,....................; total,.................... ...
3.   "   "   " withdrawn during year, -   -   "   "   "
4.   "   "   " suspended   "   "   -   - "   "   ....   "
5.   "   "   " expelled   "   "   -   "   "   "
6.   "   "   " re-entered   "   "   -   "   "   "
7.   "   "   " remaining in school close of year, "   "   "
8.   "   "   " neither tardy nor absent during year, "   "   "
9.   "   " cases of tardiness during year,   -   "   "   ....   "
10.   "   " pupils tardy during year,   -   - "   ....   "   "
11. Total days of attendance by all pupils for year,   -   -   -   -   -   -   -
12. *   "   "   " absence   " "   "   "   "   -   -   -   -   -
13. Total cases of tardiness,.................... ....   Time lost by tardiness,   -   -   -   ... ...
14. †Average daily attendance for year,   -   -   -   -   -   -
15. Per cent. of attendance—$11 \div (11 + 12)$,   -   -
16. Number of pupils promoted to   -   -   -   -   -   -
    (a) Second year,   -   -   -   -   -   -
    (b) Third   "   -   -   -   -   -   -   -
    (c) Fourth   "   -   -   -   -   -   ....
    (d) Fifth   "   -   -   -   -   -   -   ....
    (e) Sixth   "   -   -   -   -   -   -   ....
    (f) Seventh   "   -   -   -   -   -   -   —
    (g) Eighth   "   -   -   -   -   -
    (h) High School,   -   -   -   -   -   -   ....
17. Number of graduates from the common branches and receiving diplomas,
    Male,.................... ; female, ... ; total, ...
18. Number of graduates from non-commissioned township high schools,
    Male,.................... ...; female,.................... ; total,.................... ...
19. Number of graduates from commissioned township high schools,
    Male,....................; female,....................; total,........
20. How many books in school library (not including reading circle books) at beginning of year?
21. How many books were added to library (not including reading circle books) during year?
22. Total now in school library (not including reading circle books),   -   -   -   -
23. How many reading circle books were added during year?   -   -   -   -   -   ....
24. How many pupils read one or more school library or reading circle books during year?   -   ....
25. Do patrons read school library books?   -   -   -   -   -   -   -   ....
26. Number of visits to school,   Parents,....................; officials, ...; others, ...; total, ...
27. Number of teachers employed (if school be high school), Male,.............; female, ...; total,............ .. ..
28. Number of days teacher attended township institute,   -   -   "   -   -
29. Books and apparatus left in school room at end of term,   -   -   -   ....

I,.................... ...., do solemnly swear that the above report is true to the best of my knowledge and belief.

} Teacher.
} Principal.
....

NOTES:—
*(1.) After three days of absence the pupil should be withdrawn, and his absence counted no more for that period of absence. After being withdrawn, he is not a pupil of the school, and can not be again until he is re-entered, as in item 6.
†(2.) To find average daily attendance divide the whole number of days of attendance made by all the pupils by the number of days of school taught.

41ᴬ

    Wade Bros. & Wise, Printers.

TEACHER'S CONTRACT.

This Agreement, Between *A. S. Hermann* School Trustee of

Washington School Township, in Porter County, and State of Indiana,

of the first part, and *Myron Brown* a legally qualified teacher in said

County of the second part, certifies that the said teacher hereby agrees to teach the public school in District No. ____

Grade ____, in said Township, for the term commencing on the ____ 4 ____ day of *September*

A. D. 1 *905* , for the consideration of *Two* Dollars and

48 Cents per {day, year,} to be paid *When Called for* (State here when all or parts of salary will be paid.)

Consideration *437.40*

The said *Myron Brown* further agrees faithfully to perform

all the duties of teacher in said school; using only such text-books as are prescribed by the Trustees in accordance with the law, except supplementary reading, such as Young People's Reading Circle books, etc., and other works recommended by the County Superintendent, and observing all Rules and Regulations of the County Board of Education, and all instructions of the County Superintendent of Schools; that ...he will attend and participate in the exercises of each Institute or other teachers' meetings that may be appointed for the teachers of said township, or for each day's absence therefrom, forfeit a sum equal to one day's wages, unless such absence shall be occasioned by sickness, that ...he will accurately keep and use all registers and blanks placed in *his* hands by said Trustee; that ...he will make a complete and accurate report at the close of the school term, the blank for which is provided on the back of this sheet; that ...he will make all other reports required of *him* by said Trustee, the County Superintendent, or the laws of Indiana, at the proper time and manner and in good order; that ...he will exercise due diligence in the preservation of school buildings, grounds, furniture, apparatus, books, blanks and other school property committed to *his* care, and turn the same over to the Trustee, or his representative, at the close of the term of school, in as good condition as when received, damage and wear by use excepted.

The said School Trustee agrees to keep the school buildings in good repair, and to furnish the necessary fuel, furniture, apparatus, books and blanks, and such other appliances as may be necessary for the systematic and proper conduct of said school.

And the said School Trustee, for and in behalf of said Township, further agrees to pay the said *Myron Brown* for services as teacher of said school, either a sum equal to the whole number of days taught at the rate of the above named sum per day, as agreed upon, or the salary for the year in the event of a yearly consideration, as agreed upon, when the said teacher shall have filled all the stipulations of this contract.

The said School Trustee further agrees to pay said teacher one day's wages for each day's attendance at the Township Institute, according to the Acts of 1889.

PROVIDED, That in case the said *Myron Brown* should be dismissed from said school by said Trustee, or his successor in office, for incompetency, cruelty, gross immorality, neglect of business, or a violation of any of the stipulations of this contract, or in case *his* license should be annulled by the County Superintendent or State Superintendent, ...he shall not be entitled to any compensation after notice of dismissal, or notice of annulment of license.

PROVIDED FURTHER, That the teacher shall have a duplicate of this Contract.

IN WITNESS WHEREOF, We have hereunto subscribed our names, this *28*

day of *Aug* A. D. 1 *905*

Myron P Brown Teacher.

A. S. Hermann School Trustee.

NOTES:—
(1.) Full authority is given the Trustee to substitute the words "principal," "supervisor" or "superintendent" for the word "teacher" in the event the Contract should be so made.
(2.) This Contract is the official blank, made by the State Superintendent of Public Instruction, under the provisions of H. B. N. Acts of 1899.

Teacher's or Principal's Report to Township Trustee.

NOTE.—This report must be made by each teacher having charge of the attendance of pupils. A high school teacher who works under the direction of a principal will not need to make the report in case the principal reports for the entire high school. In graded grammar schools each teacher should report for the pupils directly under his charge. The principal of a graded grammar school should report only for the pupils directly under his charge.

REPORT of............ .... { teacher } of.......................District
.... { principal }

WASHINGTON TOWNSHIP, PORTER COUNTY, INDIANA,

to the Township Trustee, for the school term beginning.... ....and

closing ....

FOR ALL TEACHERS WHO HAVE CHARGE OF ATTENDANCE OF PUPILS.

1. Number of days school was in session,   -   -   -   -   -   -   -
2. "   " pupils enrolled during year,   -   Male, ...; female,...................; total,................ ...
3. "   "   " withdrawn during year, -   -   "   "   "
4. "   "   " suspended   "   "   -   "   " ....   "
5. "   "   " expelled   "   "   -   "   "   "
6. "   "   " re-entered   "   "   -   "   "   "
7. "   "   " remaining in school close of year, "   "   "
8. "   "   " neither tardy nor absent during year, "   "   "
9. "   " cases of tardiness,   -   "   " ....   "
10. "   " pupils tardy during year,   -   -   " ....   "   "
11. Total days of attendance by all pupils for year,   -   -   -   -   -   -
12. * "   "   " absence   "   "   "   "   "   -   -   -   -   -
13. Total cases of tardiness, ... Time lost by tardiness,   -   -   -   ... .. — ...
14. †Average daily attendance for year,   -   -   -   -   -
15. Per cent. of attendance—11÷(11+12),   -   -   -
16. Number of pupils promoted to   -   -   -   -   -
     (a) Second year,   -   -   -   -   -
     (b) Third   "   -   -   -   -   -
     (c) Fourth   "   -   -   -   -   ....
     (d) Fifth   "   -   -   -   -   ....
     (e) Sixth   "   -   -   -   -   -   ....
     (f) Seventh   "   -   -   -   -   -   —
     (g) Eighth   "   -   -   -   -   -
     (h) High School,   -   -   -   -   ....
17. Number of graduates from the common branches and receiving diplomas,
     Male,.................; female,...................; total,... .. ..
18. Number of graduates from non-commissioned township high schools,
     Male,.................; female,...................; total,......... ... -
19. Number of graduates from commissioned township high schools,
     Male,...................; female,...................; total,........
20. How many books in school library (not including reading circle books) at beginning of year?
21. How many books were added to library (not including reading circle books) during year?
22. Total now in school library (not including reading circle books),   -   -   -   -
23. How many reading circle books were added during year?   -   -   ....
24. How many pupils read one or more school library or reading circle books during year?   -   ....
25. Do patrons read school library books?   -   -   -   -   -   ....
26. Number of visits to school,   Parents,.................; officials, ...; others, ...; total,.........................
27. Number of teachers employed (if school be high school), Male,...............; female, ...; total, ...
28. Number of days teacher attended township institute,   -   -   -   -
29. Books and apparatus left in school room at end of term,   -   -   -   ....

I,.. .. . ., do solemnly swear that the above report is true to the best of my knowledge and belief.

                                            { Teacher.
.... { Principal.

NOTES:—
*(1.) After three days of absence the pupil should be withdrawn, and his absence counted no more for that period of absence. After being withdrawn, he is not a pupil of the school, and can not be again until he is re-entered, as in item 6.
†(2.) To find average daily attendance divide the whole number of days of attendance made by all the pupils by the number of days of school taught.

42 A

TEACHER'S CONTRACT.

This Agreement, Between _A. S. Hermann_ School Trustee of

Washington School Township, in Porter County, and State of Indiana,

of the first part, and _Jennie Keding_ a legally qualified teacher in said

County of the second part, certifies that the said teacher hereby agrees to teach the public school in District No. _____

Grade _____, in said Township, for the term commencing on the _9_ day of _September_

A. D. 1_905_ , for the consideration of _Two_ Dollars and

_28_/_0 0_ Cents per {day, year,} to be paid _When Called for_ (state here when all or parts of salary will be paid.)

Consideration _$11.40_

The said _Jennie Keding_ further agrees faithfully to perform all the duties of teacher in said school; using only such text-books as are prescribed by the Trustees in accordance with the law, except supplementary reading, such as Young People's Reading Circle books, etc., and other works recommended by the County Superintendent, and observing all Rules and Regulations of the County Board of Education, and all instructions of the County Superintendent of Schools; that _s_he will attend and participate in the exercises of each Institute or other teachers' meetings that may be appointed for the teachers of said township, or for each day's absence therefrom, forfeit a sum equal to one day's wages, unless such absence shall be occasioned by sickness, that _s_he will accurately keep and use all registers and blanks placed in _her_ hands by said Trustee; that _s_he will make a complete and accurate report at the close of the school term, the blank for which is provided on the back of this sheet; that _s_he will make all other reports required of _her_ by said Trustee, the County Superintendent, or the laws of Indiana, at the proper time and manner and in good order; that _s_he will exercise due diligence in the preservation of school buildings, grounds, furniture, apparatus, books, blanks and other school property committed to _her_ care, and turn the same over to the Trustee, or his representative, at the close of the term of school, in as good condition as when received, damage and wear by use excepted.

The said School Trustee agrees to keep the school buildings in good repair, and to furnish the necessary fuel, furniture, apparatus, books and blanks, and such other appliances as may be necessary for the systematic and proper conduct of said school.

And the said School Trustee, for and in behalf of said Township, further agrees to pay the said _Jennie Keding_ for services as teacher of said school, either a sum equal to the whole number of days taught at the rate of the above named sum per day, as agreed upon, or the salary for the year in the event of a yearly consideration, as agreed upon, when the said teacher shall have filled all the stipulations of this contract.

The said School Trustee further agrees to pay said teacher one day's wages for each day's attendance at the Township Institute, according to the Acts of 1889.

PROVIDED, That in case the said _Jennie Keding_ should be dismissed from said school by said Trustee, or his successor in office, for incompetency, cruelty, gross immorality, neglect of business, or a violation of any of the stipulations of this contract, or in case _her_ license should be annulled by the County Superintendent or State Superintendent, _s_he shall not be entitled to any compensation after notice of dismissal, or notice of annulment of license.

PROVIDED FURTHER, That the teacher shall have a duplicate of this Contract.

IN WITNESS WHEREOF, We have hereunto subscribed our names, this _28_

day of _Aug_ A. D. 1_905_

Jennie Keding Teacher.

A. S. Hermann School Trustee.

NOTES:—
    (1.) Full authority is given the Trustee to substitute the words "principal," "supervisor" or "superintendent" for the word "teacher" in the event the Contract should be so made.
    (2.) This Contract is the official blank, made by the State Superintendent of Public Instruction, under the provisions of H. B. No. 139, Acts of 1899.

Teacher's or Principal's Report to Township Trustee.

NOTE.—This report must be made by each teacher having charge of the attendance of pupils. A high school teacher who works under the direction of a principal will not need to make the report in case the principal reports for the entire high school. In graded grammar schools each teacher should report for the pupils directly under his charge. The principal of a graded grammar school should report only for the pupils directly under his charge.

REPORT of...................... .... { teacher } { principal } of......................District

WASHINGTON TOWNSHIP, PORTER COUNTY, INDIANA,

to the Township Trustee, for the school term beginning.... .... .and

closing ....

FOR ALL TEACHERS WHO HAVE CHARGE OF ATTENDANCE OF PUPILS.

1. Number of days school was in session,   -   -   -   -   -   -   -   -
2. "   " pupils enrolled during year,   -   Male, ...; female,.....................; total,................ ...
3. "   "   " withdrawn during year, -   -   "   "   "
4. "   "   " suspended "   "   -   - "   "   .... "
5. "   "   " expelled "   "   .   - "   "   "
6. "   "   " re-entered "   "   .   "   "   "
7. "   "   " remaining in school close of year, "   "   "
8. "   "   " neither tardy nor absent during year, "   "   "
9. "   " cases of tardiness during year,   -   "   " .... "
10. "   " pupils tardy during year,   -   - " .... " "   "
11. Total days of attendance by all pupils for year,   -   -   -   -   -
12. * "   "   " absence "   "   "   "   "   -   -   -   -
13. Total cases of tardiness, ...   Time lost by tardiness,   -   -   -   ... - - ..
14. †Average daily attendance for year,   -   .   .   .   .   -
15. Per cent. of attendance—$11\div(11+12)$,   -   -   -
16. Number of pupils promoted to   -   -   -   -   -   ....
        (a) Second year,   -   -   -   -   -
        (b) Third " -   -   -   -   -
        (c) Fourth "   -   -   -   -   -   ....
        (d) Fifth " -   -   -   -   -   ....
        (e) Sixth "   -   -   -   -   -   ....
        (f) Seventh " -   -   -   -   -   —
        (g) Eighth "   -   -   -   -   -
        (h) High School,   -   -   -   -   -   ....- .- ...
17. Number of graduates from the common branches and receiving diplomas,
        Male,...................; female,..................; total,.... .. ..
18. Number of graduates from non-commissioned township high schools,
        Male,................ .; female,...................; total,........... ... .
19. Number of graduates from commissioned township high schools,
        Male,...................; female,..................; total,........
20. How many books in school library (not including reading circle books) at beginning of year?
21. How many books were added to library (not including reading circle books) during year?
22. Total now in school library (not including reading circle books),   -   -   -   -   -
23. How many reading circle books were added during year?   -   -   -   .   -   ....
24. How many pupils read one or more school library or reading circle books during year?   -   ....
25. Do patrons read school library books?   -   -   -   -   -   -   ....
26. Number of visits to school,   Parents,................; officials, ...; others, ...; total, ...
27. Number of teachers employed (if school be high school), Male,...............; female, ...; total, ...
28. Number of days teacher attended township institute,   -   -   .   .   .   .
29. Books and apparatus left in school room at end of term,   -   .   -   -   ....

I,... . ..., do solemnly swear that the above report is true to the best of my knowledge and belief.

{ Teacher.
{ Principal.
....

NOTES:—
*(1.) After three days of absence the pupil should be withdrawn, and his absence counted no more for that period of absence. After being withdrawn, he is not a pupil of the school, and can not be again until he is re-entered, as in item 6.
†(2.) To find average daily attendance divide the whole number of days of attendance made by all the pupils by the number of days of school taught.

43A

TEACHER'S CONTRACT.

This Agreement, Between _A. S. Hermann_ School Trustee of

Washington School Township, in Porter County, and State of Indiana,

of the first part, and _Olive Freer_ a legally qualified teacher in said

County of the second part, certifies that the said teacher hereby agrees to teach the public school in District No. _____

Grade _____ , in said Township, for the term commencing on the _9_ day of _September_

A. D. 1 _905_ , for the consideration of _One_ Dollars and

_96_ Cents per { day, year, } to be paid _When Called for_ (State here when all or parts of salary will be paid.)

Consideration 343 96

The said _Olive A. Freer_ further agrees faithfully to perform

all the duties of teacher in said school; using only such text-books as are prescribed by the Trustees in accordance with the law, except supplementary reading, such as Young People's Reading Circle books, etc., and other works recommended by the County Superintendent, and observing all Rules and Regulations of the County Board of Education, and all instructions of the County Superintendent of Schools; that _he_ he will attend and participate in the exercises of each Institute or other teachers' meetings that may be appointed for the teachers of said township, or for each day's absence therefrom, forfeit a sum equal to one day's wages, unless such absence shall be occasioned by sickness, that _he_ he will accurately keep and use all registers and blanks placed in _her_ hands by said Trustee; that _he_ he will make a complete and accurate report at the close of the school term, the blank for which is provided on the back of this sheet; that _he_ he will make all other reports required of _her_ by said Trustee, the County Superintendent, or the laws of Indiana, at the proper time and manner and in good order; that _he_ he will exercise due diligence in the preservation of school buildings, grounds, furniture, apparatus, books, blanks and other school property committed to _her_ care, and turn the same over to the Trustee, or his representative, at the close of the term of school, in as good condition as when received, damage and wear by use excepted.

The said School Trustee agrees to keep the school buildings in good repair, and to furnish the necessary fuel, furniture, apparatus, books and blanks, and such other appliances as may be necessary for the systematic and proper conduct of said school.

And the said School Trustee, for and in behalf of said Township, further agrees to pay the said _Olive A. Freer_ for services as teacher of said school, either a sum equal to the whole number of days taught at the rate of the above named sum per day, as agreed upon, or the salary for the year in the event of a yearly consideration, as agreed upon, when the said teacher shall have filled all the stipulations of this contract.

The said School Trustee further agrees to pay said teacher one day's wages for each day's attendance at the Township Institute, according to the Acts of 1889.

PROVIDED, That in case the said _Olive A. Freer_ should be dismissed from said school by said Trustee, or his successor in office, for incompetency, cruelty, gross immorality, neglect of business, or a violation of any of the stipulations of this contract, or in case _she_ license should be annulled by the County Superintendent or State Superintendent, _she_ he shall not be entitled to any compensation after notice of dismissal, or notice of annulment of license.

PROVIDED FURTHER, That the teacher shall have a duplicate of this Contract.

IN WITNESS WHEREOF, We have hereunto subscribed our names, this _25_

day of _Aug_ A. D. 1 _905_

Olive A. Freer Teacher.

A. S. Hermann School Trustee.

NOTES:—
(1.) Full authority is given the Trustee to substitute the words "principal," "supervisor" or "superintendent" for the word "teacher" in the event the Contract should be so made.
(2.) This Contract is the official blank, made by the State Superintendent of Public Instruction, under the provisions of H. B. No. 139, Acts of 1899.

Teacher's or Principal's Report to Township Trustee.

NOTE.—This report must be made by each teacher having charge of the attendance of pupils. A high school teacher who works under the direction of a principal will not need to make the report in case the principal reports for the entire high school. In graded grammar schools each teacher should report for the pupils directly under his charge. The principal of a graded grammar school should report only for the pupils directly under his charge.

REPORT of........................ .... { teacher } of........................District
{ principal }

WASHINGTON TOWNSHIP, PORTER COUNTY, INDIANA,

to the Township Trustee, for the school term beginning.................... ....and

closing ....

FOR ALL TEACHERS WHO HAVE CHARGE OF ATTENDANCE OF PUPILS.

1. Number of days school was in session,   -   -   -   -   -   -   -   -
2. "   " pupils enrolled during year,   -   Male, ...; female, ...; total,........................ ...
3. "   "   " withdrawn during year, -   -   "   "   "
4. "   "   " suspended   "   "   -   -   "   "   "
5. "   "   " expelled   "   "   -   "   "   "
6. "   "   " re-entered   "   "   -   "   "   "
7. "   "   " remaining in school close of year, "   "   "
8. "   "   " neither tardy nor absent during year, "   "   "
9. "   " cases of tardiness during year,   -   "   "   "
10. "   " pupils tardy during year,   -   -   "   ....   "   "
11. Total days of attendance by all pupils for year,   -   -   -   -   -   -
12. * "   "   " absence   "   "   "   "   "   -   -   -   -   -
13. Total cases of tardiness,...................   Time lost by tardiness,   -   -   -   ... ...
14. †Average daily attendance for year,   -   -   -   -   -
15. Per cent. of attendance—$11 \div (11 + 12)$,   -   -   -
16. Number of pupils promoted to   -   -   -   -   -   -
     (a) Second year,   -   -   -   -   -   -   -
     (b) Third   "   -   -   -   -   -   -   -
     (c) Fourth   "   -   -   -   -   -   ....
     (d) Fifth   "   -   -   -   -   ....
     (e) Sixth   "   -   -   -   -   -   ....
     (f) Seventh   "   -   -   -   -   -   ....
     (g) Eighth   "   -   -   -   -   -   -   _
     (h) High School,   -   -   -   -   -   ....
17. Number of graduates from the common branches and receiving diplomas,
     Male,...................; female, ...; total,.... . ...   ..
18. Number of graduates from non-commissioned township high schools,
     Male,.................. ....; female,............... .....; total,............ ... .
19. Number of graduates from commissioned township high schools,
     Male,...................; female, ...; total,........
20. How many books in school library (not including reading circle books) at beginning of year?
21. How many books were added to library (not including reading circle books) during year?
22. Total now in school library (not including reading circle books),   -   -   -   -
23. How many reading circle books were added during year?   -   -   -   -   -   ....
24. How many pupils read one or more school library or reading circle books during year?   -   ....
25. Do patrons read school library books?   -   -   -   -   -   -   ....
26. Number of visits to school,   Parents,...................; officials, ...; others, ...; total,........................
27. Number of teachers employed (if school be high school), Male,...................; female, ...; total,........... ..
28. Number of days teacher attended township institute,   -   -   "   -   "   "   -
29. Books and apparatus left in school room at end of term,   -   -   -   -   ....

I,........................ ...., do solemnly swear that the above report is true to the best of my knowledge and belief.

.... { Teacher.
{ Principal.

NOTES:—
    *(1.) After three days of absence the pupil should be withdrawn, and his absence counted no more for that period of absence. After being withdrawn, he is not a pupil of the school, and can not be again until he is re-entered, as in item 6.
    †(2.) To find average daily attendance divide the whole number of days of attendance made by all the pupils by the number of days of school taught.

44A

Wade Bros. & Wise, Printers.

TEACHER'S CONTRACT.

This Agreement, Between......*O. S. Herman*......School Trustee of

Washington School Township, in Porter County, and State of Indiana,

of the first part, and ......*Grace Pierce*...... a legally qualified teacher in said

County of the second part, certifies that the said teacher hereby agrees to teach the public school in District No.....,

Grade.........., in said Township, for the term commencing on the .....*9*..... day of *September*

A. D. 1 *905* ......, for the consideration of ......*Two*...... Dollars and

......*18/90*...... Cents per { day, { year, } to be paid ......*When Called for*......

(State here when all or parts of salary will be paid.)

Consideration $ *94 20*

The said ......*Grace Pierce*......further agrees faithfully to perform

all the duties of teacher in said school; using only such text-books as are prescribed by the Trustees in accordance with
the law, except supplementary reading, such as Young People's Reading Circle books, etc., and other works recommended by the County Superintendent, and observing all Rules and Regulations of the County Board of Education,
and all instructions of the County Superintendent of Schools; that she will attend and participate in the exercises of
each Institute or other teachers' meetings that may be appointed for the teachers of said township, or for each day's
absence therefrom, forfeit a sum equal to one day's wages, unless such absence shall be occasioned by sickness, that
she will accurately keep and use all registers and blanks placed in her hands by said Trustee; that she will
make a complete and accurate report at the close of the school term, the blank for which is provided on the back of
this sheet; that she will make all other reports required of her by said Trustee, the County Superintendent, or
the laws of Indiana, at the proper time and manner and in good order; that she will exercise due diligence in the
preservation of school buildings, grounds, furniture, apparatus, books, blanks and other school property committed to
her care, and turn the same over to the Trustee, or his representative, at the close of the term of school, in as
good condition as when received, damage and wear by use excepted.

The said School Trustee agrees to keep the school buildings in good repair, and to furnish the necessary fuel,
furniture, apparatus, books and blanks, and such other appliances as may be necessary for the systematic and proper
conduct of said school.

And the said School Trustee, for and in behalf of said Township, further agrees to pay the said......*Grace*

......*Pierce*...... for services as teacher of said school, either a sum equal to the whole
number of days taught at the rate of the above named sum per day, as agreed upon, or the salary for the year in the
event of a yearly consideration, as agreed upon, when the said teacher shall have filled all the stipulations of this contract.

The said School Trustee further agrees to pay said teacher one day's wages for each day's attendance at the Township Institute, according to the Acts of 1889.

PROVIDED, That in case the said......*Grace Pierce*......should be
dismissed from said school by said Trustee, or his successor in office, for incompetency, cruelty, gross immorality,
neglect of business, or a violation of any of the stipulations of this contract, or in case her license should be
annulled by the County Superintendent or State Superintendent, she shall not be entitled to any compensation after
notice of dismissal, or notice of annulment of license.

PROVIDED FURTHER, That the teacher shall have a duplicate of this Contract.

IN WITNESS WHEREOF, We have hereunto subscribed our names, this......*28*......

day of......*Aug*......A. D. 1 *905* ......

......*Grace Pierce*...... Teacher.

......*O. S. Herman*...... School Trustee.

NOTES:—
(1.) Full authority is given the Trustee to substitute the words "principal," "supervisor" or "superintendent" for the word "teacher"
in the event the Contract should be so made.
(2.) This Contract is the official blank, made by the State Superintendent of Public Instruction, under the provisions of H. B. No. 139,
Acts of 1899.

Teacher's or Principal's Report to Township Trustee.

NOTE.—This report must be made by each teacher having charge of the attendance of pupils. A high school teacher who works under the direction of a principal will not need to make the report in case the principal reports for the entire high school. In graded grammar schools each teacher should report for the pupils directly under his charge. The principal of a graded grammar school should report only for the pupils directly under his charge.

REPORT of............................ .... { teacher } { principal } of............................District

WASHINGTON TOWNSHIP, PORTER COUNTY, INDIANA,

to the Township Trustee, for the school term beginning...and

closing ....

FOR ALL TEACHERS WHO HAVE CHARGE OF ATTENDANCE OF PUPILS.

1. Number of days school was in session,
2. " " pupils enrolled during year, - Male, ...; female,.....................; total,.................
3. " " " withdrawn during year, - " " "
4. " " " suspended " " - " " "
5. " " " expelled " " - " " "
6. " " " re-entered " " . " " "
7. " " " remaining in school close of year, " " "
8. " " " neither tardy nor absent during year, " " "
9. " " cases of tardiness during year, - " " "
10. " " pupils tardy during year, - " " "
11. Total days of attendance by all pupils for year,
12. * " " " absence " " " " "
13. Total cases of tardiness,................. Time lost by tardiness,
14. †Average daily attendance for year,
15. Per cent. of attendance—11÷(11+12),
16. Number of pupils promoted to
    (a) Second year,
    (b) Third "
    (c) Fourth "
    (d) Fifth "
    (e) Sixth "
    (f) Seventh "
    (g) Eighth "
    (h) High School,
17. Number of graduates from the common branches and receiving diplomas,
    Male,..............; female, ...; total, ...
18. Number of graduates from non-commissioned township high schools,
    Male,.................; female,...............; total,..........
19. Number of graduates from commissioned township high schools,
    Male,.................; female,...................; total,..........
20. How many books in school library (not including reading circle books) at beginning of year?
21. How many books were added to library (not including reading circle books) during year?
22. Total now in school library (not including reading circle books),
23. How many reading circle books were added during year?
24. How many pupils read one or more school library or reading circle books during year?
25. Do patrons read school library books?
26. Number of visits to school, Parents,.................; officials, ...; others, ...; total,...................
27. Number of teachers employed (if school be high school), Male,.............; female, ...; total,...........
28. Number of days teacher attended township institute,
29. Books and apparatus left in school room at end of term,

I,.. , do solemnly swear that the above report is true to the best of my knowledge and belief.

{ Teacher.
....
{ Principal.

NOTES:—
*(1.) After three days of absence the pupil should be withdrawn, and his absence counted no more for that period of absence. After being withdrawn, he is not a pupil of the school, and can not be again until he is re-entered, as in item 6.
†(2.) To find average daily attendance divide the whole number of days of attendance made by all the pupils by the number of days of school taught.

45 A

TEACHER'S CONTRACT.

This Agreement, Between _O. S. Hermann_ School Trustee of

Washington School Township, In Porter County, and State of Indiana,

of the first part, and _Cora Benham_ a legally qualified teacher in said

County of the second part, certifies that the said teacher hereby agrees to teach the public school in District No. ....

Grade ......, in said Township, for the term commencing on the ..... _7_ day of _September_

A. D. 1 _905_ , for the consideration of _Two_ Dollars and

_70/00_ Cents per { day, / year, } to be paid _When called for_ (State here when all or parts of salary will be paid.)

Consideration _486 00_

The said _Cora Benham_ further agrees faithfully to perform

all the duties of teacher in said school; using only such text-books as are prescribed by the Trustees in accordance with the law, except supplementary reading, such as Young People's Reading Circle books, etc., and other works recommended by the County Superintendent, and observing all Rules and Regulations of the County Board of Education, and all instructions of the County Superintendent of Schools; that _s_ he will attend and participate in the exercises of each Institute or other teachers' meetings that may be appointed for the teachers of said township, or for each day's absence therefrom, forfeit a sum equal to one day's wages, unless such absence shall be occasioned by sickness, that _s_ he will accurately keep and use all registers and blanks placed in _her_ hands by said Trustee; that _s_ he will make a complete and accurate report at the close of the school term, the blank for which is provided on the back of this sheet; that _s_ he will make all other reports required of _her_ by said Trustee, the County Superintendent, or the laws of Indiana, at the proper time and manner and in good order; that _s_ he will exercise due diligence in the preservation of school buildings, grounds, furniture, apparatus, books, blanks and other school property committed to _her_ care, and turn the same over to the Trustee, or his representative, at the close of the term of school, in as good condition as when received, damage and wear by use excepted.

The said School Trustee agrees to keep the school buildings in good repair, and to furnish the necessary fuel, furniture, apparatus, books and blanks, and such other appliances as may be necessary for the systematic and proper conduct of said school.

And the said School Trustee, for and in behalf of said Township, further agrees to pay the said _Cora Benham_ for services as teacher of said school, either a sum equal to the whole number of days taught at the rate of the above named sum per day, as agreed upon, or the salary for the year in the event of a yearly consideration, as agreed upon, when the said teacher shall have filled all the stipulations of this contract.

The said School Trustee further agrees to pay said teacher one day's wages for each day's attendance at the Township Institute, according to the Acts of 1889.

PROVIDED, That in case the said _Cora Benham_ should be dismissed from said school by said Trustee, or his successor in office, for incompetency, cruelty, gross immorality, neglect of business, or a violation of any of the stipulations of this contract, or in case _her_ license should be annulled by the County Superintendent or State Superintendent, _s_ he shall not be entitled to any compensation after notice of dismissal, or notice of annulment of license.

PROVIDED FURTHER, That the teacher shall have a duplicate of this Contract.

IN WITNESS WHEREOF, We have hereunto subscribed our names, this _25_

day of _Aug_ A. D. 1 _905_

Cora Benham .... Teacher.

O. S. Hermann School Trustee.

NOTES:—

(1.) Full authority is given the Trustee to substitute the words "principal," "supervisor" or "superintendent" for the word "teacher" in the event the Contract should be so made.

(2.) This Contract is the official blank, made by the State Superintendent of Public Instruction, under the provisions of H. B. No. 139, Acts of 1899.

Teacher's or Principal's Report to Township Trustee.

NOTE.—This report must be made by each teacher having charge of the attendance of pupils. A high school teacher who works under the direction of a principal will not need to make the report in case the principal reports for the entire high school. In graded grammar schools each teacher should report for the pupils directly under his charge. The principal of a graded grammar school should report only for the pupils directly under his charge.

REPORT of........................ ....{ teacher | principal } of........................District

WASHINGTON TOWNSHIP, PORTER COUNTY, INDIANA,

to the Township Trustee, for the school term beginning.................. ....and

closing ....: ....

FOR ALL TEACHERS WHO HAVE CHARGE OF ATTENDANCE OF PUPILS.

1. Number of days school was in session,   -   -   -   -   -   -   -   -   -   -
2. " " pupils enrolled during year,   - Male, ...; female,.....................; total,............. ...
3. " " " withdrawn during year, -   -   "   " "
4. " " " suspended " "   -   - "   " .... "
5. " " " expelled " "   - "   " "
6. " " " re-entered " "   - "   " "
7. " " " remaining in school close of year, "   " "
8. " " " neither tardy nor absent during year, "   " "
9. " " cases of tardiness during year,   - "   " .... "
10. " " pupils tardy during year,   - "   - " .... "   " "
11. Total days of attendance by all pupils for year,   -   -   -   -   -
12. * " " " absence " " " " "   -   -   -   -   -
13. Total cases of tardiness,................. Time lost by tardiness,   -   -   -   ... ...
14. †Average daily attendance for year,   -   -   -   -   -
15. Per cent. of attendance—11÷(11+12),   -   _____ -   -   -
16. Number of pupils promoted to   -   -   -   -   -   -
   (a) Second year,   -   -   -   -   -   -
   (b) Third "   -   -   -   -   -   -
   (c) Fourth "   -   -   -   -   -
   (d) Fifth "   -   -   -   -   -
   (e) Sixth "   -   -   -   -   -
   (f) Seventh "   -   -   -   -   -   -
   (g) Eighth "   -   -   -   -   -
   (h) High School,   -   -   -   -   -   -
17. Number of graduates from the common branches and receiving diplomas,
    Male,.................; female, ...; total,.... .. ..
18. Number of graduates from non-commissioned township high schools,
    Male,.................; female,.................; total,............ ..
19. Number of graduates from commissioned township high schools,
    Male,.................; female,.................; total,.......
20. How many books in school library (not including reading circle books) at beginning of year?
21. How many books were added to library (not including reading circle books) during year?
22. Total now in school library (not including reading circle books),   -   -   -   -   -
23. How many reading circle books were added during year?   -   -   -   -   -
24. How many pupils read one or more school library or reading circle books during year?   -   ....
25. Do patrons read school library books?   -   -   -   -   -   -   -
26. Number of visits to school,   Parents,.................; officials,.................; others, ...; total, ...
27. Number of teachers employed (if school be high school), Male,.................; female, ...; total,............. .. ..
28. Number of days teacher attended township institute,   -   -   "   "   "
29. Books and apparatus left in school room at end of term,   -   -   -   -   ....

I,... .. . ., do solemnly swear that the above report is true to the best of my knowledge and belief.

....{ Teacher. | Principal.

NOTES:—
*(1.) After three days of absence the pupil should be withdrawn, and his absence counted no more for that period of absence. After being withdrawn, he is not a pupil of the school, and can not be again until he is re-entered, as in item 6.
†(2.) To find average daily attendance divide the whole number of days of attendance made by all the pupils by the number of days of school taught.

TEACHER'S CONTRACT.

This Agreement, Between _A. S. Hermann_ School Trustee of

Washington School Township, in Porter County, and State of Indiana,

of the first part, and _Grace Maxwell_ a legally qualified teacher in said

County of the second part, certifies that the said teacher hereby agrees to teach the public school in District No. ....

Grade ...., in said Township, for the term commencing on the _9_ day of _September_

A. D. 1 _905_ , for the consideration of _Two_ Dollars and

_83_ Cents per day, year, to be paid _When Called for_

(State here when all or parts of salary will be paid.)

Consideration 913-40

The said _Grace Maxwell_ further agrees faithfully to perform

all the duties of teacher in said school; using only such text-books as are prescribed by the Trustees in accordance with
the law, except supplementary reading, such as Young People's Reading Circle books, etc., and other works recommended by the County Superintendent, and observing all Rules and Regulations of the County Board of Education,
and all instructions of the County Superintendent of Schools; that _s_ he will attend and participate in the exercises of
each Institute or other teachers' meetings that may be appointed for the teachers of said township, or for each day's
absence therefrom, forfeit a sum equal to one day's wages, unless such absence shall be occasioned by sickness, that
_s_ he will accurately keep and use all registers and blanks placed in _her_ hands by said Trustee; that _s_ he will
make a complete and accurate report at the close of the school term, the blank for which is provided on the back of
this sheet; that _s_ he will make all other reports required of _her_ by said Trustee, the County Superintendent, or
the laws of Indiana, at the proper time and manner and in good order; that _s_ he will exercise due diligence in the
preservation of school buildings, grounds, furniture, apparatus, books, blanks and other school property committed to
her care, and turn the same over to the Trustee, or his representative, at the close of the term of school, in as
good condition as when received, damage and wear by use excepted.

The said School Trustee agrees to keep the school buildings in good repair, and to furnish the necessary fuel,
furniture, apparatus, books and blanks, and such other appliances as may be necessary for the systematic and proper
conduct of said school.

And the said School Trustee, for and in behalf of said Township, further agrees to pay the said _Grace_

Maxwell for services as teacher of said school, either a sum equal to the whole
number of days taught at the rate of the above named sum per day, as agreed upon, or the salary for the year in the
event of a yearly consideration, as agreed upon, when the said teacher shall have filled all the stipulations of this contract.

The said School Trustee further agrees to pay said teacher one day's wages for each day's attendance at the Township Institute, according to the Acts of 1889.

PROVIDED, That in case the said _Grace Maxwell_ should be
dismissed from said school by said Trustee, or his successor in office, for incompetency, cruelty, gross immorality,
neglect of business, or a violation of any of the stipulations of this contract, or in case _her_ license should be
annulled by the County Superintendent or State Superintendent, _s_ he shall not be entitled to any compensation after
notice of dismissal, or notice of annulment of license.

PROVIDED FURTHER, That the teacher shall have a duplicate of this Contract.

IN WITNESS WHEREOF, We have hereunto subscribed our names, this _28_

day of _Aug_ A. D. 1 _905_

Grace Maxwell Teacher.

A. S. Hermann School Trustee.

NOTES:—
    (1.) Full authority is given the Trustee to substitute the words "principal," "supervisor" or "superintendent" for the word "teacher"
in the event the Contract should be so made.
    (2.) This Contract is the official blank, made by the State Superintendent of Public Instruction, under the provisions of H. B. No. 139,
Acts of 1899.

Teacher's or Principal's Report to Township Trustee.

NOTE.—This report must be made by each teacher having charge of the attendance of pupils. A high school teacher who works under the direction of a principal will not need to make the report in case the principal reports for the entire high school. In graded grammar schools each teacher should report for the pupils directly under his charge. The principal of a graded grammar school should report only for the pupils directly under his charge.

REPORT of .... { teacher } of .... District
                                                                       { principal }

WASHINGTON TOWNSHIP, PORTER COUNTY, INDIANA,

to the Township Trustee, for the school term beginning .... and

closing ... :   ....

FOR ALL TEACHERS WHO HAVE CHARGE OF ATTENDANCE OF PUPILS.

1. Number of days school was in session,   -   -   -   -   -   -   -   -
2. "   " pupils enrolled during year,   -   Male, ...; female, ...; total, ...
3. "   "   " withdrawn during year, -   -   "   "   "
4. "   "   " suspended   "   "   -   -   "   "   ....   "
5. "   "   " expelled   "   "   -   "   "   "
6. "   "   " re-entered   "   "   -   "   "   "
7. "   "   " remaining in school close of year, "   "   "
8. "   "   " "neither tardy nor absent during year, "   "   "
9. "   "   " cases of tardiness during year,   -   "   "   ....   "
10. "   "   " pupils tardy during year,   -   -   "   ....   "   "
11. Total days of attendance by all pupils for year,   -   -   -   -   -   -
12. * "   "   " absence   "   "   "   "   "   -   -   -   -
13. Total cases of tardiness, ...   Time lost by tardiness,   -   -   ... .
14. †Average daily attendance for year,   -   -   -   -   -   -
15. Per cent. of attendance—11÷(11+12),   -   -   -
16. Number of pupils promoted to   -   -   -   -   -   -   -
        (a) Second year,   -   -   -   -   -   -
        (b) Third   "   -   -   -   -   -   -
        (c) Fourth   "   -   -   -   -   -   -
        (d) Fifth   "   -   -   -   -   -   -
        (e) Sixth   "   -   -   -   -   -   -
        (f) Seventh   "   -   -   -   -   -   -
        (g) Eighth   "   -   -   -   -   -   -
        (h) High School,   -   -   -   -   -   -
17. Number of graduates from the common branches and receiving diplomas,
        Male, ...; female, ...; total, ...
18. Number of graduates from non-commissioned township high schools,
        Male, ...; female, ...; total, ...
19. Number of graduates from commissioned township high schools,
        Male, ...; female, ...; total, ...
20. How many books in school library (not including reading circle books) at beginning of year?
21. How many books were added to library (not including reading circle books) during year?
22. Total now in school library (not including reading circle books),   -   -   -   -
23. How many reading circle books were added during year?   -   -   -   -
24. How many pupils read one or more school library or reading circle books during year?   -
25. Do patrons read school library books?   -   -   -   -   -
26. Number of visits to school,   Parents, ...; officials, ...; others, ...; total, ...
27. Number of teachers employed (if school be high school), Male, ...; female, ...; total, ...
28. Number of days teacher attended township institute,   -   "   -   "   -   -
29. Books and apparatus left in school room at end of term,   -   -   -   -   -

I, ..., do solemnly swear that the above report is true to the best of my knowledge and belief.

                                                                { Teacher.
....   { Principal.

NOTES:—
*(1.) After three days of absence the pupil should be withdrawn, and his absence counted no more for that period of absence. After being withdrawn, he is not a pupil of the school, and can not be again until he is re-entered, as in item 6.
†(2.) To find average daily attendance divide the whole number of days of attendance made by all the pupils by the number of days of school taught.

47A

TEACHER'S CONTRACT.

This Agreement, Between _A. S. Hermanel_ School Trustee of

Washington School Township, in Porter County, and State of Indiana,

of the first part, and _Iva Miller_ ....a legally qualified teacher in said

County of the second part, certifies that the said teacher hereby agrees to teach the public school in District No. _4_,

Grade _____, in said Township, for the term commencing on the _second_ day of _January_

A. D. 1 _906_ ..., for the consideration of ...._Two_............................Dollars and

_57_ ... Cents per { day, year, } to be paid _When Collected for_
(State here when all or parts of salary will be paid.)

100 Days Teaching   Consideration $257 00

The said _Iva Miller_ ....further agrees faithfully to perform

all the duties of teacher in said school; using only such text-books as are prescribed by the Trustees in accordance with the law, except supplementary reading, such as Young People's Reading Circle books, etc., and other works recommended by the County Superintendent, and observing all Rules and Regulations of the County Board of Education, and all instructions of the County Superintendent of Schools; that _s_he will attend and participate in the exercises of each Institute or other teachers' meetings that may be appointed for the teachers of said township, or for each day's absence therefrom, forfeit a sum equal to one day's wages, unless such absence shall be occasioned by sickness, that _s_he will accurately keep and use all registers and blanks placed in _her_ hands by said Trustee; that _s_he will make a complete and accurate report at the close of the school term, the blank for which is provided on the back of this sheet; that _s_he will make all other reports required of _her_ by said Trustee, the County Superintendent, or the laws of Indiana, at the proper time and manner and in good order; that _s_he will exercise due diligence in the preservation of school buildings, grounds, furniture, apparatus, books, blanks and other school property committed to _her_ care, and turn the same over to the Trustee, or his representative, at the close of the term of school, in as good condition as when received, damage and wear by use excepted.

The said School Trustee agrees to keep the school buildings in good repair, and to furnish the necessary fuel, furniture, apparatus, books and blanks, and such other appliances as may be necessary for the systematic and proper conduct of said school.

And the said School Trustee, for and in behalf of said Township, further agrees to pay the said _Iva Miller_ ....for services as teacher of said school, either a sum equal to the whole number of days taught at the rate of the above named sum per day, as agreed upon, or the salary for the year in the event of a yearly consideration, as agreed upon, when the said teacher shall have filled all the stipulations of this contract.

The said School Trustee further agrees to pay said teacher one day's wages for each day's attendance at the Township Institute, according to the Acts of 1889.

PROVIDED, That in case the said _Iva Miller_ ....should be dismissed from said school by said Trustee, or his successor in office, for incompetency, cruelty, gross immorality, neglect of business, or a violation of any of the stipulations of this contract, or in case _her_ license should be annulled by the County Superintendent or State Superintendent, _s_he shall not be entitled to any compensation after notice of dismissal, or notice of annulment of license.

PROVIDED FURTHER, That the teacher shall have a duplicate of this Contract.

IN WITNESS WHEREOF, We have hereunto subscribed our names, this _2_

day of _January_ A. D. 1 _906_

Ivy Miller .Teacher.

A. S. Hermanel School Trustee.

NOTES:—
(1.) Full authority is given the Trustee to substitute the words "principal," "supervisor" or "superintendent" for the word "teacher" in the event the Contract should be so made.
(2.) This Contract is the official blank, made by the State Superintendent of Public Instruction, under the provisions of H. B. No. Acts of 1899.

TEACHER'S CONTRACT.

This Agreement, Between *A. S. Hermanee* School Trustee of

Washington School Township, in Porter County, and State of Indiana,

of the first part, and *Jennie Weddle* ....a legally qualified teacher in said

County of the second part, certifies that the said teacher hereby agrees to teach the public school in District No. *No 5,*

Grade........., in said Township, for the term commencing on the *Third* day of *September*

A. D. : *905* , for the consideration of.... *Two* Dollars and

Seventy five. Cents per { day, } to be paid *As Called for 180* year, } (State here when all or part of salary will be paid.)

Days Consideration 995.00

The said *Jennie Weddle* ....further agrees faithfully to perform

all the duties of teacher in said school; using only such text-books as are prescribed by the Trustees in accordance with the law, except supplementary reading, such as Young People's Reading Circle books, etc., and other works recommended by the County Superintendent, and observing all Rules and Regulations of the County Board of Education, and all instructions of the County Superintendent of Schools; that *S* he will attend and participate in the exercises of each Institute or other teachers' meetings that may be appointed for the teachers of said township, or for each day's absence therefrom, forfeit a sum equal to one day's wages, unless such absence shall be occasioned by sickness, that *S* he will accurately keep and use all registers and blanks placed in *her* hands by said Trustee; that *S* he will make a complete and accurate report at the close of the school term, the blank for which is provided on the back of this sheet; that *S* he will make all other reports required of *her* by said Trustee, the County Superintendent, or the laws of Indiana, at the proper time and manner and in good order; that *S* he will exercise due diligence in the preservation of school buildings, grounds, furniture, apparatus, books, blanks and other school property committed to *her* care, and turn the same over to the Trustee, or his representative, at the close of the term of school, in as good condition as when received, damage and wear by use excepted.

The said School Trustee agrees to keep the school buildings in good repair, and to furnish the necessary fuel, furniture, apparatus, books and blanks, and such other appliances as may be necessary for the systematic and proper conduct of said school.

And the said School Trustee, for and in behalf of said Township, further agrees to pay the said....

Jennie Weddle ....for services as teacher of said school, either a sum equal to the whole number of days taught at the rate of the above named sum per day, as agreed upon, or the salary for the year in the event of a yearly consideration, as agreed upon, when the said teacher shall have filled all the stipulations of this contract.

The said School Trustee further agrees to pay said teacher one day's wages for each day's attendance at the Township Institute, according to the Acts of 1889.

PROVIDED, That in case the said *Jennie Weddle* ....should be dismissed from said school by said Trustee, or his successor in office, for incompetency, cruelty, gross immorality, neglect of business, or a violation of any of the stipulations of this contract, or in case *her* license should be annulled by the County Superintendent or State Superintendent, *S* he shall not be entitled to any compensation after notice of dismissal, or notice of annulment of license.

PROVIDED FURTHER, That the teacher shall have a duplicate of this Contract.

IN WITNESS WHEREOF, We have hereunto subscribed our names, this *Third*

day of *September,* A. D. *1905*

Jennie Weddle ....Teacher.

A. S. Hermanee ....School Trustee.

NOTES:—

(1.) Full authority is given the Trustee to substitute the words "principal," "supervisor" or "superintendent" for the word "teacher" in the event the Contract should be so made. ·

(2.) This Contract is the official blank, made by the State Superintendent of Public Instruction, under the provisions of H. B. No. 139, Acts of 1899.

Teacher's or Principal's Report to Township Trustee.

NOTE.—This report must be made by each teacher having charge of the attendance of pupils. A high school teacher who works under the direction of a principal will not need to make the report in case the principal reports for the entire high school. In graded grammar schools each teacher should report for the pupils directly under his charge. The principal of a graded grammar school should report only for the pupils directly under his charge.

REPORT of.......................... .... { teacher } of...........................District
{ principal }

WASHINGTON TOWNSHIP, PORTER COUNTY, INDIANA,

to the Township Trustee, for the school term beginning.................................... ....and

closing ....:

FOR ALL TEACHERS WHO HAVE CHARGE OF ATTENDANCE OF PUPILS.

1. Number of days school was in session,
2. " " pupils enrolled during year, Male, ...; female,..............; total,..............
3. " " " withdrawn during year, " " "
4. " " " suspended " " " " "
5. " " " expelled " " " " "
6. " " " re-entered " " " " "
7. " " " remaining in school close of year, " " "
8. " " " " neither tardy nor absent during year, " " "
9. " " " cases of tardiness during year, " " "
10. " " pupils tardy during year, " " "
11. Total days of attendance by all pupils for year,
12. * " " " absence " " " " "
13. Total cases of tardiness,.................... Time lost by tardiness,
14. †Average daily attendance for year,
15. Per cent. of attendance—11÷(11+12),
16. Number of pupils promoted to
    (a) Second year,
    (b) Third "
    (c) Fourth "
    (d) Fifth "
    (e) Sixth "
    (f) Seventh "
    (g) Eighth "
    (h) High School,
17. Number of graduates from the common branches and receiving diplomas,
    Male,..............; female,..............; total,..............
18. Number of graduates from non-commissioned township high schools,
    Male,..............; female,..............; total,..............
19. Number of graduates from commissioned township high schools,
    Male,..............; female,..............; total,..............
20. How many books in school library (not including reading circle books) at beginning of year?
21. How many books were added to library (not including reading circle books) during year?
22. Total now in school library (not including reading circle books),
23. How many reading circle books were added during year?
24. How many pupils read one or more school library or reading circle books during year?
25. Do patrons read school library books?
26. Number of visits to school, Parents,..............; officials,..............; others,..............; total,..............
27. Number of teachers employed (if school be high school), Male,..............; female,..............; total,..............
28. Number of days teacher attended township institute,
29. Books and apparatus left in school room at end of term,

I,... ...., do solemnly swear that the above report is true to the best of my knowledge and belief.

{ Teacher.
.... { Principal.

NOTES:—
   *(1.) After three days of absence the pupil should be withdrawn, and his absence counted no more for that period of absence. After being withdrawn, he is not a pupil of the school, and can not be again until he is re-entered, as in item 6.
   †(2.) To find average daily attendance divide the whole number of days of attendance made by all the pupils by the number of days of school taught.

TEACHER'S CONTRACT.

This Agreement, Between _A. S. Herman_ School Trustee of

Washington School Township, in Porter County, and State of Indiana,

of the first part, and _Bertha Coburn_ a legally qualified teacher in said

County of the second part, certifies that the said teacher hereby agrees to teach the public school in District No. _2_,

Grade ..., in said Township, for the term commencing on the _third_ day of _Sep._

A. D. 1_906_, for the consideration of _Two_ Dollars and

Seventy five Cents per { day, year, } to be paid _As Called For_ (State here when all or part of salary will be paid.)

For 180 days Teaching Consideration 495=00.

The said _Bertha Coburn_ further agrees faithfully to perform

all the duties of teacher in said school; using only such text-books as are prescribed by the Trustees in accordance with the law, except supplementary reading, such as Young People's Reading Circle books, etc., and other works recommended by the County Superintendent, and observing all Rules and Regulations of the County Board of Education, and all instructions of the County Superintendent of Schools; that _S_he will attend and participate in the exercises of each Institute or other teachers' meetings that may be appointed for the teachers of said township, or for each day's absence therefrom, forfeit a sum equal to one day's wages, unless such absence shall be occasioned by sickness, that _S_he will accurately keep and use all registers and blanks placed in _her_ hands by said Trustee; that _S_he will make a complete and accurate report at the close of the school term, the blank for which is provided on the back of this sheet; that _S_he will make all other reports required of _her_ by said Trustee, the County Superintendent, or the laws of Indiana, at the proper time and manner and in good order; that _S_he will exercise due diligence in the preservation of school buildings, grounds, furniture, apparatus, books, blanks and other school property committed to _her_ care, and turn the same over to the Trustee, or his representative, at the close of the term of school, in as good condition as when received, damage and wear by use excepted.

The said School Trustee agrees to keep the school buildings in good repair, and to furnish the necessary fuel, furniture, apparatus, books and blanks, and such other appliances as may be necessary for the systematic and proper conduct of said school.

And the said School Trustee, for and in behalf of said Township, further agrees to pay the said _Bertha Coburn_ for services as teacher of said school, either a sum equal to the whole number of days taught at the rate of the above named sum per day, as agreed upon, or the salary for the year in the event of a yearly consideration, as agreed upon, when the said teacher shall have filled all the stipulations of this contract.

The said School Trustee further agrees to pay said teacher one day's wages for each day's attendance at the Township Institute, according to the Acts of 1889.

PROVIDED, That in case the said _Bertha Coburn_ should be dismissed from said school by said Trustee, or his successor in office, for incompetency, cruelty, gross immorality, neglect of business, or a violation of any of the stipulations of this contract, or in case _her_ license should be annulled by the County Superintendent or State Superintendent, _S_he shall not be entitled to any compensation after notice of dismissal, or notice of annulment of license.

PROVIDED FURTHER, That the teacher shall have a duplicate of this Contract.

IN WITNESS WHEREOF, We have hereunto subscribed our names, this _Third_

day of _September_ A. D. 1_906_

Bertha Coburn Teacher.

A. S. Herman School Trustee.

NOTES:—
(1.) Full authority is given the Trustee to substitute the words "principal," "supervisor" or "superintendent" for the word "teacher" in the event the Contract should be so made.
(2.) This Contract is the official blank, made by the State Superintendent of Public Instruction, under the provisions of H. B. No. 139, Acts of 1899.

Teacher's or Principal's Report to Township Trustee.

NOTE.—This report must be made by each teacher having charge of the attendance of pupils. A high school teacher who works under the direction of a principal will not need to make the report in case the principal reports for the entire high school. In graded grammar schools each teacher should report for the pupils directly under his charge. The principal of a graded grammar school should report only for the pupils directly under his charge.

REPORT of............................ .... { teacher } of..........................District
{ principal }

WASHINGTON TOWNSHIP, PORTER COUNTY, INDIANA,

to the Township Trustee, for the school term beginning.................... ....and

closing ....

FOR ALL TEACHERS WHO HAVE CHARGE OF ATTENDANCE OF PUPILS.

1. Number of days school was in session, - - - - - - - - -
2. " " pupils enrolled during year, - Male, ...; female,....................; total,................
3. " " " withdrawn during year, - - " " "
4. " " " suspended " " - - " " "
5. " " " expelled " " - . " " "
6. " " " re-entered " " - " " "
7. " " " remaining in school close of year, " " "
8. " " " neither tardy nor absent during year, " " "
9. " " cases of tardiness during year, - " " "
10. " " pupils tardy during year, - - " " "
11. Total days of attendance by all pupils for year, - - - - - -
12. * " " " absence " " " " " - - - - -
13. Total cases of tardiness,.................... Time lost by tardiness, - - - . . . - - -
14. †Average daily attendance for year, - - - - - -
15. Per cent. of attendance—11÷(11+12), - - - -
16. Number of pupils promoted to - - - - - - -
    (a) Second year, - - - - -
    (b) Third " - - - - - -
    (c) Fourth " - - - - - ....
    (d) Fifth " - - - - - ....
    (e) Sixth " - - - - - ....
    (f) Seventh " - - - - - ....
    (g) Eighth " - - - - - -
    (h) High School, - - - - - ....
17. Number of graduates from the common branches and receiving diplomas,
    Male,....................; female, ...; total,.... ..
18. Number of graduates from non-commissioned township high schools,
    Male,.....................; female,..................; total, ...
19. Number of graduates from commissioned township high schools,
    Male,....................; female,..................; total,..........
20. How many books in school library (not including reading circle books) at beginning of year?
21. How many books were added to library (not including reading circle books) during year?
22. Total now in school library (not including reading circle books), - - - - ....
23. How many reading circle books were added during year? - - - ....
24. How many pupils read one or more school library or reading circle books during year? - ....
25. Do patrons read school library books? - - - ....
26. Number of visits to school, Parents,...................; officials, ...; others, ...; total, ...
27. Number of teachers employed (if school be high school), Male, ...; female, ...; total, ...
28. Number of days teacher attended township institute, - - - - -
29. Books and apparatus left in school room at end of term, - - - ....

I,... ...., do solemnly swear that the above report is true to the best of my knowledge and belief.

{ Teacher.
{ Principal.
....

NOTES:—

*(1.) After three days of absence the pupil should be withdrawn, and his absence counted no more for that period of absence. After being withdrawn, he is not a pupil of the school, and can not be again until he is re-entered, as in item 6.

†(2.) To find average daily attendance divide the whole number of days of attendance made by all the pupils by the number of days of school taught.

For Township Trustees.   Wade Bros. & Wise, Printers.

TEACHER'S CONTRACT.

This Agreement, Between _Wm. A. Bond_ School Trustee of

Washington School Township, In Porter County, and State of Indiana,

of the first part, and _____ a legally qualified teacher in said

County of the second part, certifies that the said teacher hereby agrees to teach the public school in District No. _3_,

Grade _____, in said Township, for the term commencing on the _4th_ day of _____

A. D. 1 _899_, for the consideration of _____ _Two_ Dollars and

_____ Cents per { day, year, } to be paid _When Called for_
(State here when all or parts of salary will be paid.)

The said _Nellie Galbreath_ further agrees faithfully to perform
all the duties of teacher in said school; using only such text-books as are prescribed by the Trustees in accordance with
the law, except supplementary reading, such as Young People's Reading Circle books, etc., and other works recommended by the County Superintendent, and observing all Rules and Regulations of the County Board of Education,
and all instructions of the County Superintendent of Schools; that _S_he will attend and participate in the exercises of
each Institute or other teachers' meetings that may be appointed for the teachers of said township, or for each day's
absence therefrom, forfeit a sum equal to one day's wages, unless such absence shall be occasioned by sickness, that
_S_he will accurately keep and use all registers and blanks placed in _her_ hands by said Trustee; that _S_he will
make a complete and accurate report at the close of the school term, the blank for which is provided on the back of
this sheet; that _S_he will make all other reports required of _her_ by said Trustee, the County Superintendent, or
the laws of Indiana, at the proper time and manner and in good order; that _S_he will exercise due diligence in the
preservation of school buildings, grounds, furniture, apparatus, books, blanks and other school property committed to
her care, and turn the same over to the Trustee, or his representative, at the close of the term of school, in as
good condition as when received, damage and wear by use excepted.

The said School Trustee agrees to keep the school buildings in good repair, and to furnish the necessary fuel,
furniture, apparatus, books and blanks, and such other appliances as may be necessary for the systematic and proper
conduct of said school.

And the said School Trustee, for and in behalf of said Township, further agrees to pay the said _____
Nellie Galbreath for services as teacher of said school, either a sum equal to the whole
number of days taught at the rate of the above named sum per day, as agreed upon, or the salary for the year in the
event of a yearly consideration, as agreed upon, when the said teacher shall have filled all the stipulations of this contract.

The said School Trustee further agrees to pay said teacher one day's wages for each day's attendance at the Township Institute, according to the Acts of 1889.

PROVIDED, That in case the said _Nellie Galbreath_ should be
dismissed from said school by said Trustee, or his successor in office, for incompetency, cruelty, gross immorality,
neglect of business, or a violation of any of the stipulations of this contract, or in case _her_ license should be
annulled by the County Superintendent or State Superintendent, _S_he shall not be entitled to any compensation after
notice of dismissal, or notice of annulment of license.

PROVIDED FURTHER, That the teacher shall have a duplicate of this Contract.

IN WITNESS WHEREOF, We have hereunto subscribed our names, this _2nd_

day of _Sep_ A. D. 1 _899_

Nellie Galbreath Teacher.

Wm. A. Bond School Trustee.

NOTES:—
(1.) Full authority is given the Trustee to substitute the words "principal," "supervisor" or "superintendent" for the word "teacher"
in the event the Contract should be so made.
(2.) This Contract is the official blank, made by the State Superintendent of Public Instruction, under the provisions of H. B. No. 139,
Acts of 1899.

Teacher's or Principal's Report to Township Trustee.

NOTE.—This report must be made by each teacher having charge of the attendance of pupils. A high school teacher who works under the direction of a principal will not need to make the report in case the principal reports for the entire high school. In graded grammar schools each teacher should report for the pupils directly under his charge. The principal of a graded grammar school should report only for the pupils directly under his charge.

REPORT of.......................... { teacher } { principal } of..........................District

WASHINGTON TOWNSHIP, PORTER COUNTY, INDIANA,

to the Township Trustee, for the school term beginning...and closing .....

FOR ALL TEACHERS WHO HAVE CHARGE OF ATTENDANCE OF PUPILS.

1. Number of days school was in session,
2. " " pupils enrolled during year, Male, ...; female,.................; total,.................
3. " " " withdrawn during year, - " " "
4. " " " suspended " " - " " "
5. " " " expelled " " - " " "
6. " " " re-entered " " - " " "
7. " " " remaining in school close of year, " " "
8. " " " " neither tardy nor absent during year, " " "
9. " " cases of tardiness during year, - " " "
10. " " pupils tardy during year, - " " "
11. Total days of attendance by all pupils for year, -
12. * " " " absence " " " " " -
13. Total cases of tardiness,..................... Time lost by tardiness, -
14. †Average daily attendance for year, -
15. Per cent. of attendance—$11 \div (11 + 12)$, -
16. Number of pupils promoted to -
    (a) Second year, -
    (b) Third " -
    (c) Fourth " -
    (d) Fifth " -
    (e) Sixth " -
    (f) Seventh " -
    (g) Eighth " -
    (h) High School, -
17. Number of graduates from the common branches and receiving diplomas,
    Male,...............; female, ...; total,...............
18. Number of graduates from non-commissioned township high schools,
    Male,...............; female,...............; total,...............
19. Number of graduates from commissioned township high schools,
    Male,...............; female,...............; total,...............
20. How many books in school library (not including reading circle books) at beginning of year?
21. How many books were added to library (not including reading circle books) during year?
22. Total now in school library (not including reading circle books), - -
23. How many reading circle books were added during year? - -
24. How many pupils read one or more school library or reading circle books during year? -
25. Do patrons read school library books?
26. Number of visits to school, Parents,...............; officials, ...; others, ...; total,...............
27. Number of teachers employed (if school be high school), Male,...............; female, ...; total,...............
28. Number of days teacher attended township institute, - - - - -
29. Books and apparatus left in school room at end of term, -

I,.., do solemnly swear that the above report is true to the best of my knowledge and belief.

{ Teacher.
{ Principal.
....

NOTES:—
*(1.) After three days of absence the pupil should be withdrawn, and his absence counted no more for that period of absence. After being withdrawn, he is not a pupil of the school, and can not be again until he is re-entered, as in item 6.
†(2.) To find average daily attendance divide the whole number of days of attendance made by all the pupils by the number of days of school taught.

TEACHER'S CONTRACT.

This Agreement, Between _C. S. Hermanee_ School Trustee of

Washington School Township, in Porter County, and State of Indiana,

of the first part, and _Bertha Coburn_ a legally qualified teacher in said

County of the second part, certifies that the said teacher hereby agrees to teach the public school in District No. _2_,

Grade_____, in said Township, for the term commencing on the _Third_ day of _Sep_

A. D. _1906_, for the consideration of _Two_ Dollars and

Seventy five Cents per { day, { year, } to be paid _as Called for_

(State here when all or parts of salary will be paid.)

For 180 Days Teaching   Consideration 495 00

The said _Bertha Coburn_ further agrees faithfully to perform

all the duties of teacher in said school; using only such text-books as are prescribed by the Trustees in accordance with the law, except supplementary reading, such as Young People's Reading Circle books, etc., and other works recommended by the County Superintendent, and observing all Rules and Regulations of the County Board of Education, and all instructions of the County Superintendent of Schools; that _she_ will attend and participate in the exercises of each Institute or other teachers' meetings that may be appointed for the teachers of said township, or for each day's absence therefrom, forfeit a sum equal to one day's wages, unless such absence shall be occasioned by sickness; that _she_ will accurately keep and use all registers and blanks placed in _her_ hands by said Trustee; that _she_ will make a complete and accurate report at the close of the school term, the blank for which is provided on the back of this sheet; that _she_ will make all other reports required of _her_ by said Trustee, the County Superintendent, or the laws of Indiana, at the proper time and manner and in good order; that _she_ will exercise due diligence in the preservation of school buildings, grounds, furniture, apparatus, books, blanks and other school property committed to _her's_ care, and turn the same over to the Trustee, or his representative, at the close of the term of school, in as good condition as when received, damage and wear by use excepted.

The said School Trustee agrees to keep the school buildings in good repair, and to furnish the necessary fuel, furniture, apparatus, books and blanks, and such other appliances as may be necessary for the systematic and proper conduct of said school.

And the said School Trustee, for and in behalf of said Township, further agrees to pay the said _Bertha Coburn_ for services as teacher of said school, either a sum equal to the whole number of days taught at the rate of the above named sum per day, as agreed upon, or the salary for the year in the event of a yearly consideration, as agreed upon, when the said teacher shall have filled all the stipulations of this contract.

The said School Trustee further agrees to pay said teacher one day's wages for each day's attendance at the Township Institute, according to the Acts of 1889.

PROVIDED, That in case the said _Bertha Coburn_ should be dismissed from said school by said Trustee, or his successor in office, for incompetency, cruelty, gross immorality, neglect of business, or a violation of any of the stipulations of this contract, or in case _her_ license should be annulled by the County Superintendent or State Superintendent, _she_ shall not be entitled to any compensation after notice of dismissal, or notice of annulment of license.

PROVIDED FURTHER, That the teacher shall have a duplicate of this Contract.

IN WITNESS WHEREOF, We have hereunto subscribed our names, this _Third_ day of _September_ A. D. 1906

....Teacher.

C. S. Hermanee School Trustee.

NOTES:—
(1.) Full authority is given the Trustee to substitute the words "principal," "supervisor" or "superintendent" for the word "teacher" in the event the Contract should be so made.
(2.) This Contract is the official blank, made by the State Superintendent of Public Instruction, under the provisions of H. B. No. 139, Acts of 1899.

Teacher's or Principal's Report to Township Trustee.

NOTE.—This report must be made by each teacher having charge of the attendance of pupils. A high school teacher who works under the direction of a principal will not need to make the report in case the principal reports for the entire high school. In graded grammar schools each teacher should report for the pupils directly under his charge. The principal of a graded grammar school should report only for the pupils directly under his charge.

REPORT of.................... .... { teacher } of............................District
                                           { principal }

WASHINGTON TOWNSHIP, PORTER COUNTY, INDIANA,

to the Township Trustee, for the school term beginning...and

closing ....: ....

FOR ALL TEACHERS WHO HAVE CHARGE OF ATTENDANCE OF PUPILS.

1. Number of days school was in session,   -   -   -   -   -   -   -   -   -
2.   "   " pupils enrolled during year,   -   Male, ...; female,..............; total,..................
3.   "   "   " withdrawn during year, -   -   "   "   "
4.   "   "   " suspended "   "   -   - "   "   "
5.   "   "   " expelled   "   "   -   . "   "   "
6.   "   "   " re-entered   "   "   -   "   "   "
7.   "   "   " remaining in school close of year, "   "   "
8.   "   "   " " neither tardy nor absent during year, "   "   "
9.   "   " cases of tardiness during year,   -   "   "   "
10.   "   " pupils tardy during year,   -   - "   ....   "   "
11. Total days of attendance by all pupils for year,   -   -   -   -
12. * "   "   " absence   "   "   "   "   "   -   -   -   -   -
13. Total cases of tardiness,.................   Time lost by tardiness,   -   -   -
14. †Average daily attendance for year,   -   -   -   -   -   -
15. Per cent. of attendance—11÷(11+12),   -   -   -
16. Number of pupils promoted to   -   -   -   -   -
    (a) Second year,   -   -   -   -   -
    (b) Third "   -   -   -   -
    (c) Fourth "   -   -   -   -
    (d) Fifth "   -   -   -
    (e) Sixth "   -   -   -   -
    (f) Seventh "   -   -   -   -
    (g) Eighth "   -   -   -   -
    (h) High School,   -   -   -   -   -
17. Number of graduates from the common branches and receiving diplomas,
                          Male,.................; female,..............; total,.........
18. Number of graduates from non-commissioned township high schools,
                          Male,.................; female,..............; total,.........
19. Number of graduates from commissioned township high schools,
                          Male,.................; female,..............; total,.........
20. How many books in school library (not including reading circle books) at beginning of year?
21. How many books were added to library (not including reading circle books) during year?
22. Total now in school library (not including reading circle books),   -   -   -
23. How many reading circle books were added during year?   -   -   -
24. How many pupils read one or more school library or reading circle books during year?   -
25. Do patrons read school library books?   -   -   -   -
26. Number of visits to school,   Parents,.................; officials,..............; others,...........; total,..............
27. Number of teachers employed (if school be high school), Male,..............; female,..............; total,.........
28. Number of days teacher attended township institute,   -   -   -   -
29. Books and apparatus left in school room at end of term,   -   -   -

I,.., do solemnly swear that the above report is true to the best of my knowledge and belief.

                                           { Teacher.
.... { Principal.

NOTES:—
    *(1.) After three days of absence the pupil should be withdrawn, and his absence counted no more for that period of absence. After being withdrawn, he is not a pupil of the school, and can not be again until he is re-entered, as in item 6.
    †(2.) To find average daily attendance divide the whole number of days of attendance made by all the pupils by the number of days of school taught.

TEACHER'S CONTRACT.

This Agreement, Between _A. S. Hermance_ School Trustee of

Washington School Township, in Porter County, and State of Indiana,

of the first part, and _Ivy Miller_ ....a legally qualified teacher in said

County of the second part, certifies that the said teacher hereby agrees to teach the public school in District No. _4_,

Grade_____, in said Township, for the term commencing on the _third_ day of _Sep_

A. D. 1 _906_ _____, for the consideration of _Two_ ....Dollars and

Seventy five Cents per { day, / year, } to be paid _as Called for_ ____
(State here when all or parts of salary will be paid.)

For 180 Days Teaching Consideration 495 ⁰⁰

The said _Ivy Miller_ ....further agrees faithfully to perform

all the duties of teacher in said school; using only such text-books as are prescribed by the Trustees in accordance with the law, except supplementary reading, such as Young People's Reading Circle books, etc., and other works recommended by the County Superintendent, and observing all Rules and Regulations of the County Board of Education, and all instructions of the County Superintendent of Schools; that _s_ he will attend and participate in the exercises of each Institute or other teachers' meetings that may be appointed for the teachers of said township, or for each day's absence therefrom, forfeit a sum equal to one day's wages, unless such absence shall be occasioned by sickness, that _s_ he will accurately keep and use all registers and blanks placed in _her_ hands by said Trustee; that _s_ he will make a complete and accurate report at the close of the school term, the blank for which is provided on the back of this sheet; that _s_ he will make all other reports required of _her_ by said Trustee, the County Superintendent, or the laws of Indiana, at the proper time and manner and in good order; that _s_ he will exercise due diligence in the preservation of school buildings, grounds, furniture, apparatus, books, blanks and other school property committed to _her_ care, and turn the same over to the Trustee, or his representative, at the close of the term of school, in as good condition as when received, damage and wear by use excepted.

The said School Trustee agrees to keep the school buildings in good repair, and to furnish the necessary fuel, furniture, apparatus, books and blanks, and such other appliances as may be necessary for the systematic and proper conduct of said school.

And the said School Trustee, for and in behalf of said Township, further agrees to pay the said _Ivy Miller_ for services as teacher of said school, either a sum equal to the whole number of days taught at the rate of the above named sum per day, as agreed upon, or the salary for the year in the event of a yearly consideration, as agreed upon, when the said teacher shall have filled all the stipulations of this contract.

The said School Trustee further agrees to pay said teacher one day's wages for each day's attendance at the Township Institute, according to the Acts of 1889.

PROVIDED, That in case the said _Ivy Miller_ should be dismissed from said school by said Trustee, or his successor in office, for incompetency, cruelty, gross immorality, neglect of business, or a violation of any of the stipulations of this contract, or in case _her_ license should be annulled by the County Superintendent or State Superintendent, _s_ he shall not be entitled to any compensation after notice of dismissal, or notice of annulment of license.

PROVIDED FURTHER, That the teacher shall have a duplicate of this Contract.

IN WITNESS WHEREOF, We have hereunto subscribed our names, this _third_

day of _September_ A. D. 1 _906_

Ivy Miller ....Teacher.

A. S. Hermance School Trustee.

NOTES:—
(1.) Full authority is given the Trustee to substitute the words "principal," "supervisor" or "superintendent" for the word "teacher" in the event the Contract should be so made.
(2.) This Contract is the official blank, made by the State Superintendent of Public Instruction, under the provisions of H. B. No. 139, Acts of 1899.

Teacher's or Principal's Report to Township Trustee.

NOTE.—This report must be made by each teacher having charge of the attendance of pupils. A high school teacher who works under the direction of a principal will not need to make the report in case the principal reports for the entire high school. In graded grammar schools each teacher should report for the pupils directly under his charge. The principal of a graded grammar school should report only for the pupils directly under his charge.

REPORT of.. .... { teacher } of.........................District
{ principal }

WASHINGTON TOWNSHIP, PORTER COUNTY, INDIANA,

to the Township Trustee, for the school term beginning..and

closing ....

FOR ALL TEACHERS WHO HAVE CHARGE OF ATTENDANCE OF PUPILS.

1. Number of days school was in session, - - - - - - - - - -
2. " " pupils enrolled during year, - Male, ...; female,................; total,...............
3. " " " withdrawn during year, - - " " "
4. " " " suspended " " - - " " "
5. " " " expelled " " - - " " "
6. " " " re-entered " " - " " "
7. " " " remaining in school close of year, " " "
8. " " " " neither tardy nor absent during year, " " "
9. " " cases of tardiness during year, - " " "
10. " " pupils tardy during year, - - " " "
11. Total days of attendance by all pupils for year, - - - -
12. * " " " absence " " " " " - - - -
13. Total cases of tardiness,...................... Time lost by tardiness, - - -
14. †Average daily attendance for year, - - - - - -
15. Per cent. of attendance—11÷(11+12), - - -
16. Number of pupils promoted to - - - -
      (a) Second year, - - -
      (b) Third " -
      (c) Fourth " - - -
      (d) Fifth " - - -
      (e) Sixth " - - - -
      (f) Seventh " - - - -
      (g) Eighth " - - - -
      (h) High School, - - - -
17. Number of graduates from the common branches and receiving diplomas,
      Male,...............; female,................; total,........
18. Number of graduates from non-commissioned township high schools,
      Male,...............; female,................; total,........
19. Number of graduates from commissioned township high schools,
      Male,...............; female,................; total,........
20. How many books in school library (not including reading circle books) at beginning of year?
21. How many books were added to library (not including reading circle books) during year?
22. Total now in school library (not including reading circle books), - - - -
23. How many reading circle books were added during year? - - -
24. How many pupils read one or more school library or reading circle books during year? -
25. Do patrons read school library books? - - - - - -
26. Number of visits to school, Parents,...............; officials,................; others,...............; total,...............
27. Number of teachers employed (if school be high school), Male,................; female,................; total,...............
28. Number of days teacher attended township institute, - - - - -
29. Books and apparatus left in school room at end of term, -

I,..., do solemnly swear that the above report is true to the best of my knowledge and belief.

{ Teacher.
.... { Principal.

NOTES:—
   *(1.) After three days of absence the pupil should be withdrawn, and his absence counted no more for that period of absence. After being withdrawn, he is not a pupil of the school, and can not be again until he is re-entered, as in item 6.
   †(2.) To find average daily attendance divide the whole number of days of attendance made by all the pupils by the number of days of school taught.

Teacher's or Principal's Report to Township Trustee.

NOTE.—This report must be made by each teacher having charge of the attendance of pupils. A high school teacher who works under the direction of a principal will not need to make the report in case the principal reports for the entire high school. In graded grammar schools each teacher should report for the pupils directly under his charge. The principal of a graded grammar school should report only for the pupils directly under his charge.

REPORT of .... { teacher | principal } of ....District

WASHINGTON TOWNSHIP, PORTER COUNTY, INDIANA,

to the Township Trustee, for the school term beginning...and

closing ....

FOR ALL TEACHERS WHO HAVE CHARGE OF ATTENDANCE OF PUPILS.

1. Number of days school was in session,
2. " " pupils enrolled during year,   Male, ...; female, ...; total, ...
3. " " " withdrawn during year, - - "   "   "
4. " " " suspended   "   " - - "   "   "
5. " " " expelled   "   " - - "   "   "
6. " " " re-entered   "   " - "   "   "
7. " " " remaining in school close of year, "   "   "
8. " " " neither tardy nor absent during year, "   "   "
9. " " cases of tardiness during year, - "   "   "
10. " " pupils tardy during year, - - "   "   "
11. Total days of attendance by all pupils for year, - - - -
12. * " " " absence " " " " " - - - -
13. Total cases of tardiness, ... Time lost by tardiness, - - -
14. †Average daily attendance for year, - - - -
15. Per cent. of attendance—$11 \div (11+12)$, - - -
16. Number of pupils promoted to - - - -
    (a) Second year, - - - -
    (b) Third   " - - - -
    (c) Fourth   " - - - -
    (d) Fifth   " - - - -
    (e) Sixth   " - - - -
    (f) Seventh   " - - -
    (g) Eighth   " - - -
    (h) High School, - - - -
17. Number of graduates from the common branches and receiving diplomas,
    Male, ...; female, ...; total, ...
18. Number of graduates from non-commissioned township high schools,
    Male, ...; female, ...; total, ...
19. Number of graduates from commissioned township high schools,
    Male, ...; female, ...; total, ...
20. How many books in school library (not including reading circle books) at beginning of year?
21. How many books were added to library (not including reading circle books) during year?
22. Total now in school library (not including reading circle books), - - -
23. How many reading circle books were added during year? - - -
24. How many pupils read one or more school library or reading circle books during year? -
25. Do patrons read school library books? - - - -
26. Number of visits to school, Parents, ...; officials, ...; others, ...; total, ...
27. Number of teachers employed (if school be high school), Male, ...; female, ...; total, ...
28. Number of days teacher attended township institute, - - - -
29. Books and apparatus left in school room at end of term, - - -

I, ..., do solemnly swear that the above report is true to the best of my knowledge and belief.

{ Teacher. | Principal. }

NOTES:—
*(1.) After three days of absence the pupil should be withdrawn, and his absence counted no more for that period of absence. After being withdrawn, he is not a pupil of the school, and can not be again until he is re-entered, as in item 6.
†(2.) To find average daily attendance divide the whole number of days of attendance made by all the pupils by the number of days of school taught.

TEACHER'S CONTRACT.

This Agreement, Between _A. S. Hermans_ School Trustee of

Washington School Township, in Porter County, and State of Indiana,

of the first part, and _Grace Pierce_ a legally qualified teacher in said

County of the second part, certifies that the said teacher hereby agrees to teach the public school in District No. _1_,

Grade ____, in said Township, for the term commencing on the _third_ day of _Sep_

A. D. 1 _906_ , for the consideration of _Two_ Dollars and

Twenty Two Cents per { day, year, } to be paid _As Called For_ (State here when all or parts of salary will be paid.)

For 180 Days Teaching Consideration 899 00

The said _Grace Pierce_ further agrees faithfully to perform

all the duties of teacher in said school; using only such text-books as are prescribed by the Trustees in accordance with the law, except supplementary reading, such as Young People's Reading Circle books, etc., and other works recommended by the County Superintendent, and observing all Rules and Regulations of the County Board of Education, and all instructions of the County Superintendent of Schools; that _s_ he will attend and participate in the exercises of each Institute or other teachers' meetings that may be appointed for the teachers of said township, or for each day's absence therefrom, forfeit a sum equal to one day's wages, unless such absence shall be occasioned by sickness, that _s_ he will accurately keep and use all registers and blanks placed in _her_ hands by said Trustee; that _s_ he will make a complete and accurate report at the close of the school term, the blank for which is provided on the back of this sheet; that _s_ he will make all other reports required of _her_ by said Trustee, the County Superintendent, or the laws of Indiana, at the proper time and manner and in good order; that _s_ he will exercise due diligence in the preservation of school buildings, grounds, furniture, apparatus, books, blanks and other school property committed to _her_ care, and turn the same over to the Trustee, or his representative, at the close of the term of school, in as good condition as when received, damage and wear by use excepted.

The said School Trustee agrees to keep the school buildings in good repair, and to furnish the necessary fuel, furniture, apparatus, books and blanks, and such other appliances as may be necessary for the systematic and proper conduct of said school.

And the said School Trustee, for and in behalf of said Township, further agrees to pay the said _Grace Pierce_ for services as teacher of said school, either a sum equal to the whole number of days taught at the rate of the above named sum per day, as agreed upon, or the salary for the year in the event of a yearly consideration, as agreed upon, when the said teacher shall have filled all the stipulations of this contract.

The said School Trustee further agrees to pay said teacher one day's wages for each day's attendance at the Township Institute, according to the Acts of 1889.

PROVIDED, That in case the said _Grace Pierce_ should be dismissed from said school by said Trustee, or his successor in office, for incompetency, cruelty, gross immorality, neglect of business, or a violation of any of the stipulations of this contract, or in case _her_ license should be annulled by the County Superintendent or State Superintendent, _s_ he shall not be entitled to any compensation after notice of dismissal, or notice of annulment of license.

PROVIDED FURTHER, That the teacher shall have a duplicate of this Contract.

IN WITNESS WHEREOF, We have hereunto subscribed our names, this _Third_

day of _September_ A. D. 1 _906_

Grace Pierce Teacher.

A. S. Hermans School Trustee.

NOTES:—

(1.) Full authority is given the Trustee to substitute the words "principal," "supervisor" or "superintendent" for the word "teacher" in the event the Contract should be so made.

(2.) This Contract is the official blank, made by the State Superintendent of Public Instruction, under the provisions of H. B. No. 139, Acts of 1899.

Teacher's or Principal's Report to Township Trustee.

NOTE.—This report must be made by each teacher having charge of the attendance of pupils. A high school teacher who works under the direction of a principal will not need to make the report in case the principal reports for the entire high school. In graded grammar schools each teacher should report for the pupils directly under his charge. The principal of a graded grammar school should report only for the pupils directly under his charge.

REPORT of... .... { teacher } { principal } of............................District

WASHINGTON TOWNSHIP, PORTER COUNTY, INDIANA,

to the Township Trustee, for the school term beginning.................................. ....and

closing ...: ....

FOR ALL TEACHERS WHO HAVE CHARGE OF ATTENDANCE OF PUPILS.

1. Number of days school was in session, - - - - - - - - - - -
2. " " pupils enrolled during year, - Male, ...; female,.................; total,.................
3. " " " withdrawn during year, - - " " "
4. " " " suspended " " - - " " .... "
5. " " " expelled " " - - " " "
6. " " " re-entered " " - " " "
7. " " " remaining in school close of year, " " "
8. " " " " neither tardy nor absent during year, " " "
9. " " " cases of tardiness during year, - " " .... "
10. " " " pupils tardy during year, - - " .... " "
11. Total days of attendance by all pupils for year, - - - - -
12. * " " " absence " " " " " - - - -
13. Total cases of tardiness, ... Time lost by tardiness, - - - ... ... - ..
14. †Average daily attendance for year, - - - - -
15. Per cent. of attendance—11÷(11+12), - - -
16. Number of pupils promoted to - - - -
    (a) Second year, - - - -
    (b) Third " - - - - -
    (c) Fourth " - - - - - ....
    (d) Fifth " - - - - - ....
    (e) Sixth " - - - - - ....
    (f) Seventh " - - - - - - _
    (g) Eighth " - - - - - -
    (h) High School, - - - - - ....
17. Number of graduates from the common branches and receiving diplomas,
    Male,.................; female, ...; total,.. .. ...
18. Number of graduates from non-commissioned township high schools,
    Male,.................; female,.................; total,.................
19. Number of graduates from commissioned township high schools,
    Male,.................; female,.................; total,.........
20. How many books in school library (not including reading circle books) at beginning of year?
21. How many books were added to library (not including reading circle books) during year?
22. Total now in school library (not including reading circle books), - - - -
23. How many reading circle books were added during year? - - - - - ....
24. How many pupils read one or more school library or reading circle books during year? - ....
25. Do patrons read school library books? - - - - - - ....
26. Number of visits to school, Parents,.................; officials, ...; others, ...; total,.................
27. Number of teachers employed (if school be high school), Male,.................; female, ...; total,.................
28. Number of days teacher attended township institute, - - -
29. Books and apparatus left in school room at end of term, - - - - ....

I,.. ...., do solemnly swear that the above report is true to the best of my knowledge and belief.

                                  { Teacher.
.... { Principal.

NOTES:—
*(1.) After three days of absence the pupil should be withdrawn, and his absence counted no more for that period of absence. After being withdrawn, he is not a pupil of the school, and can not be again until he is re-entered, as in item 6.
†(2.) To find average daily attendance divide the whole number of days of attendance made by all the pupils by the number of days of school taught.

TEACHER'S CONTRACT.

This Agreement, Between _A. D. Hermance_ School Trustee of

Washington School Township, in Porter County, and State of Indiana,

of the first part, and _Florence Lupold_ a legally qualified teacher in said

County of the second part, certifies that the said teacher hereby agrees to teach the public school in District No. _3_,

Grade _____, in said Township, for the term commencing on the _____ day of _____

A. D. 1 _906_ , for the consideration of _Two_ Dollars and

Twenty Cents per { day, year, } to be paid _as Called for_ (State here when all or part of salary will be paid.)

For 180 Days Teaching Consideration $96.00

The said _Florence Lupold_ further agrees faithfully to perform

all the duties of teacher in said school; using only such text-books as are prescribed by the Trustees in accordance with the law, except supplementary reading, such as Young People's Reading Circle books, etc., and other works recommended by the County Superintendent, and observing all Rules and Regulations of the County Board of Education, and all instructions of the County Superintendent of Schools; that _s_he will attend and participate in the exercises of each Institute or other teachers' meetings that may be appointed for the teachers of said township, or for each day's absence therefrom, forfeit a sum equal to one day's wages, unless such absence shall be occasioned by sickness, that _s_he will accurately keep and use all registers and blanks placed in _her_ hands by said Trustee; that _s_he will make a complete and accurate report at the close of the school term, the blank for which is provided on the back of this sheet; that _s_he will make all other reports required of _her_ by said Trustee, the County Superintendent, or the laws of Indiana, at the proper time and manner and in good order; that _s_he will exercise due diligence in the preservation of school buildings, grounds, furniture, apparatus, books, blanks and other school property committed to _her_ care, and turn the same over to the Trustee, or his representative, at the close of the term of school, in as good condition as when received, damage and wear by use excepted.

The said School Trustee agrees to keep the school buildings in good repair, and to furnish the necessary fuel, furniture, apparatus, books and blanks, and such other appliances as may be necessary for the systematic and proper conduct of said school.

And the said School Trustee, for and in behalf of said Township, further agrees to pay the said _Florence Lupold_ for services as teacher of said school, either a sum equal to the whole number of days taught at the rate of the above named sum per day, as agreed upon, or the salary for the year in the event of a yearly consideration, as agreed upon, when the said teacher shall have filled all the stipulations of this contract.

The said School Trustee further agrees to pay said teacher one day's wages for each day's attendance at the Township Institute, according to the Acts of 1889.

PROVIDED, That in case the said _Florence Lupold_ should be dismissed from said school by said Trustee, or his successor in office, for incompetency, cruelty, gross immorality, neglect of business, or a violation of any of the stipulations of this contract, or in case _her_ license should be annulled by the County Superintendent or State Superintendent, _s_he shall not be entitled to any compensation after notice of dismissal, or notice of annulment of license.

PROVIDED FURTHER, That the teacher shall have a duplicate of this Contract.

IN WITNESS WHEREOF, We have hereunto subscribed our names, this _Third_

day of _September_ A. D. 1 906

Florence Lupold Teacher.

A. D. Hermance School Trustee.

NOTES:—

(1.) Full authority is given the Trustee to substitute the words "principal," "supervisor" or "superintendent" for the word "teacher" in the event the Contract should be so made.

(2.) This Contract is the official blank, made by the State Superintendent of Public Instruction, under the provisions of H. B. No. 139, Acts of 1899.

Teacher's or Principal's Report to Township Trustee.

NOTE.—This report must be made by each teacher having charge of the attendance of pupils. A high school teacher who works under the direction of a principal will not need to make the report in case the principal reports for the entire high school. In graded grammar schools each teacher should report for the pupils directly under his charge. The principal of a graded grammar school should report only for the pupils directly under his charge.

REPORT of............................ .... { teacher } { principal } of........................District

WASHINGTON TOWNSHIP, PORTER COUNTY, INDIANA,

to the Township Trustee, for the school term beginning.................. ....-and

closing ....:

FOR ALL TEACHERS WHO HAVE CHARGE OF ATTENDANCE OF PUPILS.

1. Number of days school was in session, - - - - - - - - - -
2. " " pupils enrolled during year, - Male, ...; female,....................; total,............
3. " " " withdrawn during year, - - " " "
4. " " " suspended " " - - " " "
5. " " " expelled " " - " " "
6. " " " re-entered " " - " " "
7. " " " remaining in school close of year, " " "
8. " " " neither tardy nor absent during year, " " "
9. " " cases of tardiness during year, - " " "
10. " " pupils tardy during year, - - " " "
11. Total days of attendance by all pupils for year, - - - - -
12. * " " " absence " " " " " - - - -
13. Total cases of tardiness,................... Time lost by tardiness, - - - -
14. †Average daily attendance for year, - - - - -
15. Per cent. of attendance—$11 \div (11 + 12)$, - - -
16. Number of pupils promoted to - - - - - -
    (a) Second year, - - - - - -
    (b) Third " - - - - - -
    (c) Fourth " - - - - - -
    (d) Fifth " - - - - -
    (e) Sixth " - - - - -
    (f) Seventh " - - - - - -
    (g) Eighth " - - - - - -
    (h) High School, - - - - - -
17. Number of graduates from the common branches and receiving diplomas,
    Male,.................; female,..................; total,.............
18. Number of graduates from non-commissioned township high schools,
    Male,.................; female,..................; total,.............
19. Number of graduates from commissioned township high schools,
    Male,.................; female,..................; total,.............
20. How many books in school library (not including reading circle books) at beginning of year?
21. How many books were added to library (not including reading circle books) during year?
22. Total now in school library (not including reading circle books), - - - -
23. How many reading circle books were added during year? - - - -
24. How many pupils read one or more school library or reading circle books during year? -
25. Do patrons read school library books? - - - - - -
26. Number of visits to school, Parents,.............; officials,.............; others,.............; total,.............
27. Number of teachers employed (if school be high school), Male,.............; female,.............; total,.............
28. Number of days teacher attended township institute, - - - -
29. Books and apparatus left in school room at end of term, - -

I,..., do solemnly swear that the above report is true to the best of my knowledge and belief.

{ Teacher.
.... { Principal.

NOTES:—
*(1.) After three days of absence the pupil should be withdrawn, and his absence counted no more for that period of absence. After being withdrawn, he is not a pupil of the school, and can not be again until he is re-entered, as in item 6.
†(2.) To find average daily attendance divide the whole number of days of attendance made by all the pupils by the number of days of school taught.

TEACHER'S CONTRACT.

This Agreement, Between *A. S. Hermance* School Trustee of

Washington School Township, In Porter County, and State of Indiana,

of the first part, and *Leah Hataling* a legally qualified teacher in said

County of the second part, certifies that the said teacher hereby agrees to teach the public school in District No. *7*,

Grade........., in said Township, for the term commencing on the *third* day of *Sep.*

A. D. 1 *906* , for the consideration of.... *Two* ....Dollars and

Twenty five Cents per { day, year, } to be paid *as Called for* (State here when all or parts of salary will be paid.)

For 180 Days Teaching Consideration 405.00

The said *Leah Hataling* ....further agrees faithfully to perform

all the duties of teacher in said school; using only such text-books as are prescribed by the Trustees in accordance with the law, except supplementary reading, such as Young People's Reading Circle books, etc., and other works recommended by the County Superintendent, and observing all Rules and Regulations of the County Board of Education, and all instructions of the County Superintendent of Schools; that *S*he will attend and participate in the exercises of each Institute or other teachers' meetings that may be appointed for the teachers of said township, or for each day's absence therefrom, forfeit a sum equal to one day's wages, unless such absence shall be occasioned by sickness, that *S*he will accurately keep and use all registers and blanks placed in *her* hands by said Trustee; that *S*he will make a complete and accurate report at the close of the school term, the blank for which is provided on the back of this sheet; that *S*he will make all other reports required of *her* by said Trustee, the County Superintendent, or the laws of Indiana, at the proper time and manner and in good order; that *S*he will exercise due diligence in the preservation of school buildings, grounds, furniture, apparatus, books, blanks and other school property committed to *her* care, and turn the same over to the Trustee, or his representative, at the close of the term of school, in as good condition as when received, damage and wear by use excepted.

The said School Trustee agrees to keep the school buildings in good repair, and to furnish the necessary fuel, furniture, apparatus, books and blanks, and such other appliances as may be necessary for the systematic and proper conduct of said school.

And the said School Trustee, for and in behalf of said Township, further agrees to pay the said *Leah Hataling* .... for services as teacher of said school, either a sum equal to the whole number of days taught at the rate of the above named sum per day, as agreed upon, or the salary for the year in the event of a yearly consideration, as agreed upon, when the said teacher shall have filled all the stipulations of this contract.

The said School Trustee further agrees to pay said teacher one day's wages for each day's attendance at the Township Institute, according to the Acts of 1889.

PROVIDED, That in case the said....... *Leah Hataling* ....should be dismissed from said school by said Trustee, or his successor in office, for incompetency, cruelty, gross immorality, neglect of business, or a violation of any of the stipulations of this contract, or in case *her* license should be annulled by the County Superintendent or State Superintendent, *S*he shall not be entitled to any compensation after notice of dismissal, or notice of annulment of license.

PROVIDED FURTHER, That the teacher shall have a duplicate of this Contract.

IN WITNESS WHEREOF, We have hereunto subscribed our names, this *third*

day of *September* A. D. 1 *906*

Leah Hotaling ....Teacher.

A. S. Hermance School Trustee.

NOTES:—

(1.) Full authority is given the Trustee to substitute the words "principal," "supervisor" or "superintendent" for the word "teacher" in the event the Contract should be so made.

(2.) This Contract is the official blank, made by the State Superintendent of Public Instruction, under the provisions of H. B. No. 139, Acts of 1899.

Teacher's or Principal's Report to Township Trustee.

NOTE.—This report must be made by each teacher having charge of the attendance of pupils. A high school teacher who works under the direction of a principal will not need to make the report in case the principal reports for the entire high school. In graded grammar schools each teacher should report for the pupils directly under his charge. The principal of a graded grammar school should report only for the pupils directly under his charge.

REPORT of............................ .... { teacher } of........................District
{ principal }

WASHINGTON TOWNSHIP, PORTER COUNTY, INDIANA,

to the Township Trustee, for the school term beginning...and

closing ...: ....

FOR ALL TEACHERS WHO HAVE CHARGE OF ATTENDANCE OF PUPILS.

1. Number of days school was in session, - - - - - - - - -
2. "   " pupils enrolled during year, - Male, ...; female,......................; total,..............
3. "   "   "   withdrawn during year, - - "   "   "
4. "   "   "   suspended   "   "   - - "   "   "
5. "   "   "   expelled   "   "   - . "   "   "
6. "   "   "   re-entered   "   "   - "   "   "
7. "   "   "   remaining in school close of year, "   "   "
8. "   "   "   " neither tardy nor absent during year, "   "   "
9. "   "   cases of tardiness during year, - "   "   "
10. "   "   pupils tardy during year, - - "   .... "   "
11. Total days of attendance by all pupils for year, - - - - - -
12. * "   "   "   absence   "   "   "   "   "   - - - - - -
13. Total cases of tardiness, ... Time lost by tardiness, - - - ... .
14. †Average daily attendance for year, - - - - -
15. Per cent. of attendance—11÷(11+12), - -
16. Number of pupils promoted to - - - - - - -
    (a) Second year, - - - - - - -
    (b) Third   "   - - - - - -
    (c) Fourth "   - - - - ....
    (d) Fifth   "   - - - - ....
    (e) Sixth   "   - - - - - ....
    (f) Seventh "   - - - - - - _
    (g) Eighth "   - - - - - -
    (h) High School, - - - - - ....
17. Number of graduates from the common branches and receiving diplomas,
    Male,......................; female,...................; total,.. ..   ....
18. Number of graduates from non-commissioned township high schools,
    Male,......................; female,...................; total,.............. ..
19. Number of graduates from commissioned township high schools,
    Male,......................; female,...................; total,...........
20. How many books in school library (not including reading circle books) at beginning of year?
21. How many books were added to library (not including reading circle books) during year?
22. Total now in school library (not including reading circle books), - - - - -
23. How many reading circle books were added during year? - - - - - ....
24. How many pupils read one or more school library or reading circle books during year? - ....
25. Do patrons read school library books? - - - - - - - ....
26. Number of visits to school, Parents,...................; officials, ...; others, ...; total,...........................
27. Number of teachers employed (if school be high school), Male,...............; female, ...; total,.................. ..
28. Number of days teacher attended township institute, * - - -
29. Books and apparatus left in school room at end of term, - - - - ....

I,..., do solemnly swear that the above report is
true to the best of my knowledge and belief.
                                                        { Teacher.
.... { Principal.

NOTES:—
*(1.) After three days of absence the pupil should be withdrawn, and his absence counted no more for that period of absence. After being withdrawn, he is not a pupil of the school, and can not be again until he is re-entered, as in item 6.
†(2.) To find average daily attendance divide the whole number of days of attendance made by all the pupils by the number of days of school taught.

502

For Township Trustees.   Wade Bros. & Wise, Printers.

TEACHER'S CONTRACT.

This Agreement, Between _C. S. Hermance_ School Trustee of

Washington School Township, In Porter County, and State of Indiana,

of the first part, and _Jennie Keding_ a legally qualified teacher in said
County of the second part, certifies that the said teacher hereby agrees to teach the public school in District No. _6_
Grade_____, in said Township, for the term commencing on the _Second_ day of _September_
A. D. 1 _907_ , for the consideration of _Two_ Dollars and
Fifty Cents per { day, year, } to be paid _When Called for_ (State here when all or parts of salary will be paid.)
For 180 days Teaching. Consideration 450 00

The said _Jennie Keding_ further agrees faithfully to perform
all the duties of teacher in said school; using only such text-books as are prescribed by the Trustees in accordance with
the law, except supplementary reading, such as Young People's Reading Circle books, etc., and other works recommended by the County Superintendent, and observing all Rules and Regulations of the County Board of Education,
and all instructions of the County Superintendent of Schools; that _S_he will attend and participate in the exercises of
each Institute or other teachers' meetings that may be appointed for the teachers of said township, or for each, day's
absence therefrom, forfeit a sum equal to one day's wages, unless such absence shall be occasioned by sickness, that
_S_he will accurately keep and use all registers and blanks placed in _her_ hands by said Trustee; that _S_he will
make a complete and accurate report at the close of the school term, the blank for which is provided on the back of
this sheet; that _S_he will make all other reports required of _her_ by said Trustee, the County Superintendent, or
the laws of Indiana, at the proper time and manner and in good order; that _S_he will exercise due diligence in the
preservation of school buildings, grounds, furniture, apparatus, books, blanks and other school property committed to
her care, and turn the same over to the Trustee, or his representative, at the close of the term of school, in as
good condition as when received, damage and wear by use excepted.

The said School Trustee agrees to keep the school buildings in good repair, and to furnish the necessary fuel,
furniture, apparatus, books and blanks, and such other appliances as may be necessary for the systematic and proper
conduct of said school.

And the said School Trustee, for and in behalf of said Township, further agrees to pay the said _Jennie_
Keding for services as teacher of said school, either a sum equal to the whole
number of days taught at the rate of the above named sum per day, as agreed upon, or the salary for the year in the
event of a yearly consideration, as agreed upon, when the said teacher shall have filled all the stipulations of this contract.

The said School Trustee further agrees to pay said teacher one day's wages for each day's attendance at the Township Institute, according to the Acts of 1889.

PROVIDED, That in case the said _Jennie Keding_ should be
dismissed from said school by said Trustee, or his successor in office, for incompetency, cruelty, gross immorality,
neglect of business, or a violation of any of the stipulations of this contract, or in case _her_ license should be
annulled by the County Superintendent or State Superintendent, _s_he shall not be entitled to any compensation after
notice of dismissal, or notice of annulment of license.

PROVIDED FURTHER, That the teacher shall have a duplicate of this Contract.

IN WITNESS WHEREOF, We have hereunto subscribed our names, this _2_
day of _Sept_ A. D. 1 _907_

Jennie Keding Teacher.
C. S. Hermance School Trustee.

NOTES:—
(1.) Full authority is given the Trustee to substitute the words "principal," "supervisor" or "superintendent" for the word "teacher"
in the event the Contract should be so made.
(2.) This Contract is the official blank, made by the State Superintendent of Public Instruction, under the provisions of H. B. No. 139,
Acts of 1899.

Teacher's or Principal's Report to Township Trustee.

NOTE.—This report must be made by each teacher having charge of the attendance of pupils. A high school teacher who works under the direction of a principal will not need to make the report in case the principal reports for the entire high school. In graded grammar schools each teacher should report for the pupils directly under his charge. The principal of a graded grammar school should report only for the pupils directly under his charge.

REPORT of................................. .... { teacher } { principal } of....................District

WASHINGTON TOWNSHIP, PORTER COUNTY, INDIANA,

to the Township Trustee, for the school term beginning...and

closing ....: ....

FOR ALL TEACHERS WHO HAVE CHARGE OF ATTENDANCE OF PUPILS.

1. Number of days school was in session, -   -   -   -   -   -   -   -   -   -
2. "   " pupils enrolled during year,   -   Male, ...; female,.......................; total,.............
3. "   "   "   " withdrawn during year, -   -   "   -   "   -   "
4. "   "   "   " suspended   "   "   -   - "   -   "   ....   "
5. "   "   "   " expelled   "   "   -   - "   -   "   -   "
6. "   "   "   " re-entered   "   "   -   "   -   "   -   "
7. "   "   "   " remaining in school close of year, "   "   "
8. "   "   "   " neither tardy nor absent during year, "   "   "
9. "   "   " cases of tardiness during year,   -   "   -   "   ....   "
10. "   "   " pupils tardy during year,   -   - "   ....   "   -   "
11. Total days of attendance by all pupils for year,   -   -   -   -   -
12. * "   "   " absence   "   "   "   "   "   -   -   -   -   -
13. Total cases of tardiness, ...   Time lost by tardiness,   -   -   -   ....
14. †Average daily attendance for year,   -   -   -   -   -   -
15. Per cent. of attendance—11÷(11+12),   -   -   -   -   -
16. Number of pupils promoted to   -   -   -   -   -   -
     (a) Second year,   -   -   -   -   -   -
     (b) Third   "   -   -   -   -   -   -
     (c) Fourth   "   -   -   -   -   -   ....
     (d) Fifth   "   -   -   -   -   -   ....
     (e) Sixth   "   -   -   -   -   -   ....
     (f) Seventh   "   -   -   -   -   -   __
     (g) Eighth   "   -   -   -   -   -   -
     (h) High School,   -   -   -   -   -   ....
17. Number of graduates from the common branches and receiving diplomas,
     Male,...........................; female,..................... ; total,.........
18. Number of graduates from non-commissioned township high schools,
     Male,..........................; female,......................; total,.................
19. Number of graduates from commissioned township high schools,
     Male,.........................; female,......................; total,.........
20. How many books in school library (not including reading circle books) at beginning of year?
21. How many books were added to library (not including reading circle books) during year?
22. Total now in school library (not including reading circle books),   -   -   -   -
23. How many reading circle books were added during year?   -   -   -   -   -   ....
24. How many pupils read one or more school library or reading circle books during year?   -   ....
25. Do patrons read school library books?   -   -   -   -   -   -   -   ....
26. Number of visits to school,   Parents,..........................; officials, ...; others, ...; total, ...
27. Number of teachers employed (if school be high school), Male,.....................; female, ...; total,.................
28. Number of days teacher attended township institute,   -   -   -   -   -
29. Books and apparatus left in school room at end of term,   -   -   -   -   ....

I,.. ...., do solemnly swear that the above report is true to the best of my knowledge and belief.

           { Teacher.
.... { Principal.

NOTES:—

*(1.) After three days of absence the pupil should be withdrawn, and his absence counted no more for that period of absence. After being withdrawn, he is not a pupil of the school, and can not be again until he is re-entered, as in item 6.

†(2.) To find average daily attendance divide the whole number of days of attendance made by all the pupils by the number of days of school taught.

TEACHER'S CONTRACT.

This Agreement, Between.... _C. S. Hermance_ ....School Trustee of

Washington School Township, in Porter County, and State of Indiana,

of the first part, and _Ethel Dodd_ ....a legally qualified teacher in said

County of the second part, certifies that the said teacher hereby agrees to teach the public school in District No. _5_,

Grade........., in said Township, for the term commencing on the _Second_ day of _Sept_

A. D. 1 _907_ .., for the consideration of..............._Two_ .... Dollars and

Sixty ......Cents per { day, / year, } to be paid _When Called for_ ....

(State here when all or parts of salary will be paid.)

For 180 Days Teaching Consideration 468 ≡

The said........._Ethel Dodd_ ....further agrees faithfully to perform

all the duties of teacher in said school; using only such text-books as are prescribed by the Trustees in accordance with
the law, except supplementary reading, such as Young People's Reading Circle books, etc., and other works recommended by the County Superintendent, and observing all Rules and Regulations of the County Board of Education,
and all instructions of the County Superintendent of Schools; that _S_he will attend and participate in the exercises of
each Institute or other teachers' meetings that may be appointed for the teachers of said township, or for each day's
absence therefrom, forfeit a sum equal to one day's wages, unless such absence shall be occasioned by sickness, that
_S_he will accurately keep and use all registers and blanks placed in _her_ hands by said Trustee; that _S_he will
make a complete and accurate report at the close of the school term, the blank for which is provided on the back of
this sheet; that _S_he will make all other reports required of _her_ by said Trustee, the County Superintendent, or
the laws of Indiana, at the proper time and manner and in good order; that _S_he will exercise due diligence in the
preservation of school buildings, grounds, furniture, apparatus, books, blanks and other school property committed to
her care, and turn the same over to the Trustee, or his representative, at the close of the term of school, in as
good condition as when received, damage and wear by use excepted.

The said School Trustee agrees to keep the school buildings in good repair, and to furnish the necessary fuel,
furniture, apparatus, books and blanks, and such other appliances as may be necessary for the systematic and proper
conduct of said school.

And the said School Trustee, for and in behalf of said Township, further agrees to pay the said.. _Ethel_ ..

.._Dodd_ ....for services as teacher of said school, either a sum equal to the whole
number of days taught at the rate of the above named sum per day, as agreed upon, or the salary for the year in the
event of a yearly consideration, as agreed upon, when the said teacher shall have filled all the stipulations of this contract.

The said School Trustee further agrees to pay said teacher one day's wages for each day's attendance at the Township Institute, according to the Acts of 1889.

PROVIDED, That in case the said................._Ethel Dodd_ ....should be
dismissed from said school by said Trustee, or his successor in office, for incompetency, cruelty, gross immorality,
neglect of business, or a violation of any of the stipulations of this contract, or in case _her_ license should be
annulled by the County Superintendent or State Superintendent, _S_he shall not be entitled to any compensation after
notice of dismissal, or notice of annulment of license.

PROVIDED FURTHER, That the teacher shall have a duplicate of this Contract.

IN WITNESS WHEREOF, We have hereunto subscribed our names, this _Second_

day of.....__Sept_ ....A. D. 1 _907_

...................._Ethel A. Dodd,_ ....Teacher.

...................._C. S. Hermance_ ....School Trustee.

NOTES:—

　　　　(1.) Full authority is given the Trustee to substitute the words "principal," "supervisor" or "superintendent" for the word "teacher"
in the event the Contract should be so made.

　　　　(2.) This Contract is the official blank, made by the State Superintendent of Public Instruction, under the provisions of H. B. No. 139,
Acts of 1899.

Teacher's or Principal's Report to Township Trustee.

NOTE.—This report must be made by each teacher having charge of the attendance of pupils. A high school teacher who works under the direction of a principal will not need to make the report in case the principal reports for the entire high school. In graded grammar schools each teacher should report for the pupils directly under his charge. The principal of a graded grammar school should report only for the pupils directly under his charge.

REPORT of......................... .... { teacher } of......................District
{ principal }

WASHINGTON TOWNSHIP, PORTER COUNTY, INDIANA,

to the Township Trustee, for the school term beginning.................. ....and

closing ....

FOR ALL TEACHERS WHO HAVE CHARGE OF ATTENDANCE OF PUPILS.

1. Number of days school was in session, - - - - - - - - - -
2. " " pupils enrolled during year, - Male, ...; female,......................; total,............ ..
3. " " " withdrawn during year, - - " " "
4. " " " suspended " " - - " " "
5. " " " expelled " " - - " " "
6. " " " re-entered " " - " " "
7. " " " remaining in school close of year, " " "
8. " " " neither tardy nor absent during year, " " "
9. " " cases of tardiness during year, - " " "
10. " " pupils tardy during year, - - " " "
11. Total days of attendance by all pupils for year, - - - - -
12. * " " " absence " " " " " - - - -
13. Total cases of tardiness,................. Time lost by tardiness, - ... ...
14. †Average daily attendance for year, - - - - -
15. Per cent. of attendance—$11 \div (11 + 12)$, - - -
16. Number of pupils promoted to - - - -
    (a) Second year, - - - - -
    (b) Third " - - - - -
    (c) Fourth " - - - - -
    (d) Fifth " - - - - -
    (e) Sixth " - - - - -
    (f) Seventh " - - - - -
    (g) Eighth " - - - - -
    (h) High School, - - - - -
17. Number of graduates from the common branches and receiving diplomas,
    Male,................; female,................ ; total, ...
18. Number of graduates from non-commissioned township high schools,
    Male,................; female,................; total,............ .
19. Number of graduates from commissioned township high schools,
    Male,................; female,................; total,........
20. How many books in school library (not including reading circle books) at beginning of year?
21. How many books were added to library (not including reading circle books) during year?
22. Total now in school library (not including reading circle books), - - - -
23. How many reading circle books were added during year? - - -
24. How many pupils read one or more school library or reading circle books during year? -
25. Do patrons read school library books? - - -
26. Number of visits to school, Parents,................; officials,................; others,............; total,............
27. Number of teachers employed (if school be high school), Male,............; female,............; total,............
28. Number of days teacher attended township institute, - - -
29. Books and apparatus left in school room at end of term, - - -

I,.. ...., do solemnly swear that the above report is
true to the best of my knowledge and belief.

{ Teacher.
.... { Principal.

58 A

TEACHER'S CONTRACT.

This Agreement, Between _A. S. Hermance_ School Trustee of

Washington School Township, in Porter County, and State of Indiana,

of the first part, and _Bertha Sweet_ ....a legally qualified teacher in said

County of the second part, certifies that the said teacher hereby agrees to teach the public school in District No. _4_,

Grade_____, in said Township, for the term commencing on the _Second_ day of _Sept_

A. D. 1 _907_ , for the consideration of _Two_ _____Dollars and

Seventy five Cents per { day, / year, } to be paid _When Called For_ (State here when all or part of salary will be paid.)

For 180 days Teaching Consideration 495 00

The said _Bertha Sweet_ ....further agrees faithfully to perform

all the duties of teacher in said school; using only such text-books as are prescribed by the Trustees in accordance with
the law, except supplementary reading, such as Young People's Reading Circle books, etc., and other works recommended by the County Superintendent, and observing all Rules and Regulations of the County Board of Education,
and all instructions of the County Superintendent of Schools; that _S_ he will attend and participate in the exercises of
each Institute or other teachers' meetings that may be appointed for the teachers of said township, or for each day's
absence therefrom, forfeit a sum equal to one day's wages, unless such absence shall be occasioned by sickness, that
_S_ he will accurately keep and use all registers and blanks placed in _her_ hands by said Trustee; that _S_ he will
make a complete and accurate report at the close of the school term, the blank for which is provided on the back of
this sheet; that _S_ he will make all other reports required of _her_ by said Trustee, the County Superintendent, or
the laws of Indiana, at the proper time and manner and in good order; that _S_ he will exercise due diligence in the
preservation of school buildings, grounds, furniture, apparatus, books, blanks and other school property committed to
her care, and turn the same over to the Trustee, or his representative, at the close of the term of school, in as
good condition as when received, damage and wear by use excepted.

The said School Trustee agrees to keep the school buildings in good repair, and to furnish the necessary fuel,
furniture, apparatus, books and blanks, and such other appliances as may be necessary for the systematic and proper
conduct of said school.

And the said School Trustee, for and in behalf of said Township, further agrees to pay the said _Bertha
Sweet_ ....for services as teacher of said school, either a sum equal to the whole
number of days taught at the rate of the above named sum per day, as agreed upon, or the salary for the year in the
event of a yearly consideration, as agreed upon, when the said teacher shall have filled all the stipulations of this contract.

The said School Trustee further agrees to pay said teacher one day's wages for each day's attendance at the Township Institute, according to the Acts of 1889.

PROVIDED, That in case the said _Bertha Sweet_ ....should be
dismissed from said school by said Trustee, or his successor in office, for incompetency, cruelty, gross immorality,
neglect of business, or a violation of any of the stipulations of this contract, or in case _her_ license should be
annulled by the County Superintendent or State Superintendent, _S_ he shall not be entitled to any compensation after
notice of dismissal, or notice of annulment of license.

PROVIDED FURTHER, That the teacher shall have a duplicate of this Contract.

IN WITNESS WHEREOF, We have hereunto subscribed our names, this _Second_

day of _Sept_ .... A. D. 1 _907_

Bertha Sweet ....Teacher.

A. S. Hermance ....School Trustee.

NOTES:—
    (1.) Full authority is given the Trustee to substitute the words "principal," "supervisor" or "superintendent" for the word "teacher"
in the event the Contract should be so made.
    (2.) This Contract is the official blank, made by the State Superintendent of Public Instruction, under the provisions of H. B. No. 139,
Acts of 1899.

Teacher's or Principal's Report to Township Trustee.

NOTE.—This report must be made by each teacher having charge of the attendance of pupils. A high school teacher who works under the direction of a principal will not need to make the report in case the principal reports for the entire high school. In graded grammar schools each teacher should report for the pupils directly under his charge. The principal of a graded grammar school should report only for the pupils directly under his charge.

REPORT of.................... .... { teacher } of........................District
                                                                                                            { principal }

WASHINGTON TOWNSHIP, PORTER COUNTY, INDIANA,

to the Township Trustee, for the school term beginning.................... ....and

closing ....:   ....

FOR ALL TEACHERS WHO HAVE CHARGE OF ATTENDANCE OF PUPILS.

1. Number of days school was in session,   -   -   -   -   -   -   -   -   -

2. "   " pupils enrolled during year,   -   Male, ...; female,.....................; total,...................... ...

3. "   "   " withdrawn during year, -   -   "   "   "

4. "   "   " suspended   "   "   -   - "   "   ....   "

5. "   "   " expelled   "   " -   - "   "   "

6. "   "   " re-entered   "   "   -   "   "   "

7. "   "   " remaining in school close of year, "   "   "

8. "   "   " " neither tardy nor absent during year, "   "   "

9. "   " cases of tardiness during year,   -   "   "   ....   "

10. "   " pupils tardy during year,   -   - "   ....   "   "

11. Total days of attendance by all pupils for year,   -   -   -   -   -   -

12. * "   "   " absence   " "   "   "   "   -   -   -   -   -

13. Total cases of tardiness,.................   Time lost by tardiness,   -   -   -   ... .

14. †Average daily attendance for year,   -   -   -   -   -   -

15. Per cent. of attendance—11÷(11+12),   -   -   -   -   -   -

16. Number of pupils promoted to   -   -   -   -   -   -   -

      (a) Second year,   -   -   -   -   -   -   -

      (b) Third   "   -   -   -   -   -   -   -

      (c) Fourth   "   -   -   -   -   -   -   -   ....

      (d) Fifth   " -   -   -   -   -   -   ....

      (e) Sixth   "   -   -   -   -   -   -   ....

      (f) Seventh " -   -   -   -   -   -   -   __

      (g) Eighth   "   -   -   -   -   -   -

      (h) High School,   -   -   -   -   -   -   ....

17. Number of graduates from the common branches and receiving diplomas,

                        Male,.................... ; female,................. ; total,.... ..   ..

18. Number of graduates from non-commissioned township high schools,

                        Male,.................... ; female,................. ; total,................ ...

19. Number of graduates from commissioned township high schools,

                        Male,....................; female,....................; total,..............

20. How many books in school library (not including reading circle books) at beginning of year?

21. How many books were added to library (not including reading circle books) during year?

22. Total now in school library (not including reading circle books),   -   -   -   -   -

23. How many reading circle books were added during year?   -   -   -   -   -   ....

24. How many pupils read one or more school library or reading circle books during year?   -   ....

25. Do patrons read school library books?   -   -   -   -   -   -

26. Number of visits to school,   Parents,....................; officials, ...; others, ... ; total,.....................

27. Number of teachers employed (if school be high school), Male,...................; female, ...; total,.....................

28. Number of days teacher attended township institute,   -   *   -   -   -

29. Books and apparatus left in school room at end of term, -   -   -   -   ....

I,... .. .., do solemnly swear that the above report is true to the best of my knowledge and belief.

                                                                              { Teacher.
                        .... { Principal.

NOTES:—

      *(1.) After three days of absence the pupil should be withdrawn, and his absence counted no more for that period of absence. After being withdrawn, he is not a pupil of the school, and can not be again until he is re-entered, as in item 6.

      †(2.) To find average daily attendance divide the whole number of days of attendance made by all the pupils by the number of days of school taught.

TEACHER'S CONTRACT.

This Agreement, Between _A. S. Hermann_ School Trustee of

Washington School Township, in Porter County, and State of Indiana,

of the first part, and _Ada Douglas_ a legally qualified teacher in said

County of the second part, certifies that the said teacher hereby agrees to teach the public school in District No. _3_,

Grade _____, in said Township, for the term commencing on the _Second_ day of _Sept_

A. D. 1 _907_, for the consideration of _Two_ • Dollars and

Sixty Cents per { day, year, } to be paid _When Called For_ (State here when all or parts of salary will be paid.)

For 180 Days Teaching Consideration 468.00

The said _Ada Douglas_ further agrees faithfully to perform

all the duties of teacher in said school; using only such text-books as are prescribed by the Trustees in accordance with the law, except supplementary reading, such as Young People's Reading Circle books, etc., and other works recommended by the County Superintendent, and observing all Rules and Regulations of the County Board of Education, and all instructions of the County Superintendent of Schools; that _s_he will attend and participate in the exercises of each Institute or other teachers' meetings that may be appointed for the teachers of said township, or for each day's absence therefrom, forfeit a sum equal to one day's wages, unless such absence shall be occasioned by sickness, that _s_he will accurately keep and use all registers and blanks placed in _her_ hands by said Trustee; that _s_he will make a complete and accurate report at the close of the school term, the blank for which is provided on the back of this sheet; that _s_he will make all other reports required of _her_ by said Trustee, the County Superintendent, or the laws of Indiana, at the proper time and manner and in good order; that _s_he will exercise due diligence in the preservation of school buildings, grounds, furniture, apparatus, books, blanks and other school property committed to _her_ care, and turn the same over to the Trustee, or his representative, at the close of the term of school, in as good condition as when received, damage and wear by use excepted.

The said School Trustee agrees to keep the school buildings in good repair, and to furnish the necessary fuel, furniture, apparatus, books and blanks, and such other appliances as may be necessary for the systematic and proper conduct of said school.

And the said School Trustee, for and in behalf of said Township, further agrees to pay the said _Ada Douglas_ for services as teacher of said school, either a sum equal to the whole number of days taught at the rate of the above named sum per day, as agreed upon, or the salary for the year in the event of a yearly consideration, as agreed upon, when the said teacher shall have filled all the stipulations of this contract.

The said School Trustee further agrees to pay said teacher one day's wages for each day's attendance at the Township Institute, according to the Acts of 1889.

PROVIDED, That in case the said _Ada Douglas_ should be dismissed from said school by said Trustee, or his successor in office, for incompetency, cruelty, gross immorality, neglect of business, or a violation of any of the stipulations of this contract, or in case _her_ license should be annulled by the County Superintendent or State Superintendent, _s_he shall not be entitled to any compensation after notice of dismissal, or notice of annulment of license.

PROVIDED FURTHER, That the teacher shall have a duplicate of this Contract.

IN WITNESS WHEREOF, We have hereunto subscribed our names, this _Second_

day of _Sept_ A. D. 1 _907_

Ada Douglas .Teacher.

A. S. Hermann School Trustee.

NOTES:—
(1.) Full authority is given the Trustee to substitute the words "principal," "supervisor" or "superintendent" for the word "teacher" in the event the Contract should be so made.
(2.) This Contract is the official blank, made by the State Superintendent of Public Instruction, under the provisions of H. B. No. 139, Acts of 1899.

Teacher's or Principal's Report to Township Trustee.

NOTE.—This report must be made by each teacher having charge of the attendance of pupils. A high school teacher who works under the direction of a principal will not need to make the report in case the principal reports for the entire high school. In graded grammar schools each teacher should report for the pupils directly under his charge. The principal of a graded grammar school should report only for the pupils directly under his charge.

REPORT of.................................. .... { teacher } { principal } of.....................................District

WASHINGTON TOWNSHIP, PORTER COUNTY, INDIANA,

to the Township Trustee, for the school term beginning............................ ....and

closing ....

FOR ALL TEACHERS WHO HAVE CHARGE OF ATTENDANCE OF PUPILS.

1. Number of days school was in session, - - - - - - - - - - -
2. " " pupils enrolled during year, - Male, ...; female,..................; total,.................
3. " " " withdrawn during year, - - " " "
4. " " " suspended " " - - " " ....   "
5. " " " expelled " " - " " "
6. " " " re-entered " " - " " "
7. " " " remaining in school close of year, " " "
8. " " " neither tardy nor absent during year, " " "
9. " " cases of tardiness during year, - " " ....   "
10. " " pupils tardy during year, - - " ....   " "
11. Total days of attendance by all pupils for year, - - - - -
12. * " " " absence " " " " " - - - - -
13. Total cases of tardiness,.................... Time lost by tardiness, - - - ... ...
14. †Average daily attendance for year, - - - - -
15. Per cent. of attendance—11÷(11+12), - - -
16. Number of pupils promoted to - - - - - - -
   (a) Second year, - - - - - - -
   (b) Third " - - - - - - -
   (c) Fourth " - - - - - ....
   (d) Fifth " - - - - - ....
   (e) Sixth " - - - - - ....
   (f) Seventh " - - - - - -
   (g) Eighth " - - - - - -
   (h) High School, - - - - - ....
17. Number of graduates from the common branches and receiving diplomas,
   Male,.................; female, ... ; total,.........
18. Number of graduates from non-commissioned township high schools,
   Male,................; female,..................; total,.............
19. Number of graduates from commissioned township high schools,
   Male,................; female,..................; total,.........
20. How many books in school library (not including reading circle books) at beginning of year?
21. How many books were added to library (not including reading circle books) during year?
22. Total now in school library (not including reading circle books), - - - - -
23. How many reading circle books were added during year? - - - - -
24. How many pupils read one or more school library or reading circle books during year? - ....
25. Do patrons read school library books? - - - - - - -
26. Number of visits to school, Parents,.................; officials, ...; others, ...; total,.................
27. Number of teachers employed (if school be high school), Male,............; female, ...; total,..............
28. Number of days teacher attended township institute, - - - - *
29. Books and apparatus left in school room at end of term, - - - ....

I,.. ...., do solemnly swear that the above report is true to the best of my knowledge and belief.

.... { Teacher. { Principal.

NOTES:—
*(11.) After three days of absence the pupil should be withdrawn, and his absence counted no more for that period of absence. After being withdrawn, he is not a pupil of the school, and can not be again until he is re-entered, as in item 6.
†(12.) To find average daily attendance divide the whole number of days of attendance made by all the pupils by the number of days of school taught.

5ª

TEACHER'S CONTRACT.

This Agreement, Between _Wm. A. Bond_ School Trustee of

Washington School Township, in Porter County, and State of Indiana,

of the first part, and _Maud Casbon_ a legally qualified teacher in said

County of the second part, certifies that the said teacher hereby agrees to teach the public school in District No. _4_,

Grade_____, in said Township, for the term commencing on the _4th_ day of _Sept._

A. D. 18_99_, for the consideration of _Two_ Dollars and

_____ Cents per {day, / year,} to be paid _when Called for_ (State here when all or parts of salary will be paid.)

The said _Maud Casbon_ further agrees faithfully to perform
all the duties of teacher in said school; using only such text-books as are prescribed by the Trustees in accordance with
the law, except supplementary reading, such as Young People's Reading Circle books, etc., and other works recommended by the County Superintendent, and observing all Rules and Regulations of the County Board of Education,
and all instructions of the County Superintendent of Schools; that _S_he will attend and participate in the exercises of
each Institute or other teachers' meetings that may be appointed for the teachers of said township, or for each day's
absence therefrom, forfeit a sum equal to one day's wages, unless such absence shall be occasioned by sickness, that
_S_he will accurately keep and use all registers and blanks placed in _her_ hands by said Trustee; that _S_he will
make a complete and accurate report at the close of the school term, the blank for which is provided on the back of
this sheet; that _S_he will make all other reports required of _her_ by said Trustee, the County Superintendent, or
the laws of Indiana, at the proper time and manner and in good order; that _S_he will exercise due diligence in the
preservation of school buildings, grounds, furniture, apparatus, books, blanks and other school property committed to
her care, and turn the same over to the Trustee, or his representative, at the close of the term of school, in as
good condition as when received, damage and wear by use excepted.

The said School Trustee agrees to keep the school buildings in good repair, and to furnish the necessary fuel,
furniture, apparatus, books and blanks, and such other appliances as may be necessary for the systematic and proper
conduct of said school.

And the said School Trustee, for and in behalf of said Township, further agrees to pay the said_____
Maud Casbon for services as teacher of said school, either a sum equal to the whole
number of days taught at the rate of the above named sum per day, as agreed upon, or the salary for the year in the
event of a yearly consideration, as agreed upon, when the said teacher shall have filled all the stipulations of this contract.

The said School Trustee further agrees to pay said teacher one day's wages for each day's attendance at the Township Institute, according to the Acts of 1889.

PROVIDED, That in case the said _Maud Casbon_ should be
dismissed from said school by said Trustee, or his successor in office, for incompetency, cruelty, gross immorality,
neglect of business, or a violation of any of the stipulations of this contract, or in case _her_ license should be
annulled by the County Superintendent or State Superintendent, _S_he shall not be entitled to any compensation after
notice of dismissal, or notice of annulment of license.

PROVIDED FURTHER, That the teacher shall have a duplicate of this Contract.

IN WITNESS WHEREOF, We have hereunto subscribed our names, this _5th_

day of _Aug_ A. D. 18_99_

Maud Casbon .Teacher.

Wm. A. Bond .School Trustee.

NOTES:—
     (1.) Full authority is given the Trustee to substitute the words "principal," "supervisor" or "superintendent" for the word "teacher"
in the event the Contract should be so made.
     (2.) This Contract is the official blank, made by the State Superintendent of Public Instruction, under the provisions of H. B. No. 139,
Acts of 1899.

Teacher's or Principal's Report to Township Trustee.

NOTE.—This report must be made by each teacher having charge of the attendance of pupils. A high school teacher who works under the direction of a principal will not need to make the report in case the principal reports for the entire high school. In graded grammar schools each teacher should report for the pupils directly under his charge. The principal of a graded grammar school should report only for the pupils directly under his charge.

REPORT of............................ .... { teacher } of..........................District
.... { principal }

WASHINGTON TOWNSHIP, PORTER COUNTY, INDIANA,

to the Township Trustee, for the school term beginning...and

closing ....

FOR ALL TEACHERS WHO HAVE CHARGE OF ATTENDANCE OF PUPILS.

1. Number of days school was in session, - - - - - - - -
2. " " pupils enrolled during year, - Male, ...; female,...........................; total,........... ...
3. " " " withdrawn during year, - - " " "
4. " " " suspended " " - - " " ....   "
5. " " " expelled " " - " " "
6. " " " re-entered " " - " " "
7. " " " remaining in school close of year, " " "
8. " " " neither tardy nor absent during year, " " "
9. " " cases of tardiness during year, - " " ....   "
10. " " pupils tardy during year, - " ....   " "
11. Total days of attendance by all pupils for year, - - - - -
12. * " " " absence " " " " " - - - -
13. Total cases of tardiness,........................ Time lost by tardiness, - - ... ...
14. †Average daily attendance for year, - - - - -
15. Per cent. of attendance—11÷(11+12), - -
16. Number of pupils promoted to - - - - -
     (a) Second year, - - - -
     (b) Third " - - - -
     (c) Fourth " - - - ....
     (d) Fifth " - - - ....
     (e) Sixth " - - - - -
     (f) Seventh " - - - - —
     (g) Eighth " - - - -
     (h) High School, - - - - ....
17. Number of graduates from the common branches and receiving diplomas,
     Male,........................; female,........................; total,........ .. ..
18. Number of graduates from non-commissioned township high schools,
     Male,........................; female,........................; total,............ .
19. Number of graduates from commissioned township high schools,
     Male,........................; female,........................; total,........
20. How many books in school library (not including reading circle books) at beginning of year?
21. How many books were added to library (not including reading circle books) during year?
22. Total now in school library (not including reading circle books), - - - - -
23. How many reading circle books were added during year? - - - - ....
24. How many pupils read one or more school library or reading circle books during year? - ....
25. Do patrons read school library books? - - - - - ....
26. Number of visits to school, Parents,........................; officials,....................; others,....................; total,...........................
27. Number of teachers employed (if school be high school), Male,....................; female,....................; total,............ .. ..
28. Number of days teacher attended township institute, - - * * *
29. Books and apparatus left in school room at end of term, - - - ....

I,.., do solemnly swear that the above report is true to the best of my knowledge and belief.

{ Teacher.
.... { Principal.

NOTES:—
*(1.) After three days of absence the pupil should be withdrawn, and his absence counted no more for that period of absence. After being withdrawn, he is not a pupil of the school, and can not be again until he is re-entered, as in item 6.
†(2.) To find average daily attendance divide the whole number of days of attendance made by all the pupils by the number of days of school taught.

For Township Trustees.   Wade Bros. & Wise, Printers.

TEACHER'S CONTRACT.

This Agreement, Between _A. S. Hermann_ School Trustee of

Washington School Township, In Porter County, and State of Indiana,

of the first part, and _Avis Adams_ .... a legally qualified teacher in said

County of the second part, certifies that the said teacher hereby agrees to teach the public school in District No. _7_ ,

Grade _____ , in said Township, for the term commencing on the _Second_ day of _Sept_

A. D. 1 _907_ , for the consideration of _Two_ Dollars and

Sixty .... Cents per { day, year, } to be paid _When Called for_ (State here when all or parts of salary will be paid.)

For 180 Days Teaching Consideration 468 ⁰⁰

The said _Avis Adams_ .... further agrees faithfully to perform

all the duties of teacher in said school; using only such text-books as are prescribed by the Trustees in accordance with the law, except supplementary reading, such as Young People's Reading Circle books, etc., and other works recommended by the County Superintendent, and observing all Rules and Regulations of the County Board of Education, and all instructions of the County Superintendent of Schools; that _S_ he will attend and participate in the exercises of each Institute or other teachers' meetings that may be appointed for the teachers of said township, or for each day's absence therefrom, forfeit a sum equal to one day's wages, unless such absence shall be occasioned by sickness, that _S_ he will accurately keep and use all registers and blanks placed in _her_ hands by said Trustee; that _S_ he will make a complete and accurate report at the close of the school term, the blank for which is provided on the back of this sheet; that _S_ he will make all other reports required of _her_ by said Trustee, the County Superintendent, or the laws of Indiana, at the proper time and manner and in good order; that _S_ he will exercise due diligence in the preservation of school buildings, grounds, furniture, apparatus, books, blanks and other school property committed to _her_ care, and turn the same over to the Trustee, or his representative, at the close of the term of school, in as good condition as when received, damage and wear by use excepted.

The said School Trustee agrees to keep the school buildings in good repair, and to furnish the necessary fuel, furniture, apparatus, books and blanks, and such other appliances as may be necessary for the systematic and proper conduct of said school.

And the said School Trustee, for and in behalf of said Township, further agrees to pay the said _Avis_ _Adams_ .... for services as teacher of said school, either a sum equal to the whole number of days taught at the rate of the above named sum per day, as agreed upon, or the salary for the year in the event of a yearly consideration, as agreed upon, when the said teacher shall have filled all the stipulations of this contract.

The said School Trustee further agrees to pay said teacher one day's wages for each day's attendance at the Township Institute, according to the Acts of 1889.

PROVIDED, That in case the said _Avis Adams_ should be dismissed from said school by said Trustee, or his successor in office, for incompetency, cruelty, gross immorality, neglect of business, or a violation of any of the stipulations of this contract, or in case _her_ license should be annulled by the County Superintendent or State Superintendent _she_ he shall not be entitled to any compensation after notice of dismissal, or notice of annulment of license.

PROVIDED FURTHER, That the teacher shall have a duplicate of this Contract.

IN WITNESS WHEREOF, We have hereunto subscribed our names, this _Second_

day of _Sept_ .... A. D. 1 _907_

Lois Adams .Teacher.

A. S. Herman School Trustee.

NOTES:—

(1.) Full authority is given the Trustee to substitute the words "principal," "supervisor" or "superintendent" for the word "teacher" in the event the Contract should be so made.

(2.) This Contract is the official blank, made by the State Superintendent of Public Instruction, under the provisions of H. B. No. 139, Acts of 1899.

Teacher's or Principal's Report to Township Trustee.

NOTE.—This report must be made by each teacher having charge of the attendance of pupils. A high school teacher who works under the direction of a principal will not need to make the report in case the principal reports for the entire high school. In graded grammar schools each teacher should report for the pupils directly under his charge. The principal of a graded grammar school should report only for the pupils directly under his charge.

REPORT of .... ⎰ teacher ⎱ of ....District
⎱ principal ⎰

WASHINGTON TOWNSHIP, PORTER COUNTY, INDIANA,

to the Township Trustee, for the school term beginning..and

closing ....: ....

FOR ALL TEACHERS WHO HAVE CHARGE OF ATTENDANCE OF PUPILS.

1. Number of days school was in session, - - - - - - - -
2. " " pupils enrolled during year, - Male, ...; female,....................; total,.................
3. " " " withdrawn during year, - - " " "
4. " " " suspended " " - " " "
5. " " " expelled " " - " " "
6. " " " re-entered " " - " " "
7. " " " remaining in school close of year, " " "
8. " " " " neither tardy nor absent during year, " " "
9. " " " cases of tardiness during year, - " " "
10. " " " pupils tardy during year, - - " " "
11. Total days of attendance by all pupils for year, - - - - -
12. * " " " absence " " " " " - - - -
13. Total cases of tardiness, ... Time lost by tardiness, - - -
14. †Average daily attendance for year, - - - -
15. Per cent. of attendance—$11 \div (11+12)$, - - -
16. Number of pupils promoted to - - - - -
    (a) Second year, - - - - -
    (b) Third " - - - -
    (c) Fourth " - - - -
    (d) Fifth " - - -
    (e) Sixth " - - -
    (f) Seventh " - - -
    (g) Eighth " - -
    (h) High School, - - - -
17. Number of graduates from the common branches and receiving diplomas,
    Male,.................; female, ...; total, ...
18. Number of graduates from non-commissioned township high schools,
    Male,.................; female,..................; total,..............
19. Number of graduates from commissioned township high schools,
    Male,.................; female,..................; total,........
20. How many books in school library (not including reading circle books) at beginning of year?
21. How many books were added to library (not including reading circle books) during year?
22. Total now in school library (not including reading circle books), - - - -
23. How many reading circle books were added during year? - - -
24. How many pupils read one or more school library or reading circle books during year? -
25. Do patrons read school library books? - - - - - -
26. Number of visits to school, Parents,.................; officials, ...; others, ...; total,......................
27. Number of teachers employed (if school be high school), Male,................; female, ...; total,......
28. Number of days teacher attended township Institute, - " " "
29. Books and apparatus left in school room at end of term, - - -

I,..., do solemnly swear that the above report is true to the best of my knowledge and belief.

.... ⎰ Teacher.
⎱ Principal.

NOTES:—
*(1.) After three days of absence the pupil should be withdrawn, and his absence counted no more for that period of absence. After being withdrawn, he is not a pupil of the school, and can not be again until he is re-entered, as in item 6.
†(2.) To find average daily attendance divide the whole number of days of attendance made by all the pupils by the number of days of school taught.

6 1 A

TEACHER'S CONTRACT.

This Agreement, Between *C. S. Herman* School Trustee of

Washington School Township, in Porter County, and State of Indiana,

of the first part, and *Julia Stephan* a legally qualified teacher in said County of the second part, certifies that the said teacher hereby agrees to teach the public school in District No. *1*, Grade____, in said Township, for the term commencing on the *Second* day of *Sept* A. D. 1*907*, for the consideration of *Two* Dollars and *Twenty five* Cents per { day, } { year, } to be paid *When Called for* (State here when all or parts of salary will be paid.)

For 180 days Teaching Consideration 405⁰⁰

The said *Julia Stephan* further agrees faithfully to perform all the duties of teacher in said school; using only such text-books as are prescribed by the Trustees in accordance with the law, except supplementary reading, such as Young People's Reading Circle books, etc., and other works recommended by the County Superintendent, and observing all Rules and Regulations of the County Board of Education, and all instructions of the County Superintendent of Schools; that *S*he will attend and participate in the exercises of each Institute or other teachers' meetings that may be appointed for the teachers of said township, or for each day's absence therefrom, forfeit a sum equal to one day's wages, unless such absence shall be occasioned by sickness, that *S*he will accurately keep and use all registers and blanks placed in *her* hands by said Trustee; that *S*he will make a complete and accurate report at the close of the school term, the blank for which is provided on the back of this sheet; that *S*he will make all other reports required of *her* by said Trustee, the County Superintendent, or the laws of Indiana, at the proper time and manner and in good order; that *S*he will exercise due diligence in the preservation of school buildings, grounds, furniture, apparatus, books, blanks and other school property committed to *her* care, and turn the same over to the Trustee, or his representative, at the close of the term of school, in as good condition as when received, damage and wear by use excepted.

The said School Trustee agrees to keep the school buildings in good repair, and to furnish the necessary fuel, furniture, apparatus, books and blanks, and such other appliances as may be necessary for the systematic and proper conduct of said school.

And the said School Trustee, for and in behalf of said Township, further agrees to pay the said *Julia Stephan* for services as teacher of said school, either a sum equal to the whole number of days taught at the rate of the above named sum per day, as agreed upon, or the salary for the year in the event of a yearly consideration, as agreed upon, when the said teacher shall have filled all the stipulations of this contract.

The said School Trustee further agrees to pay said teacher one day's wages for each day's attendance at the Township Institute, according to the Acts of 1889.

PROVIDED, That in case the said *Julia Stephan* should be dismissed from said school by said Trustee or his successor in office, for incompetency, cruelty, gross immorality, neglect of business, or a violation of any of the stipulations of this contract, or in case *her* license should be annulled by the County Superintendent or State Superintendent, *S*he shall not be entitled to any compensation after notice of dismissal, or notice of annulment of license.

PROVIDED FURTHER, That the teacher shall have a duplicate of this Contract.

IN WITNESS WHEREOF, We have hereunto subscribed our names, this *second* day of *Sept* A. D. 19*07*

Julia Stephan Teacher.

C. S. Herman School Trustee.

NOTES:—
(1.) Full authority is given the Trustee to substitute the words "principal," "supervisor" or "superintendent" for the word "teacher" in the event the Contract should be so made.
(2.) This Contract is the official blank, made by the State Superintendent of Public Instruction, under the provisions of H. B. No. 139, Acts of 1899.

Teacher's or Principal's Report to Township Trustee.

NOTE.—This report must be made by each teacher having charge of the attendance of pupils. A high school teacher who works under the direction of a principal will not need to make the report in case the principal reports for the entire high school. In graded grammar schools each teacher should report for the pupils directly under his charge. The principal of a graded grammar school should report only for the pupils directly under his charge.

REPORT of.................................. .... { teacher } { principal } of..........................District

WASHINGTON TOWNSHIP, PORTER COUNTY, INDIANA,

to the Township Trustee, for the school term beginning...and

closing ....

FOR ALL TEACHERS WHO HAVE CHARGE OF ATTENDANCE OF PUPILS.

1. Number of days school was in session,   -   -   -   -   -   -   -   -   -
2. "   " pupils enrolled during year,   -   Male, ...; female,......................; total,................
3. "   "   " withdrawn during year,   -   -   "   "   "
4. "   "   " suspended   "   "   -   - "   "   "
5. "   "   " expelled   "   "   -   . "   "   "
6. "   "   " re-entered   "   "   . "   "   "
7. "   "   " remaining in school close of year, "   "   "
8. "   "   " neither tardy nor absent during year, "   "   "
9. "   " cases of tardiness during year,   -   "   "   "
10. "   " pupils tardy during year,   -   . "   .... "   "
11. Total days of attendance by all pupils for year,   -   -   -   -   -   -
12. * "   "   " absence   "   "   "   "   "   -   -   -   -   -
13. Total cases of tardiness,......................   Time lost by tardiness,   -   -   -   .   . . . .
14. †Average daily attendance for year,   -   -   -   -   -   -
15. Per cent. of attendance—$11 \div (11+12)$,   -   -   -   -
16. Number of pupils promoted to   -   -   -   -   -   -
    (a) Second year,   -   -   -   -   -
    (b) Third   "   -   -   -   -   -
    (c) Fourth   "   -   -   -   -   ....
    (d) Fifth   "   -   -   -   -   -   ....
    (e) Sixth   "   -   -   -   -   ....
    (f) Seventh   "   -   -   -   -   —
    (g) Eighth   "   -   -   -   -   -
    (h) High School,   -   -   -   -   -   ....
17. Number of graduates from the common branches and receiving diplomas,
    Male,.......................; female, ... ; total, ...
18. Number of graduates from non-commissioned township high schools,
    Male,...................; female,......................; total,....................
19. Number of graduates from commissioned township high schools,
    Male,...................; female,......................; total,...........
20. How many books in school library (not including reading circle books) at beginning of year?
21. How many books were added to library (not including reading circle books) during year?
22. Total now in school library (not including reading circle books),   -   -   -   -   -
23. How many reading circle books were added during year?   -   -   -   -   ....
24. How many pupils read one or more school library or reading circle books during year?   -   ....
25. Do patrons read school library books?   -   -   -   -   -   -   ....
26. Number of visits to school,   Parents,...................; officials, ...; others, ...; total, ...
27. Number of teachers employed (if school be high school), Male,...............; female, ...; total,............. ...
28. Number of days teacher attended township institute,   -   -   -   -   *   -
29. Books and apparatus left in school room at end of term,   -   -   -   -   ....

I,..., do solemnly swear that the above report is true to the best of my knowledge and belief.
.... { Teacher. } { Principal.

NOTES:—
    *(1.) After three days of absence the pupil should be withdrawn, and his absence counted no more for that period of absence. After being withdrawn, he is not a pupil of the school, and can not be again until he is re-entered, as in item 6.
    †(14.) To find average daily attendance divide the whole number of days of attendance made by all the pupils by the number of days of school taught.

6ᴬ

For Township Trustees.   Wade Bros. & Wise, Printers.

TEACHER'S CONTRACT.

This Agreement, Between _Wm. A. Bond_ School Trustee of

Washington School Township, in Porter County, and State of Indiana,

of the first part, and _Grace Whitcomb_ a legally qualified teacher in said

County of the second part, certifies that the said teacher hereby agrees to teach the public school in District No. _5_,

Grade ___ , in said Township, for the term commencing on the _4th_ day of _Sep_

A. D. 1 _899_ , for the consideration of _Two_ Dollars and

_____ ⸱ Cents per { day, { to be paid _When Called For_
                    { year, {   (State here when all or parts of salary will be paid.)

The said _Grace Whitcomb_ further agrees faithfully to perform

all the duties of teacher in said school; using only such text-books as are prescribed by the Trustees in accordance with
the law, except supplementary reading, such as Young People's Reading Circle books, etc., and other works recommended by the County Superintendent, and observing all Rules and Regulations of the County Board of Education,
and all instructions of the County Superintendent of Schools; that She will attend and participate in the exercises of
each Institute or other teachers' meetings that may be appointed for the teachers of said township, or for each day's
absence therefrom, forfeit a sum equal to one day's wages, unless such absence shall be occasioned by sickness, that
She will accurately keep and use all registers and blanks placed in _her_ hands by said Trustee; that She will
make a complete and accurate report at the close of the school term, the blank for which is provided on the back of
this sheet; that She will make all other reports required of _her_ by said Trustee, the County Superintendent, or
the laws of Indiana, at the proper time and manner and in good order; that She will exercise due diligence in the
preservation of school buildings, grounds, furniture, apparatus, books, blanks and other school property committed to
her care, and turn the same over to the Trustee or his representative, at the close of the term of school, in as
good condition as when received, damage and wear by use excepted.

The said School Trustee agrees to keep the school buildings in good repair, and to furnish the necessary fuel,
furniture, apparatus, books and blanks, and such other appliances as may be necessary for the systematic and proper
conduct of said school.

And the said School Trustee, for and in behalf of said Township, further agrees to pay the said
Grace Whitcomb for services as teacher of said school, either a sum equal to the whole
number of days taught at the rate of the above named sum per day, as agreed upon, or the salary for the year in the
event of a yearly consideration, as agreed upon, when the said teacher shall have filled all the stipulations of this contract.

The said School Trustee further agrees to pay said teacher one day's wages for each day's attendance at the Township Institute, according to the Acts of 1889.

PROVIDED, That in case the said _Grace Whitcomb_ should be
dismissed from said school by said Trustee, or his successor in office, for incompetency, cruelty, gross immorality,
neglect of business, or a violation of any of the stipulations of this contract, or in case _her_ license should be
annulled by the County Superintendent or State Superintendent, She shall not be entitled to any compensation after
notice of dismissal, or notice of annulment of license.

PROVIDED FURTHER, That the teacher shall have a duplicate of this Contract.

IN WITNESS WHEREOF, We have hereunto subscribed our names, this _26th_

day of _Aug_ A. D. 1 _899_

Grace Whitcomb ....Teacher.

Wm. A. Bond ....School Trustee.

NOTES:—
  (1.) Full authority is given the Trustee to substitute the words "principal," "supervisor" or "superintendent" for the word "teacher"
in the event the Contract should be so made.
  (2.) This Contract is the official blank, made by the State Superintendent of Public Instruction, under the provisions of H. B. No. 139,
Acts of 1899.

Teacher's or Principal's Report to Township Trustee.

NOTE.—This report must be made by each teacher having charge of the attendance of pupils. A high school teacher who works under the direction of a principal will not need to make the report in case the principal reports for the entire high school. In graded grammar schools each teacher should report for the pupils directly under his charge. The principal of a graded grammar school should report only for the pupils directly under his charge.

REPORT of... .... { teacher } of.............................District
{ principal }

WASHINGTON TOWNSHIP, PORTER COUNTY, INDIANA,

to the Township Trustee, for the school term beginning........................... ....-and

closing ....: ....

FOR ALL TEACHERS WHO HAVE CHARGE OF ATTENDANCE OF PUPILS.

1. Number of days school was in session,   -   -   -   -   -   -   -   -   -   -   -
2.   "   " pupils enrolled during year,   -   Male, ...; female,....................; total,.............. ...
3.   "   "   " withdrawn during year, -   -   "   "   "
4.   "   "   " suspended   "   "   -   - "   ....   "
5.   "   "   " expelled   "   "   -   "   "   "
6.   "   "   " re-entered   "   "   -   "   "   "
7.   "   "   " remaining in school close of year, "   "   "
8.   "   "   " neither tardy nor absent during year, "   "   "
9.   "   " cases of tardiness during year,   -   "   "   ....   "
10.   "   " pupils tardy during year,   -   - "   ....   "   "
11. Total days of attendance by all pupils for year,   -   -   -   -   -   -
12. * "   "   " " absence   " "   " "   " "   -   -   -   -   -
13. Total cases of tardiness, ...   Time lost by tardiness,   -   -   ... ...
14. †Average daily attendance for year,   -   -   -   -   -   -
15. Per cent. of attendance—11÷(11+12),   -   -   -   -   -
16. Number of pupils promoted to   -   -   -   -   -
    (a) Second year,   -   -   -   -   -   -
    (b) Third   "   -   -   -   -   -
    (c) Fourth   "   -   -   -   -   -   ....
    (d) Fifth   "   -   -   -   -   -   ....
    (e) Sixth   "   -   -   -   -   -   ....
    (f) Seventh   "   -   -   -   -   -   —
    (g) Eighth   "   -   -   -   -   -
    (h) High School,   -   -   -   -   -   ....
17. Number of graduates from the common branches and receiving diplomas,
    Male,..................; female,....................; total,.... ... ...
18. Number of graduates from non-commissioned township high schools,
    Male,..................; female,....................; total,............ .
19. Number of graduates from commissioned township high schools,
    Male,..................; female,....................; total,...........
20. How many books in school library (not including reading circle books) at beginning of year?
21. How many books were added to library (not including reading circle books) during year?
22. Total now in school library (not including reading circle books),   -   -   -   -
23. How many reading circle books were added during year?   -   -   -   -   ....
24. How many pupils read one or more school library or reading circle books during year?   -   ....
25. Do patrons read school library books?   -   -   -   -   -   ....
26. Number of visits to school,   Parents,..................; officials,....................; others, ...; total, ...
27. Number of teachers employed (if school be high school), Male,..................; female,.................; total,.......... ... ..
28. Number of days teacher attended township institute,   -   -   -   .   .   .
29. Books and apparatus left in school room at end of term,   -   -   -   ....

I,.. ... ., do solemnly swear that the above report is true to the best of my knowledge and belief.

{ Teacher.
.... { Principal.

NOTES:—
*(1.) After three days of absence the pupil should be withdrawn, and his absence counted no more for that period of absence. After being withdrawn, he is not a pupil of the school, and can not be again until he is re-entered, as in item 6.
†(2.) To find average daily attendance divide the whole number of days of attendance made by all the pupils by the number of days of school taught.

TEACHER'S CONTRACT.

This Agreement, Between _Wm. A. Bond_ School Trustee of

Washington School Township, in Porter County, and State of Indiana,

of the first part, and _Seth Shepard_ a legally qualified teacher in said County of the second part, certifies that the said teacher hereby agrees to teach the public school in District No. _6_, Grade _____, in said Township, for the term commencing on the _4th_ day of _Sep_ A. D. 1 _899_ , for the consideration of _____ _Two_ Dollars and _____ Cents per { day, } to be paid _When Called for_ { year, } (State here when all or parts of salary will be paid.)

The said _Seth Shepard_ further agrees faithfully to perform all the duties of teacher in said school; using only such text-books as are prescribed by the Trustees in accordance with the law, except supplementary reading, such as Young People's Reading Circle books, etc., and other works recommended by the County Superintendent, and observing all Rules and Regulations of the County Board of Education, and all instructions of the County Superintendent of Schools; that _he will attend and participate in the exercises of each Institute or other teachers' meetings that may be appointed for the teachers of said township, or for each day's absence therefrom, forfeit a sum equal to one day's wages, unless such absence shall be occasioned by sickness; that _he will accurately keep and use all registers and blanks placed in _____ hands by said Trustee; that _he will make a complete and accurate report at the close of the school term, the blank for which is provided on the back of this sheet; that _he will make all other reports required of _him_ by said Trustee, the County Superintendent, or the laws of Indiana, at the proper time and manner and in good order; that _he will exercise due diligence in the preservation of school buildings, grounds, furniture, apparatus, books, blanks and other school property committed to _his_ care, and turn the same over to the Trustee, or his representative, at the close of the term of school, in as good condition as when received, damage and wear by use excepted.

The said School Trustee agrees to keep the school buildings in good repair, and to furnish the necessary fuel, furniture, apparatus, books and blanks, and such other appliances as may be necessary for the systematic and proper conduct of said school.

And the said School Trustee, for and in behalf of said Township, further agrees to pay the said _____ _Seth Shepard_ for services as teacher of said school, either a sum equal to the whole number of days taught at the rate of the above named sum per day, as agreed upon, or the salary for the year in the event of a yearly consideration, as agreed upon, when the said teacher shall have filled all the stipulations of this contract.

The said School Trustee further agrees to pay said teacher one day's wages for each day's attendance at the Township Institute, according to the Acts of 1889.

PROVIDED, That in case the said _Seth Shepard_ should be dismissed from said school by said Trustee, or his successor in office, for incompetency, cruelty, gross immorality, neglect of business, or a violation of any of the stipulations of this contract, or in case _his_ license should be annulled by the County Superintendent or State Superintendent, _he shall not be entitled to any compensation after notice of dismissal, or notice of annulment of license.

PROVIDED FURTHER, That the teacher shall have a duplicate of this Contract.

IN WITNESS WHEREOF, We have hereunto subscribed our names, this _29th_ day of _April_ A. D. 1 _899_

Seth Shepard ....Teacher.

Wm. A. Bond School Trustee.

NOTES:—
    (1.) Full authority is given the Trustee to substitute the words "principal," "supervisor" or "superintendent" for the word "teacher" in the event the Contract should be so made.
    (2.) This Contract is the official blank, made by the State Superintendent of Public Instruction, under the provisions of H. B. No. 139, Acts of 1899.

Teacher's or Principal's Report to Township Trustee.

NOTE.—This report must be made by each teacher having charge of the attendance of pupils. A high school teacher who works under the direction of a principal will not need to make the report in case the principal reports for the entire high school. In graded grammar schools each teacher should report for the pupils directly under his charge. The principal of a graded grammar school should report only for the pupils directly under his charge.

REPORT of.................................... .... { teacher } of.......................District
{ principal }

WASHINGTON TOWNSHIP, PORTER COUNTY, INDIANA,

to the Township Trustee, for the school term beginning............................. ....and

closing ....: ....

FOR ALL TEACHERS WHO HAVE CHARGE OF ATTENDANCE OF PUPILS.

1. Number of days school was in session,   -   -   -   -   -   -   -
2. " " pupils enrolled during year,   -   Male, ...; female,.....................; total,...............
3. " " " withdrawn during year, -   -   "   "   "
4. " " " suspended "   "   -   -   "   "   "
5. " " " expelled "   "   -   "   "   "
6. " " " re-entered "   "   -   "   "   "
7. " " " remaining in school close of year, "   "   "
8. " " " neither tardy nor absent during year, "   "   "
9. " " cases of tardiness during year,   -   "   "   "
10. " " pupils tardy during year,   -   -   "   ....   "   "
11. Total days of attendance by all pupils for year,   -   -   -   -   -
12. * " " " absence " " " " "   -   -   -   -
13. Total cases of tardiness,....................   Time lost by tardiness,   -   -   -   .. .. . .
14. †Average daily attendance for year,   -   -   -   -   -
15. Per cent. of attendance—$11 \div (11+12)$,   -   -   -
16. Number of pupils promoted to   -   -   -   -   -   -
    (a) Second year,   -   -   -   -   -
    (b) Third "   -   -   -   -   -
    (c) Fourth "   -   -   -   -   -
    (d) Fifth "   -   -   -   -   -
    (e) Sixth "   -   -   -   -   -
    (f) Seventh "   -   -   -   -   -
    (g) Eighth "   -   -   -   -   -
    (h) High School,   -   -   -   -   -
17. Number of graduates from the common branches and receiving diplomas,
    Male,.......................; female, ...; total, ...
18. Number of graduates from non-commissioned township high schools,
    Male,...................; female,...................; total,.............. .
19. Number of graduates from commissioned township high schools,
    Male,...................; female,...................; total,.........
20. How many books in school library (not including reading circle books) at beginning of year?
21. How many books were added to library (not including reading circle books) during year?
22. Total now in school library (not including reading circle books),   -   -   -   -
23. How many reading circle books were added during year?   -   -   ....
24. How many pupils read one or more school library or reading circle books during year?   -   ....
25. Do patrons read school library books?   -   -   -   -   ....
26. Number of visits to school,   Parents,...................; officials, ...; others, ...; total,..................
27. Number of teachers employed (if school be high school), Male,.............; female,..............; total,..............
28. Number of days teacher attended township institute,   -   -   *   -   *   -
29. Books and apparatus left in school room at end of term,   -   -   -   ....

I,... ...., do solemnly swear that the above report is true to the best of my knowledge and belief.

.... { Teacher.
{ Principal.

NOTES:—
*(1.) After three days of absence the pupil should be withdrawn, and his absence counted no more for that period of absence. After being withdrawn, he is not a pupil of the school, and can not be again until he is re-entered, as in item 6.
†(2.) To find average daily attendance divide the whole number of days of attendance made by all the pupils by the number of days of school taught.

8 A

TEACHER'S CONTRACT.

This Agreement, Between _Wm A. Boul_ School Trustee of

Washington School Township, In Porter County, and State of Indiana,

of the first part, and _W. J. Morgan_ a legally qualified teacher in said

County of the second part, certifies that the said teacher hereby agrees to teach the public school in District No. _7_,

Grade _____ , in said Township, for the term commencing on the _4th_ day of _Sep_

A. D. 1 _899_ , for the consideration of_____ _Two_ Dollars and

_____ Cents per { day, / year, } to be paid _When called for_ (State here when all or parts of salary will be paid.)

The said _W. J. Morgan_ further agrees faithfully to perform

all the duties of teacher in said school; using only such text-books as are prescribed by the Trustees in accordance with the law, except supplementary reading, such as Young People's Reading Circle books, etc., and other works recommended by the County Superintendent, and observing all Rules and Regulations of the County Board of Education, and all instructions of the County Superintendent of Schools; that ___ he will attend and participate in the exercises of each Institute or other teachers' meetings that may be appointed for the teachers of said township, or for each day's absence therefrom, forfeit a sum equal to one day's wages, unless such absence shall be occasioned by sickness, that ___ he will accurately keep and use all registers and blanks placed in _his_ hands by said Trustee; that ___ he will make a complete and accurate report at the close of the school term, the blank for which is provided on the back of this sheet; that ___ he will make all other reports required of _him_ by said Trustee, the County Superintendent, or the laws of Indiana, at the proper time and manner and in good order; that ___ he will exercise due diligence in the preservation of school buildings, grounds, furniture, apparatus, books, blanks and other school property committed to _his_ care, and turn the same over to the Trustee, or his representative, at the close of the term of school, in as good condition as when received, damage and wear by use excepted.

The said School Trustee agrees to keep the school buildings in good repair, and to furnish the necessary fuel, furniture, apparatus, books and blanks, and such other appliances as may be necessary for the systematic and proper conduct of said school.

And the said School Trustee, for and in behalf of said Township, further agrees to pay the said_____

W. J. Morgan for services as teacher of said school, either a sum equal to the whole number of days taught at the rate of the above named sum per day, as agreed upon, or the salary for the year in the event of a yearly consideration, as agreed upon, when the said teacher shall have filled all the stipulations of this contract.

The said School Trustee further agrees to pay said teacher one day's wages for each day's attendance at the Township Institute, according to the Acts of 1889.

PROVIDED, That in case the said _W. J. Morgan_ should be dismissed from said school by said Trustee, or his successor in office, for incompetency, cruelty, gross immorality, neglect of business, or a violation of any of the stipulations of this contract, or in case _his_ license should be annulled by the County Superintendent or State Superintendent, ___ he shall not be entitled to any compensation after notice of dismissal, or notice of annulment of license.

PROVIDED FURTHER, That the teacher shall have a duplicate of this Contract.

IN WITNESS WHEREOF, We have hereunto subscribed our names, this _26th_

day of _Aug_ A. D. 1 _899_

W. J. Morgan Teacher.

Wm Ab Boul School Trustee.

NOTES:—

(1.) Full authority is given the Trustee to substitute the words "principal," "supervisor" or "superintendent" for the word "teacher" in the event the Contract should be so made.

(2.) This Contract is the official blank, made by the State Superintendent of Public Instruction, under the provisions of H. B. No. 139, Acts of 1899.

Teacher's or Principal's Report to Township Trustee.

NOTE.—This report must be made by each teacher having charge of the attendance of pupils. A high school teacher who works under the direction of a principal will not need to make the report in case the principal reports for the entire high school. In graded grammar schools each teacher should report for the pupils directly under his charge. The principal of a graded grammar school should report only for the pupils directly under his charge.

REPORT of.................... .... { teacher } of........................District
  { principal }

WASHINGTON TOWNSHIP, PORTER COUNTY, INDIANA,

to the Township Trustee, for the school term beginning...and

closing ....: ....

FOR ALL TEACHERS WHO HAVE CHARGE OF ATTENDANCE OF PUPILS.

1. Number of days school was in session, - - - - - - - -
2. " " pupils enrolled during year, - Male, ...; female,....................; total,..........
3. " " " " withdrawn during year, - - " " "
4. " " " " suspended " " - " " "
5. " " " " expelled " " - " " "
6. " " " " re-entered " " " " "
7. " " " " remaining in school close of year, " " "
8. " " " " neither tardy nor absent during year, " " "
9. " " " cases of tardiness during year, - " " "
10. " " " pupils tardy during year, - " " "
11. Total days of attendance by all pupils for year, - - - -
12. * " " " absence " " " " " - - -
13. Total cases of tardiness,................. Time lost by tardiness, - - -
14. †Average daily attendance for year, - - -
15. Per cent. of attendance—11÷(11+12), - - -
16. Number of pupils promoted to - - - -
    (a) Second year, - - - -
    (b) Third " - - -
    (c) Fourth " - - -
    (d) Fifth " - - -
    (e) Sixth " - - -
    (f) Seventh " - - -
    (g) Eighth " - - -
    (h) High School, - - - -
17. Number of graduates from the common branches and receiving diplomas,
    Male,................; female, ... ; total,.........
18. Number of graduates from non-commissioned township high schools,
    Male,................; female,................; total,..........
19. Number of graduates from commissioned township high schools,
    Male,................; female,..................; total,.......
20. How many books in school library (not including reading circle books) at beginning of year?
21. How many books were added to library (not including reading circle books) during year?
22. Total now in school library (not including reading circle books), - - - -
23. How many reading circle books were added during year? - - - -
24. How many pupils read one or more school library or reading circle books during year? -
25. Do patrons read school library books? - - - - -
26. Number of visits to school, Parents,..............; officials, ...; others, ... ; total,............
27. Number of teachers employed (if school be high school), Male,.............; female, ...; total,.........
28. Number of days teacher attended township institute, - - - -
29. Books and apparatus left in school room at end of term, - - -

I,.. do solemnly swear that the above report is true to the best of my knowledge and belief.

.... { Teacher.
  { Principal.

NOTES:—
*(1.) After three days of absence the pupil should be withdrawn, and his absence counted no more for that period of absence. After being withdrawn, he is not a pupil of the school, and can not be again until he is re-entered, as in item 6.
†(2.) To find average daily attendance divide the whole number of days of attendance made by all the pupils by the number of days of school taught.

9 A

For Township Trustees.   Wade Bros. & Wise, Printers.

TEACHER'S CONTRACT.

This Agreement, Between _W. A. Bowl_ School Trustee of

Washington School Township, in Porter County, and State of Indiana,

of the first part, and _W. J. Morgan_ a legally qualified teacher in said

County of the second part, certifies that the said teacher hereby agrees to teach the public school in District No. _7_,

Grade ____, in said Township, for the term commencing on the _3_ day of _Sep_

A. D. 1 _900_, for the consideration of _Two_ Dollars and

____ Cents per { day, year, } to be paid _As Called for_ (State here when all or parts of salary will be paid.)

The said _W. J. Morgan_ further agrees faithfully to perform
all the duties of teacher in said school; using only such text-books as are prescribed by the Trustees in accordance with
the law, except supplementary reading, such as Young People's Reading Circle books, etc., and other works recommended by the County Superintendent, and observing all Rules and Regulations of the County Board of Education,
and all instructions of the County Superintendent of Schools; that ____he will attend and participate in the exercises of
each Institute or other teachers' meetings that may be appointed for the teachers of said township, or for each day's
absence therefrom, forfeit a sum equal to one day's wages, unless such absence shall be occasioned by sickness, that
____he will accurately keep and use all registers and blanks placed in _his_ hands by said Trustee; that ____he will
make a complete and accurate report at the close of the school term, the blank for which is provided on the back of
this sheet; that ____he will make all other reports required of _him_ by said Trustee, the County Superintendent, or
the laws of Indiana, at the proper time and manner and in good order; that ____he will exercise due diligence in the
preservation of school buildings, grounds, furniture, apparatus, books, blanks and other school property committed to
his care, and turn the same over to the Trustee, or his representative, at the close of the term of school, in as
good condition as when received, damage and wear by use excepted.

The said School Trustee agrees to keep the school buildings in good repair, and to furnish the necessary fuel,
furniture, apparatus, books and blanks, and such other appliances as may be necessary for the systematic and proper
conduct of said school.

And the said School Trustee, for and in behalf of said Township, further agrees to pay the said
W. J. Morgan for services as teacher of said school, either a sum equal to the whole
number of days taught at the rate of the above named sum per day, as agreed upon, or the salary for the year in the
event of a yearly consideration, as agreed upon, when the said teacher shall have filled all the stipulations of this contract.

The said School Trustee further agrees to pay said teacher one day's wages for each day's attendance at the Township Institute, according to the Acts of 1889.

PROVIDED, That in case the said _W. J. Morgan_ should be
dismissed from said school by said Trustee, or his successor in office, for incompetency, cruelty, gross immorality,
neglect of business, or a violation of any of the stipulations of this contract, or in case _his_ license should be
annulled by the County Superintendent or State Superintendent, ____he shall not be entitled to any compensation after
notice of dismissal, or notice of annulment of license.

PROVIDED FURTHER, That the teacher shall have a duplicate of this Contract.

IN WITNESS WHEREOF, We have hereunto subscribed our names, this _3rd_

day of _Sep_ A. D. 1 _900_,

W. J. Morgan Teacher.

W. A. Bowl School Trustee.

NOTES:—
   (1.) Full authority is given the Trustee to substitute the words "principal," "supervisor" or "superintendent" for the word "teacher"
in the event the Contract should be so made.
   (2.) This Contract is the official blank, made by the State Superintendent of Public Instruction, under the provisions of H. B. No. 136,
Acts of 1899.

Teacher's or Principal's Report to Township Trustee.

NOTE.—This report must be made by each teacher having charge of the attendance of pupils. A high school teacher who works under the direction of a principal will not need to make the report in case the principal reports for the entire high school. In graded grammar schools each teacher should report for the pupils directly under his charge. The principal of a graded grammar school should report only for the pupils directly under his charge.

REPORT of.................... .... { teacher } { principal } of.....................District

WASHINGTON TOWNSHIP, PORTER COUNTY, INDIANA,

to the Township Trustee, for the school term beginning........................ ....and

closing ....: ....

FOR ALL TEACHERS WHO HAVE CHARGE OF ATTENDANCE OF PUPILS.

1. Number of days school was in session, - - - - - - - - -
2. " " pupils enrolled during year, - Male, ...; female,.................; total,.......... ...
3. " " " " withdrawn during year, - - " " "
4. " " " " suspended " " - - " " ....
5. " " " " expelled " " - - " " "
6. " " " " re-entered " " " " "
7. " " " " remaining in school close of year, " " "
8. " " " " neither tardy nor absent during year, " " "
9. " " " cases of tardiness during year, - " " ....
10. " " " pupils tardy during year, - - " .... " "
11. Total days of attendance by all pupils for year, - - - - -
12. * " " " absence " " " " " - - - -
13. Total cases of tardiness,................ Time lost by tardiness, - - ... .
14. †Average daily attendance for year, - - - -
15. Per cent. of attendance—$11 \div (11+12)$, - ____
16. Number of pupils promoted to - - - -
        (a) Second year, - - - - -
        (b) Third " - - - -
        (c) Fourth " - - - - ....
        (d) Fifth " - - - - ....
        (e) Sixth " - - - - ....
        (f) Seventh " - - - - _
        (g) Eighth " - - - - -
        (h) High School, - - - - - ....
17. Number of graduates from the common branches and receiving diplomas,
        Male,................; female,................; total,.... .. ...
18. Number of graduates from non-commissioned township high schools,
        Male,................; female,................; total,................
19. Number of graduates from commissioned township high schools,
        Male,................; female,................; total,.......
20. How many books in school library (not including reading circle books) at beginning of year?
21. How many books were added to library (not including reading circle books) during year?
22. Total now in school library (not including reading circle books), - - - -
23. How many reading circle books were added during year? - - - -
24. How many pupils read one or more school library or reading circle books during year? - ....
25. Do patrons read school library books? - - - - ....
26. Number of visits to school, Parents,................; officials, ...; others, ...; total, ...
27. Number of teachers employed (if school be high school), Male,................; female, ...; total,...........
28. Number of days teacher attended township institute, - - -
29. Books and apparatus left in school room at end of term, - - ....

I,........................ ...., do solemnly swear that the above report is true to the best of my knowledge and belief.

.... { Teacher. } { Principal.

NOTES:—
    *(1.) After three days of absence the pupil should be withdrawn, and his absence counted no more for that period of absence. After being withdrawn, he is not a pupil of the school, and can not be again until he is re-entered, as in Item 6.
    †(2.) To find average daily attendance divide the whole number of days of attendance made by all the pupils by the number of days of school taught.

www.ingramcontent.com/pod-product-compliance
Lightning Source LLC
Chambersburg PA
CBHW030629270326
41927CB00007B/1365